ENDORSEMENTS

Christians have enjoyed a remarkable tradition of prison literature, from St. Paul to John Bunyan to Dietrich Bonhoeffer. Now we can add to that tradition the story of Bulgarian pastor Christo Kulichev, whose stalwart faith during years of Communist harassment and imprisonment has already become legendary. His ringing declaration, "I prefer to be in prison with Jesus than to be free without him," will reverberate in our hearts forever, inspiring new faithfulness in every generation.

Dr. John Killinger
President, Mission For Biblical Literacy

Christo Kulichev is a contemporary Christian giant. His remarkable story will capture the heart and mind of every reader. Christo's life is a humble manifestation of the power and perseverance of a person who is totally committed to Jesus Christ as Lord. I pray that Christians of every age will be challenged by this remarkable story."

Dr. Paul A. Cedar
Chairman, Mission America Coalition
Former President, Evangelical Free Churches Of America

My first encounter with Christo was in 1978, when I first delivered Bibles (covertly) to him during the Communist years. His courage, commitment, and deep spirituality stood out as a true example of a fearless and focused Christian. His zeal and passion have not diminished with age or changing circumstances. I commend this book as a testimony to our great God and a life well-lived for God's glory.

Stuart McAllister
International Director, Ravi Zacharias International Ministries

Imprisoned for Christ is a masterfully told story. It is a troubling story of evil and injustice, and it is a triumphant story of God's grace as it sustains suffering Christians. For Christians living in free countries, the rumors of the persecuted church around the world often seem remote; this book brings the persecution close as we see and feel what it is like to be imprisoned for Christ.

Dr. Leland Ryken
Professor of English, Wheaton College

The fury of atheism and power of persecution in a Slavic culture permeated by a totalitarian regime is portrayed by Bulgarian pastor Christo Kulichev, who tells of life in one of the Soviet system's oppressive regimes. Church leaders were branded as traitors, put on trial, and imprisoned. On the 51st anniversary of the mass arrest of pastors who viewed Jesus Christ, not the state, as head of the church, the story of the reversal of hope is told in tribute to leaders of churches who found an even greater reversal in the resurrection of the crucified Jesus. Read it and count it joy that we live today under very precious freedoms.

Dr. Carl F. H. Henry
Evangelical Theologian and Author
Founding Editor, Christianity Today

The story of Christo Kulichev and his historic struggle with the Communist government and Orthdox church in Bulgaria is well worth telling. The historic Congregational churches in Bulgaria began in the 1830s and '40s. They were the first real Western contact with the Bulgarian people. Christo stands as a hero in the battle not only for Christianity but for religious freedom itself. I first met Christo at an international conference in Germany and have been with him numerous times since then. I have looked at his memoirs and heard his stories. Sometimes people exaggerate their experiences, but deeper involvement in the struggle for the church's liberty led me to check both Vatican and international legal experts. These confirmed not only the central facts of Christo's struggles, but that the struggle was well-known by government courts and judges. Even the government now recognizes him as a national hero. Christo is a tender-hearted and caring man with an inflexible commitment to Christ and the cause of religious freedom. We who have lived under the blessings of liberty need to study the model of such a Christian, for we do not know when the call to endure suffering and imprisonment for the gospel may overtake us.

Dr. Paul E. Larsen
General Secretary, International Federation of Free Evangelical Churches

I rejoice that the story of the imprisonment of my friend Christo Kulichev is now in print. Christo is a man of principle and strong convictions who was willing to suffer for what he believed. He was not "a reed shaken with the wind." Like Job, God honored him in the end and gave him back more than he lost. The church needs such men!

Clifford R. Christensen
Conference Minister, Conservative Congregational Christian Conference

The prisons of this world have embittered the spirits of most and made giants of the Spirit of only a few men who have passed through their doors. Christo Kulichev is truly a humble and courageous giant of the Spirit whose faith survived through the grace of the Lord. His story is a testament to God's grace and an inspiration for all. As a frequent visitor to the world's prisons and an admirer of Pastor Kulichev, I know beyond a doubt that he conquered the evil of unjust imprisonment and the cruelty of man with the grace and love that only God can give.

Wallace H. Cheney
Executive Vice President and General Counsel, Advocates International
Former Assistant Director and General Counsel, U.S. Federal Bureau of Prisons

Imprisoned for Christ is a compelling story of a modern-day hero of the faith. It is a story that breathes the classic prayers and spirit and passion of the historic church with a power that only the authentic story told from the heart can convey.

In the midst of my own work of reconciliation among leaders of a church that largely failed under the murderous onslaught of the Rwanda genocide, the story of Christo, pastor courageous, who did not flinch in the hour of trial, is an immense encouragement that the church of the martyrs and saints, the apostles and prophets, still stands, and that there are heroes of the faith even today in the most difficult places for Christian witness.

The story of Christo is winsomely told, in his own voice, but through the heart of a Christian brother in a free land who has identified so deeply with this compelling figure, that the story is authentic. It will renew and encourage the faith of all who read it as it has encouraged mine.

Rev. Dr. Arthur A. Rouner, Jr.
President, The Pilgrim Center for Reconciliation

Christo Kulichev's story bears witness to one who lived his faith without compromise while a prisoner of a regime bent on destroying him. Like other heroes of faith throughout history, this story demonstrates God's sovereignty in the lives of those who humbly and simply put their full trust in the Author of His-Story. In the end, God always wins.

Samuel E. Ericsson
President, Advocates International
Founder, Rule of Law Institute of Bulgaria

The story of Christo Kulichev is testimony to nothing less than the eternal nature and power of God in this generation. From the Congregational tradition freedom has involved a continuous struggle over the centuries in its assertion that it is God who calls to ministry and service individuals through the gathered church. Any interference in this process tests the commitment of both church and individuals. This story graphically reveals the unstinting commitment of one individual, Christo Kulichev, to his Lord and his church. Stripped of everything, his time in captivity exposes his faith to the closest of scrutiny, which the majority of us will never have to encounter. In his account, Michael Halcomb links the wisdom of others and Scripture that had obviously sustained Christo throughout his ordeal in testimony to the ever present presence of God. We must thank God for such servants as Christo, from whom we are able to draw immense encouragement and without whom we would be deprived of the challenge of the call of Christ in our own lives. I commend this story, which is inevitably an ongoing one.

Rev. Michael Heaney
General Secretary of the Congregational Federation (UK)

Christo's story is a compelling tale showing how God's power may work through our weakness if only we remain faithful. *Imprisoned for Christ* also reminds us of the importance of praying and working for Christians facing persecution around the world.

Baroness Cox of Queensbury
A Deputy Speaker of the House of Lords
President, Christian Solidarity Worldwide, United Kingdom

IMPRISONED FOR CHRIST

A STIRRING TESTAMENT TO GOD'S SUSTAINING GRACE IN A BALKAN PRISON

Lessons learned by a Christian pastor persecuted by an
atheistic regime that predicted Christ's church would
no longer exist in Bulgaria by the year 2000!

MICHAEL P. HALCOMB
As Told By Rev. Christo Kulichev

Tyndale House Publishers, Inc.
Wheaton, Illinois

Visit Tyndale's exciting Web site at www.tyndale.com

Edited by Jeremy P. Taylor

Designed by Zandrah Maguigad

Library of Congress Cataloging-in-Publication Data

Halcomb, Michael P.
   Imprisoned for Christ : a stirring testament to God's sustaining grace in a Balkan prison : lessons learned by a Christian pastor persecuted by an atheistic regime that predicted Christ's church would no longer exist in Bulgaria by the year 2000! / Michael P. Halcomb as told by Christo Kulichev.
      p. cm
   Includes bibliographical references (p.).
   ISBN 0-8423-5244-9
     1. Kulichev, Christo. 2. Persecution–Bulgaria–History–20th century. 3. Communism and Christianity–Bulgaria–History. 4. Protestant churches–Bulgaria–Clergy–Biography. 5. Political prisoners–Bulgaria–Biography. 6. Christian biography–Bulgaria. I. Kulichev, Christo. II. Title.

BR1608.B9 H35 2001
272′.9′092–dc21
[B]   00-054477

Printed in Bulgaria

05   04   03   02   01
5   4   3   2   1

All proceeds from the sale of this book will go to assist the ongoing ministry of the Bulgarian churches.

DEDICATION

To my dear wife, Tzvete:
with love and gratitude for her constant support
and encouragement.

To my dear children:
My daughter, Nebesna, and her husband, Toshko,
and my son, Stephan, and his wife, Daniela.

To my grandchildren:
Mimmi, Hristo, Tzvetomira, and Hristo,
with a prayer that they will always serve our Lord and Savior Jesus
Christ sincerely and faithfully all the years of their lives.

**Finally, to all who are suffering for their
faith in our Lord Jesus Christ,**
that they may learn the meaning of Philippians 1:29, that
"it has been granted to you on behalf of Christ not only to believe
on him, but also to suffer for him." This promise is the very word
of God and, as always, it does not depend upon time, place,
or circumstance but is constantly valid and unchanging.

In conclusion, I am thankful to my friend Rev. Dr. Michael
Halcomb, through whom the Lord has blessed me abundantly,
for taking the responsibility for publishing this story
in the English language.

Christo Kulichev

Reprinted
in memory of
Herta Heik Hartmann Viets
(1911 - 2002)

Both Christo Kulichev and the autor, Michael Halcomb,
express their appreciation to Dr. and Mrs. Hermann Viets for
their prayers, encouragement and generosity which made possible
the printing of this second edition of <u>Imprisioned for Christ</u>.

ACKNOWLEDGMENTS

by Michael P. Halcomb

It is both a high honor and a grave responsibility to be chosen by my dear friend Christo Kulichev to write this story, and I'm grateful for his patience and assistance in the task. Christo's godly life and unwavering commitment to Christ have left an indelible mark on my own life. The writing of the story of his imprisonment has allowed Christo and me to know one another very personally. He and his wife, Tzvete, remain, both for me and my family, not only dear friends, but also heroes of the faith.

I must also thank my wife, Bonnie, for whom this book has long been a part of our daily life. Traveling together to various mission fields of the world has changed our lives, and the global friendships gained along the way have enriched us immeasurably.

My additional acknowledgments are far too many to list, but I dare not neglect mentioning a few:

Bob and Pamela Smith were faithful in their prayers and generous support, without which the writing of this book would have been impossible.

Gary and Barbara Zaiser hosted the Kulichevs when the possibility of my writing this story was first proposed by Christo, and they have constantly encouraged and supported the effort in many ways.

Nick and Martha Athanasov were invaluable with their assistance as translators when I traveled in Bulgaria and also in advising me concerning the Slavic culture and the problems facing Christians in Bulgaria.

Panos and Roe Litsikakis first established contact with and introduced me to the evangelical congregational churches of Bulgaria.

Phaedon and Phopho Cambouropolis traveled from their home in Athens with Bonnie and me on our first visit to the Bulgarian churches and also hosted Christo and me when we met in Greece to review the final text of this book.

The process of gathering details of a story played out in another culture with its own language and customs has been more imposing than I anticipated. While I've done my best to eliminate mistakes and misunderstandings, perfection in such things is an unattainable ideal, and I bear full responsibility for any errors that remain.

CONTENTS

INTRODUCTION
by Michael P. Halcomb

It has been granted to you on behalf of Christ not only to believe on him, but also to suffer for him.
PHILIPPIANS 1:29

Dr. Mark Noll, professor of History and Christian Thought at Wheaton College, has stated that the survival of the church under communism will most likely prove to be one of five salient "turning points" for twentieth-century Christianity. He warns, "Superlatives must be used with care in talking about persecution of the church, since the long and varied history of Christianity has witnessed many bloody episodes." Noll goes on to state:

> The turning point in this situation is that Christianity survived. The story of how it survived will never in this life be fully known, for despite heroic efforts by a few chroniclers to preserve an account of oppression (like Aleksandr Solzhenitsyn in his three-volume Gulag Archipelago), most of the slain and much of what was destroyed passed away with no one to notice. What emerges as fragments, partial accounts, and occasionally with full documentation, however, is that the faith survived because traditional Christian words were refined, under deadly pressure, into a living reality of extraordinary purity.[1]

The pages that follow contain the story of Reverend Christo Kulichev, faithful pastor and evangelical leader in Bulgaria. Christo's fidelity to Christ and his willingness to endure suffering have given us a stirring testimony of God's sustaining grace that not only inspires but also instructs. It is an extraordinary story, one worthy of being added to those existing narratives that show what Christians have endured under the oppression of totalitarian regimes. It is a story that could be told of many believers—men, women, and young people— who have shown unusual faithfulness by risking their health, their freedom, and even their lives. Most of all, as Christo Kulichev will

[1] Mark Noll, *Turning Points*, Baker Books; Grand Rapids, Michigan, 1997. Page 312.

humbly tell you, it is a story of God's grace and mercy in sustaining his church.

Annus Mirabilis

On November 10, 1989, I watched with the world as the destruction of the Berlin Wall was televised live around the globe. Momentous change was in the air. As one politician stated, the falling of the Berlin Wall condemned Communism "to the dustbin of history."

The great hinges of history seldom coincide precisely with a new century or millenium. Just as World War I belatedly marked an end to the political constructs and social ideals of the nineteenth century, many have suggested that the crumbling of the Soviet bloc in early 1990 defined a new historical epoch that will carry well into the new millennium.

The fall of the Berlin Wall proved to be a momentous symbolic occasion. It was the beginning of the *Annus Mirabilis*, the year of wonders. Entrenched political systems fell, boundaries changed, and new ideas and aspirations became dominant. While I understood that the fall of Communism marked a new era, I had no comprehension of how these changes would touch my life in a personal way.

The Back Door of Bulgaria

As Secretary of Missions with the National Association of Congregational Christian Churches, I had regular contact with Reverend Panos Litsikakis, an evangelical pastor in northern Greece. In November 1991, Reverend Litsikakis told of stories filtering out of Bulgaria that Protestant churches were still active in spite of one of the most oppressive governments in the Soviet system.

Change was coming slowly to Bulgaria, where Communists had managed to stay in control, limiting political and religious freedom, after the fall of the Berlin Wall. Persecuted harshly for generations and impoverished by the economic meltdown in their country, the faithful Bulgarian Christians wondered if anyone knew or cared about them. In spite of this, they continued to witness to the power of a risen Savior. They were, however, in great need of aid.

Ignoring their own needs and the historic hostility between Greece and Bulgaria,[2] the Greek evangelical churches responded generously. Reverend Litsikakis, his small automobile loaded with clothes and food, made several trips through the Rhodope mountains to dispense aid and

---

[2] This ethnic conflict between the Greeks and Bulgarians had driven Christo Kulichev's parents from their home in Macedonia to Sofia, Bulgaria, in 1913.

spiritual encouragement. To his amazement, he discovered that many evangelical churches in Bulgaria had been established by American Congregational missionaries 150 years before. All ties with Western churches had long been severed, however, when Communism had swept through eastern Europe.

Seeing the door of Bulgaria slowly opening, Reverend Litsikakis invited my wife, Bonnie, and me to accompany him into Bulgaria. Our purpose was to assess the needs and to devise means by which Christians in the West might respond to the slowly growing number of new opportunities for providing support for the Bulgarian Church.

Reverend and Mrs. Phaedon Cambouropolis of Athens accompanied Panos Litsikakis, Bonnie, and me as we drove into Bulgaria. Leaving Panos's home in Alexandroupolos, Greece, we skirted the mountains to the north by driving east to Turkey then circling into the "back door" of Bulgaria.

Bulgaria's back door, the Turkish-Bulgarian border, is the door by which the gospel first reached Bulgaria. In 1831, missionaries who had gone to Istanbul learned of the Bulgarians, then living under Turkish control. These missionaries had quickly sent workers to share the gospel with the Bulgarian people.

Entering the central plain of Bulgaria, we visited church after church in cities such as Hoskovo, Assenovgrad, and Plovdiv. We also spent time in farming villages such as Garvanovo and Seltzi. In each place Christians gathered to greet us with tears of joy for no reason other than that we shared a common faith in Christ. Even though our schedule was already full, other impromptu services were added by churches that wouldn't let us pass without delivering greetings and a sermon. Hunger for fellowship kept us talking and praying into the wee hours of each morning.

Have You Met Christo?

In each place we visited, I was asked, "Have you met Christo?" Each time I indicated that I had not yet met Reverend Kulichev, I was told, "You must meet Christo. He's our leader. He's the one who courageously stood against the Communists, risking his life. He went to prison because of his faith in Christ." One man said, "Our churches might not be here if it had not been for Christo and his brother Dimitar. They urged us to be faithful." Another told us, "Christo and Dimitar Kulichev set up secret youth camps in the mountains. That's where I met my wife!"

It would be a year before I actually met Christo Kulichev and heard firsthand the story of his ministry and imprisonment. He later helped me piece together the many stories we had heard of how the gospel first came to Bulgaria.

A Heritage of Faithfulness

I thought it strange at first that each church I visited in Bulgaria had cracked and yellowing pictures mounted in a prominent place, usually in the lobby or near an entrance. These old pictures, we learned, were of the American missionaries who had brought the gospel to Bulgaria a century and a half earlier. These saints of old had come to Bulgaria and ministered prior to the American Civil War, yet they had not been forgotten by the Bulgarian Christians.

We heard stories of missionaries sent by the American Board of Commissioners for Foreign Missions. In 1819 Reverend and Mrs. Levi Parsons established a mission among the Armenian and Turkish people. William Goudel and Eli Smith then opened a mission station in Tzarigrad, or Constantinople, in 1831. Before long these American missionaries began hearing of other ethnic groups in the region, including the Bulgarians, who had never heard the gospel.

Actual missions work with Bulgarian people began in 1844. The famous Robert College, established in 1840 by Dr. Sirus Hamlin in Babek, Turkey, aided the work by providing a Christian education for Bulgarian students. After Bulgaria was liberated from Turkish rule, three prime ministers and many high officials in the nation's early years were graduates of Robert College.

The Astonishing Story of Dr. Elias Riggs

The story of Dr. Elias Riggs (1810–1901) stands out in Bulgarian history. Dr. Riggs, originally from Providence, New Jersey, first came into contact with the Bulgar people, as they were then called, as a young man in Smyrna (or Izmir), Turkey. He eventually dedicated his life to sharing Christ's love with the Bulgarian people and is known as the first evangelist to the Bulgarians.

The master of twelve languages, Dr. Riggs translated the entire Bible into Armenian, Turkish, and Bulgarian. He also wrote and published the first grammar books for the Bulgarian and Turkish languages, not only helping missionaries learn those languages but also greatly increasing literacy among the people of those countries. He was also the author of a widely used Bible dictionary and a three-volume work on hermeneutics entitled *Interpreting the New Testament*. He even translated 478 hymns into Bulgarian.

He died in 1901 after sixty-nine years of loyal service on this mission field. During that time, he had returned to the United States only once, in 1859, when he was offered the endowed chair of Hebrew language and culture at Union Theological Seminary in New York. He declined it, returning instead to Bulgaria and Turkey. From his mastery of Greek at nine years of age (to which he added Hebrew, Haldaic, Syrian, and Arabic by age eighteen), to his prolific list of publications in Bulgarian and Turkish during his lifetime, the story of Elias Riggs is worthy of a book in itself.

More Stories of Saints from Long Ago

Women played a prominent role in church planting. Long before the suffrage movement, women such as Helena Stone, Agnes Bert, and Inez Abbot were liberated by God's Spirit and did whatever they could to share Christ with Bulgarians. Putting aside their own desires, these godly women distributed Christian literature, trained pastors, taught the Bible, and served as preachers when needed.

In Plovdiv, Christians took us outside of their meetinghouse to see two well-kept tombstones and told us the story of William and Susan Mariam. The Mariams were sent as missionaries to Bulgaria from Boston in 1860. William was on his way home from a conference in the city of Odrin when he was attacked and killed. Susan, expecting their first child, was so stricken with grief that she went into premature labor. Complications arose, and both Susan and the baby died. Although William and Susan died in 1862 at thirty-two years of age, the story of their commitment was related to me with such emotion that it seemed as if it had happened only recently.

It became evident to me that there was good reason for such a solid connection between Bulgarian Christians today and their spiritual forerunners. Deprived by the Communists of Christian fellowship with their contemporaries, especially those abroad, they turned in the only direction they could for human encouragement—the past. Keeping alive their own history, Bulgarian believers found inspiration and exemplary models in those who had first brought the Good News of the gospel to their land.

The Pastors' Trial of 1949

One other historical event needs to be understood to put the story of Christo Kulichev into perspective. The Communists came to power in Bulgaria when Christo and his brother Dimitar were teenagers. They still vividly recall the mass arrests of pastors and church aders on November 4, 1948. The date lives on in infamy! Many vangelical ministers supported by American missions organizations ere arrested and accused of being spies or traitors.

The mass arrests were followed with a showcase trial intended) send a threatening message to anyone inclined to promote Chris- anity. With an efficiency learned from Stalin, the Communists' al was to imprison one person from each congregation, intimidat- g other Christians into silence. Four pastors were quickly given fe sentences in solitary confinement. Fifteen others were given ntences ranging from to six to fifteen years. Many simply disap- eared. Witnesses who did not cooperate were sent to concentration mps.

The mass arrests on November 4, 1948, and the trial that fol- wed in 1949 dealt severe blows to churches in Bulgaria. Christo ulichev told me, "After the trial in 1949, life in Bulgaria resembled ne large prison." To remain faithful to God under those circum- ances, believers had to be willing, at the very least, to sacrifice their ofessions, the education of their children, and the peace of living ithout the constant scrutiny of government agents. Thousands of heralded believers paid an even greater price for their faith in hrist as they were sent to prison or to their graves!

The famous Pastors' Trial of 1949 left an indelible mark upon e lives of young Christo and Dimitar Kulichev. "It was then," hristo told me, "that we resolved to live for Christ and his king- m, regardless of the price."

Evangelical Christians still face problems in Bulgaria, but circum- ances are gradually improving. In November 1999, evangelical urches in Bulgaria marked the fiftieth anniversary of the Pastors' Trial. hose faithful leaders who went to prison and laid down their lives were emorialized with affection and appreciation. The fiftieth anniversary remonies included a memorial service to honor the pastors who were prisoned for their faith in Christ. Todor Kavaldjiev, the vice president Bulgaria, who was once imprisoned by Communists for his politi- l views, spoke at the memorial service, giving thanks for the sacrifices ade by pastors. On a separate occasion, Christo Kulichev was invited meet with the president of Bulgaria.

Rev. Dr. Michael P. Halcomb
Whitefish Bay, Wisconsin
November 4, 1999 (fiftieth anniversary
of "The Pastors' Trial")

————◄◦►————

I give you thanks, Lord Jesus Christ:
In the midst of my trials and suffering
    you have granted me the strength not to waver;
By your mercy, you have given me a share of glory
    eternal.

Lord Jesus Christ, your compassion caused you to
    suffer
    to save the world.
May the heavens open and the angels receive my
    spirit,
    for I am suffering for you and your church in this
    place.
I beseech you, merciful Lord, please take me to
    yourself
and strengthen the faith of your servants who
    remain.

IRENAEUS OF SIRMIUM[3]

---

[3] Irenaeus, bishop of Sirmium (modern day Mitrovica, Serbia), was martyred there c. A.D. 304, under the Roman emperor Diocletian. Taken from *Prayers of the Martyrs,* by Duane W. H. Arnold; Zondervan Publishing House; Grand Rapids, Michigan, 1991, pg. 77.

CHAPTER ONE
Arrested for Preaching Christ

It has been granted to you on behalf of Christ not only to believe
on him, but also to suffer for him, since you are going through the
same struggle you saw I had, and now hear that I still have.
PHILIPPIANS 1:29-30

The only sacrifice is to live outside of the will of God.
AJITH FERNANDO, SRI LANKA

On January 9, 1985, the steel door of Sofia's Central Prison closed behind me with resounding finality. I would soon be locked in a cell with men who were common criminals. This was the beginning of three and one-half years when every movement and activity, indeed my very life, was rigidly controlled by the agents of a repressive atheistic regime. Arrested for preaching Christ and the freedom to worship under his authority, those years were a difficult time for me as well as for my family. But in the midst of the difficulties, God sustained us with his grace and taught us some of the most valuable lessons of our lives.

Enemies of the State

Let me assure you from the beginning that my imprisonment was not because I had done anything immoral or illegal. As is often the case under totalitarian regimes, Bulgaria's prisons and mental institutions were used routinely to hold "prisoners of conscience." A prisoner of conscience, very simply, is anyone who holds views that are different from the state's and has the temerity to talk about those views.

As pastor of the First Evangelical Church of Sofia and president of the Union of Evangelical[1] Churches, I was someone whom the government was eager to replace with their man. They wanted someone who would cooperate with their plan to keep religion under control and out of sight.

My brother Dimitar was also arrested because he was the treasurer of the Union of Evangelical Churches and because he supported me. Our "violation" was that we criticized the government when they tried to control the pulpits of our evangelical churches. This made Dimitar and me "enemies of the state."

[1] In Eastern Europe, "Evangelical" is used to describe not a theological position but all those churches that are from the "free church" tradition.

The Communist government of Bulgaria had established the Committee for Internal Religious Affairs. In spite of what the Bulgarian constitution says about freedom of religion, this committee removed any minister or church leader it disliked and appointed another in their place. The Committee worked hard to maintain absolute control of the churches. There was nothing it disliked more than our belief that Christ—rather than the totalitarian state—was the head of the church.

The Committee on Internal Religious Affairs had been watching my brother Dimitar and me for many years. We had been routinely detained for harsh and lengthy interrogations by government agents. Repeatedly the hours of questioning ended with accusations and threats of dire punishment. Although the interrogations were stressful and a terrible inconvenience, Dimitar and I were nonetheless able to continue our ministry. But not for long.

The government officials were obviously frustrated that we were not intimidated by their tactics. For some time it appeared that they were hesitant to imprison us. Claiming to be the great protector of the people, it was hard for the government to justify arresting us when we had the overwhelming support of our church members. But seeing that intimidation would not work with us, the Committee ended up sending its agents to force their way into the church and put us under arrest.

Article 274

My arrest took place on the morning of January 9, 1985. Chavdar Penkov was the name of the agent assigned to my case. He was a tall man with black hair and a thick mustache that made him appear older than his forty years. Each time I saw Penkov he was dressed in a two-piece suit, usually black. It appeared that he chose his attire to reflect the higher office to which he undoubtedly aspired.

Penkov separated me from my brother and kept me in the interrogation area of the prison for three grueling hours. His goal was to intimidate me into agreeing that the Committee had the right to replace me. Penkov and I sat opposite one another. He busied himself with some paperwork on his desk, but I could see him watching me out of the corner of his eye to see if I was becoming nervous. I sat motionless, fixing my gaze upon him and waiting for him to begin. Finally, Penkov spoke.

"You will be staying here in connection with your activities at the church located on Vasil Kolarov Street in Sofia." He paused, watching me intently, hoping to see some sign of panic, looking for some weakness he could use to break me. Other agents stood near the door, huddled in the hallway, listening to our exchanges.

Penkov finally looked away, still shuffling through the papers that lay on the desk between us. "Before me I have the notice from the Chief Prosecutor ordering us to hold you. I want to warn you, Comrade Kulichev, that signing this protocol does not necessarily mean you are guilty; it only states that we have informed you of the charges for which you are being detained in accordance with Article 274, section II of the criminal code."

Article 274 was unfamiliar to me. Mention of it came as a surprise since I had been threatened with arrest under a different law. During the many long interrogations of the previous few years, one of the agents who questioned me had been Deputy Chief Prosecutor Staikova. Staikova had threatened to charge me with impersonating a minister, using Article 324, which states that it is illegal to impersonate professionals. But now Penkov made no mention of Article 324, which I thought was significant. Perhaps he was aware that my call to preach at First Church was legitimate.

Penkov read Article 274 slowly and deliberately. "It says that anyone who 'willfully undertakes activities as a representative of society, when not properly authorized to do so . . . and in this manner illegally affects public or personal interests, will be deprived of their freedom for one year or given corrective labor.'" He watched to gauge my response.

Christ Is the Head of the Church
The charge Chavdar Penkov was making against me was very general, focusing upon my being "properly authorized," which is not as specific as "impersonating a professional." But I still found this charge surprising in light of the fact that I *had* been properly authorized as pastor by the church congregation.

Finally I spoke. "I will sign that I have been informed of the charges but not that I am guilty. There is no conceivable evidence you can bring against me that will stand up in an open and honest court," I asserted confidently.

Penkov smirked. "All that we're asking is that you recognize the authority of the Committee on Internal Religious Affairs," he reasoned. I sensed that he was playing to the other agents present.

"They want to remove me and put someone else into the pulpit, someone who will help bring the church under their control," I countered. The Committee had been attempting for some time to put their own man, Pavel Ivanov, into the pulpit of the First Evangelical Church of Sofia.

"That is their right," Penkov argued.

"Christ is the head of the church," I insisted, "not the government. You are well aware that our constitution promises freedom of worship. The Committee wants to use Pavel Ivanov to control the church politically, not to encourage it spiritually."

"You have been interfering with the life of the church," Penkov insisted. "Promise not to interfere with Pavel Ivanov and the church, and we could agree to release you!"

"The church has called me to preach God's Word and to encourage the people in their spiritual beliefs. That is precisely what I have been doing. The vote of the congregation, not the vote of the Committee, authorizes me to be their minister. I will never renounce that call because of your threats. That would be to put my own convenience ahead of my call to ministry."

Penkov was not at all interested in the evidence to be used against me. His primary concern was to go through the motions of filing a charge. He wanted to satisfy the procedural requirements so that I could be held while Pavel Ivanov was moved into the pulpit. It was obvious we were at a stalemate.

Orientation to Prison

Seeing that I wasn't going to capitulate and put myself under the Committee's control, Penkov began the orientation to prison life immediately. "You will be put on a special regimen here in the prison," Penkov informed me. "You're to have no contact whatsoever with your family. You will receive no gifts or parcels from them. This applies especially to food. The only food you will receive will be the food served within these walls."

It had long been my practice to maintain a vegetarian diet, not for religious reasons but simply because I felt it was healthier. I told Penkov, "Please bear in mind that I do not eat meat at all."

He seemed very surprised and said to me, "Well, I don't want you to look as if you are on a hunger strike. I will allow you to use the canteen." Penkov told me that my family, though they could not see me or receive mail from me, would be allowed to mail thirty *leva* (about $2.50 U.S.) to my prison account each month. This canteen account would enable me to order a small amount of food to replace the meat that I would not eat. Through it all Penkov watched me to see if I was weakening, but I was resolved never to compromise my beliefs or my principles.

Knowing how sensitive the government could be when it came to the national image presented to the outside world, I informed Penkov that I had performed a marriage ceremony for a couple the previous Sunday. I was scheduled to meet the groom that evening to give him the marriage certificate. Obviously, I wasn't able to keep the appointment because of my arrest. Making the point that this man was a foreigner, I suggested to Penkov, "If he doesn't receive his marriage certificate and learns why I'm being detained, problems could arise."

This new information caused consternation among the other agents present, and Penkov huddled briefly with them outside of the doorway. He finally reentered the room, trying to appear confident and in control. He announced, "You won't have to worry about that. Someone will see to it that the certificate is given to the proper person."

Everything was taken from prisoners upon admission to the prison. The only clothes allowed were nondescript prison clothing—a shirt, jacket, trousers, and underwear—though we were allowed to keep our own shoes after they were inspected. To prevent suicide, the prison officials did not allow any type of metal instruments or even a piece of clothing with a zipper. They also confiscated my belt, which I wore to treat a herniated disk.

As my clothing and personal articles were taken, I turned over what little money I had. It was only about thirty *leva,* but I asked if I could use it to pay for a telephone call to my wife. "I would appreciate it if you would call her to tell her that I am being held but am in good health. I know she must be worried since I've been gone for several hours."

He'll Be Staying Here

The agents had obviously anticipated my request to call my wife. One of those listening in the hallway spoke up. "Your brother has been released. I warned him that you would be held. He'll be in contact with your wife." Penkov watched to see my response. The agent's word could not be trusted, but I later learned that my brother had indeed been released—only to be arrested again later.

"Are you sure?" I asked.

"Yes," the agent replied. "In fact, I took such great pains to inform him about you that I neglected to warn him not to continue his illegal activities lest he wind up back in here with you!" The other agents chuckled.

Overlooking his attempt to sound threatening, I pursued the matter of my wife's anxiety. "My wife will be leaving for work soon, and my brother may be late in getting there. Please, won't you consider my request again? If regulations don't permit me to call her, I would be grateful if you would call her. It'll take only a minute, and I'm offering to pay for it."

Since it was already a little past noon, Penkov relented and called my wife. As he hung up, I thanked him. Penkov drew himself up ever so slightly in stature and for just a moment seemed pleased. Something in his demeanor told me he wasn't as confident as he tried to appear, that he was a man who desperately wanted to feel appreciated and important.

No sooner had I thanked Penkov than the telephone rang. As he began to speak, I realized he was talking to someone familiar with my case. "Yes, he's here with me right now. I was working on his case when you called." There was a pause. "He'll be staying here," Penkov said with finality before hanging up.

My guess was that Staikova, the Deputy Chief Prosecutor who had interrogated me on so many previous occasions, had called. He was undoubtedly interested in finding out if I was going to be cooperative or not. If it was Staikova, and if he was expecting me to agree to their plans for taking control of the church, he must have been disappointed.

The Questioning Begins in Earnest
When the conversation on the telephone concluded, the agents who had been standing around the doorway decided to leave. That left only Penkov and another agent named Vladimir Nikolov in the room with me. I had thought that the previous round of questioning was the extent of my "interview," but there was a surprise in store for me. The questioning was about to begin in earnest.

"Do you mind if we speak informally for a little while, just as friends?" Penkov began, trying to charm me with his dark eyes. I took note of his use of the informal address, only used in the Bulgarian language with someone familiar. Until that point he had used only the formal address. "That would allow us to know one another better and perhaps become closer," he wryly suggested.

"I certainly don't object to talking with you," I replied, using the formal construction again. "But I sincerely doubt it will close the distance between us. At any rate, I certainly hope it won't bring us closer than the distance of the desk between us." Government agents had a reputation for beating and torturing people, and Penkov couldn't possibly have missed the point in my remark.

Penkov looked intently at me, and the atmosphere in the room changed noticeably. His tack in questioning me changed also. Abandoning the soft-spoken, subtle approach, Penkov decided to get directly to the heart of the matter.

He stood and leaned across the desk, his white knuckles pressing upon its surface. "Do you admit your guilt?" he asked.

Dressed in the faded and ill-fitting prison clothes, with Penkov looking condescendingly down upon me, I was conscious of being at a disadvantage in many ways. It was exactly the way he wanted me to feel, but I wasn't going to be intimidated.

"No, I am not guilty," I asserted.

Feigning surprise, Penkov turned to Vladimir Nikolov. "Did you hear that, Comrade? He thinks he's not guilty!" Chuckling, he turned to face me again, then spoke seriously, "But you know that you've been conducting illegal activities in the church."

"My church activities are all related to preaching the gospel of Jesus Christ," I insisted, speaking respectfully yet firmly. "We've been conducting the same ministries for many years, and I've not been alone in leading these activities. There are many fine Christians involved, all of them upstanding citizens in the community. We've done nothing illegal."

As I concluded, the two men glanced at one another. Nikolov had apparently heard enough. Looking knowingly at Penkov, his hand on the door, Nikolov said, "I'll see you later." Nikolov closed the door behind him.

Penkov sat back down. Now he and I were alone.

Your Rights as a Pastor Have Been Taken

Penkov suddenly exclaimed, "You don't have the right to preach from the pulpit!"

"Yes, I certainly do," I said. "The congregation has recognized me as an ordained minister and has called me to be pastor. Besides, our church is a part of the free church tradition, which recognizes the right of a congregation to invite any member of the church to preach if they feel called of God to do so. The Bible tells us that Christ commands us to 'preach the gospel to every creature' (Mark 16:15, KJV)."

Penkov snorted with sarcasm and countered, "I'd be willing to wager that the Bible doesn't say 'to every creature'!"

"Do you think I would be so foolish as to twist the words of Scripture?" I said. "Or make up things that aren't actually found in the Bible? I respect the Bible as God's Word. I can assure you that those are the words used in the Bulgarian translation of the Bible."

Penkov paced back and forth. "But you know that your rights as a pastor have been taken from you."

"No," I stated. "My ordination has never been revoked, and Pavel Ivanov's appointment goes against the constitutions of both our country and the church."

Pavel Ivanov was well known to me. He had been defrocked by his own denomination some years before for adultery. Unscrupulous and ambitious, his servile cooperation with the atheistic government's agents was the only way he could reenter the ministry. Pavel Ivanov was an uneducated but gifted speaker, exactly the kind of person the government could use in controlling the churches. With the government supporting him, he was transferred to first one church and then another—trouble inevitably following him. Ivanov was serving a congregation in Assenovgrad when I became acquainted with him. We had known for months that he was working with the Committee in hopes of being relocated to the larger First Church, where I was minister. In order to ensure that I was doing what the congregation wanted, I offered to step down as pastor when I heard of Ivanov's ambitions. My offer was flatly refused by the church. The people of our congregation not only knew of Pavel Ivanov, they ardently opposed his being in ministry—especially in First Church.

What You Are Saying Is Not True

"The Committee decides what is proper and what is not!" Penkov asserted.

Now that Penkov had brought up the subject of the Committee's conduct, I was more than willing to discuss it. The details of their unscrupulous behavior would press home the point that they were violating my religious liberties and those of the church.

"What you are saying is not true," I said confidently. "My church recognized my calling to preach, and it is a calling that comes from God, not from a government committee. Only the church that has called me can dismiss me or question my right to preach the gospel. That would happen only if I failed to maintain the ethical and moral standards that evangelical churches require of their pastors."

Penkov fidgeted and adjusted his approach once again. "Is it not true that Mr. Tzvetkov called you and your brother before the Committee to tell you they wanted you to step down in favor of another man? Didn't he tell you that he wanted Pavel Ivanov because he is more reasonable and cooperative?" Tzvetkov was the Chairman of the Committee on Internal Religious Affairs, which had been investigating our church.

Penkov was forcing me to walk a fine line. I knew that I dared not show anger, which could bring a harsh reprisal. At the same time, I could not appear to be afraid. Penkov would pounce on any show of weakness and probe relentlessly. The best course was to speak respectfully, choosing words that conveyed an understanding of my rights and a firm commitment to maintaining my principles.

"It's true that we were called before the Committee, but that does not mean that I have lost my rights as a pastor. No written order forbids me to preach. Besides, I will continue to be a minister of the gospel for the rest of my life because God has called me to preach."

Penkov didn't respond, and I continued, "When Tzvetkov told us not to return to the church building, it was only an expression of his own will. His personal wishes do not define a standard of justice by which the congregation can be deprived of its rights! The congregation has the right to call a pastor of their own choosing."

Penkov was growing impatient. "Are you going to force us to document your removal by the Committee?"

"No one has done so up to this point," I insisted. "But even if you were to give me a written order right now demanding that I cease to preach, that would not be right or just. The church has ordained me, and only the church can rescind my right to preach. Put anything you want on paper; we must still talk about justice. We have very clear laws in our country guaranteeing the freedom of conscience and religion."

I'm Asking the Questions Here!

For each point that I made, my antagonist had a rejoinder. It made no difference that his reasoning went far beyond the limits of the constitution itself. "Just because we promise freedom of conscience and religion, does not mean that you can violate the *spirit* of the laws in Bulgaria," Penkov said forcefully. "And let me say another thing: you can be sure we're never going to allow your churches to be a country within a country. If we accepted your interpretation of the constitution, it would make it illegal for us to interfere with activities of which we do not approve! Don't you know you're living in an atheistic state? By now you should know we consider you 'believers' to be enemies of the state!"

"In exactly what way are believers enemies of the state?" I asked Penkov. "Is it by being honest citizens and not lying? We Christians are not thieves or murderers. We seek God's help in building strong, healthy families. Do you really have any evidence that this is causing problems in our society?"

Penkov didn't reply, so I answered for him. "No. It's just the opposite. Since the absence of religious faith has been encouraged by the government, the crime rate has risen steadily all across the land. Your own statistics will force you to admit that there are more people in prison today than at any time in our history. On the other hand, these people called believers, at whom you scoff, are doing their best to fulfill their obligations as good citizens. And you call this enemy activity?"

"I'm asking the questions here!" Penkov loudly interrupted. "You studied at the University and know the teachings of Marxism! Religion and the church have always taken the side of the ruling class. None of you can prove that God even exists!" Penkov was clearly agitated. "In fact, I challenge you to tell me of one person God has been able to help. Can he help me drive a better car than the *Moscvich*[2] I'm driving? Can he give me more money or a better apartment? You say that you believe in God and that he loves you. If that's so, why has he put you here in these miserable circumstances? Why is your God allowing you to be separated from your family if you serve him so well? Look at yourself, man! Your family is suffering out there by themselves, and you're going to suffer here in this prison!"

Turn Your Life Over in Faith to God

Knowing there is great power in Scripture, even when speaking to someone who has no faith, I turned to God's Word in formulating my answer: "The Bible says, 'It has been granted to you on behalf of Christ not only to believe on him, but also to suffer for him' (Philippians 1:29). In another place Jesus Christ himself said, 'Blessed are you when people insult you, persecute you and falsely say all kinds of evil against you because of me' (Matthew 5:11).

"You know that I'm not here as a common thief or murderer. You know I'm not a threat to society. I've been arrested solely for preaching the gospel. It frustrates the Committee because I trust faithfully in the teachings of God's Word even in the face of threats against the church, my family, and myself. As a Christian, I'm willing to suffer for Christ—even die for my faith if necessary. I'll gladly bear suffering that comes as a result of preaching Christ as Lord. My purpose in living is to bring glory to God."

Penkov had a strange look of disbelief on his face, but he said nothing.

I continued, "The reason I have no fear of your threats is because

---

[2] *Moscvich* was the name of a popular Soviet-made au tomobile in Eastern Europe, a very common and economical model.

the Bible promises that when Christians witness in Christ's name, even in the presence of powerful leaders or kings, God will give us the words to say. He will also give us the courage to speak those words."

To my amazement Penkov allowed me to continue. Expecting him to stop me at any second, I decided to risk speaking to him about his own personal responsibility before God.

"Perhaps God has brought me here before you today to speak with you about eternal life. From the depths of my heart, I feel an urge to say this: someday each one of us will be asked to stand before God and give an account for our lives.

"How will you answer? Whether you believe in God right now or not, the Bible says there will come a time when you will stand before him as he judges you. There will be no excuse for your unbelief, because I'm giving you an opportunity right now. I'm asking you to turn your life over in faith to the God who created you and loves you. Why would you want to continue in your unbelief and risk spending eternity in hell?"

Finally Penkov spoke. Rather than being belligerent, as I expected, he was almost philosophical. "Do you really believe in a life after death?"

"Oh, yes, I do," I replied. "It would be easier for me to doubt that I'm here before you now than to doubt the promises of God's Word. The Bible tells us that eternal life is given to those who believe. God wants to call everyone into relationship with himself, but he has given us free will and does not force us. When we die our decision will stand for eternity, and I know that I will go to be with God in what the Bible calls 'heaven.'"

Pavel Ivanov Is Our Man
Perhaps some seed of faith was planted by my attempt to witness to this man. Only God knows what happened in his heart. It was interesting that he didn't try to refute what I said but suddenly changed the subject away from faith and back to the Committee. "Listen, Christo. Why are you complicating this matter? Why don't you just make it easy on yourself and agree to allow Pavel Ivanov to take your place in the church as the Committee has decided?"

"The decision of who may best serve the church as pastor is not mine to make," I responded. "That's a decision that must be made by the people of the congregation. Churches of the free tradition are guided by democratic principles. It's been that way for over a hundred years, since the first day the free churches were established in Bulgaria.

Why have you and the Committee on Internal Religious Affairs suddenly decided that it's time to destroy this time-honored principle? By forcing this man Ivanov upon us, you're not only attacking these highly respected principles that have guided us well, but you are also raising a question of trust. As a result, our people are asking, 'Can our own government be trusted to treat us with proper respect?'"

"Do you really believe that?" Penkov responded.

"That's precisely where the conflict lies," I answered. "I've been preaching the gospel for thirty years, and the people have respected my leadership. I've been held in esteem in this church for ten years. My conduct has not changed. Now you're trying to convince me, after all of this time, that I'm somehow breaking the laws of the country?"

"We're protecting the public interests," Penkov insisted.

"Be honest!" I shot back. "Your only concern is that I've become an obstacle to the Committee because I don't believe their propaganda and won't cooperate with their political objectives. The Committee professes to be concerned about the will of the people, and yet I've been removed and Pavel Ivanov appointed without an election! All of this is against the will of the people."

"Still, Pavel Ivanov is our man," Penkov said. "We trust him. He will cooperate with us, and you don't want to do that." He stood and moved toward the door.

"Certainly not," I said. "As a Christian pastor, it is not my job to cooperate with you. My responsibility is to do the will of Christ, who is my Savior and the Lord of the church. That is why Jesus said, 'No man can serve two masters' (Matthew 6:24, KJV)."

Penkov motioned for me to leave. Finally the long interrogation was over.

CHAPTER TWO
Central Prison of Sofia

*But in everything and in every way we show that we truly are
God's servants. We have always been patient, though we have had
a lot of trouble, suffering, and hard times. We have been beaten,
put in jail. . . . We have been punished, but never killed,
and we are always happy, even in times of suffering.*
2 CORINTHIANS 6:4-5, 9-10 (CEV)

*Jesus did not come to explain away suffering or remove it.
He came to fill it with his Presence.*
PAUL CLAUDEL

When the guards escorted me into the dank confines of the cell block, I immediately noticed the stench of human waste. The silence was broken only by occasional whispers, the footsteps of pacing prisoners, and someone's hacking cough. Probing eyes appeared in peepholes on the doors—the metal covers cracked ajar just wide enough to provide a glimpse—watching as we passed cell after cell.

Cell 74 was already "home" to two other inmates, both younger than me. They introduced themselves as Mitko and Raijko. Hearing Mitko's name reminded me of my brother-in-law, also named Mitko. My two cellmates immediately asked why I was in prison. Eager to establish my identity as a Christian, I told them I was an evangelical pastor.

From the first hour of my imprisonment, I spoke openly of my faith in Jesus Christ. "As Savior and Lord, he died for our sins and rose again to give us new life," I told them. "Christ has changed my life, and I live according to his gospel. Because I preached these things, the government found me to be inconvenient and put me in prison. They've now appointed their own representative to the pulpit of my church."

"That's the only reason you're here?" Raijko asked incredulously. "Why didn't you just cooperate, the way the other guy is doing? Then you wouldn't be in prison!"

"That's what the agents proposed," I responded, "but I can't accept it. To stop practicing Christian beliefs in my daily living and then stand in the pulpit to tell people things that aren't true would make me a hypocrite."

Mitko and Rajko found it hard to believe I would rather be in prison and remain faithful to Christ than be outside and know I was a hypocrite. I explained I would rather be spiritually free, even if it means going to prison, than walk the streets while living a lie. It's difficult for people without faith to understand such things. As Scripture says, "The foolishness of God is wiser than man's wisdom, and the weakness of God is stronger than man's strength" (1 Corinthians 1:25).

The Pecking Order

Much has been written about the Central Prison in Sofia, all of it bad. But the greater part of the sordid history of this gray, aging prison may never be known, since a large number of those who entered it never came out alive. Many prisoners left their bones in Central Prison, and even the ones who did leave lost their health there. The temptation to sacrifice honor and dignity to preserve one's life in Central Prison was great, but many of those who did were haunted forever with memories of their cowardice and fear.

For most prisoners, the dehumanizing treatment began the first hour of imprisonment and quickly instilled deep feelings of fear and anger. Family relationships were abruptly severed. Worse, we were totally dependent upon our captors for everything. The short haircut and drab prison garb made prisoners look alike, stripping away individual identity and eroding self-esteem. Once we were dressed in the institutional garb, we were treated as less than human. Even during the initial interrogation, we prisoners weren't allowed to use words such as *comrade*, ordinarily used in Bulgarian society as a polite form of address. In these and many other subtle ways, our captors left no doubt in our minds that we were no longer a part of society.

With at least three people sharing a small cell, there was absolutely no privacy in the prison. There was no room for furniture of any kind.

Each of my two cellmates had his own mattress on the floor, and they were surprised to see I had been given one also. Most cells had three prisoners sharing two mattresses. I had also been given two blankets, one to cover the mattress and the other to cover myself.

The outside temperatures averaged well below freezing that January in Sofia, and many of the prison windows were cracked or broken. Cold drafts infiltrated the cells. Two blankets weren't sufficient to keep me warm, but I dared not complain, knowing that my mattress would most likely be taken away if I called for a guard.

There were many prison traditions about which I soon learned. I learned the first on my very first night: the newcomer slept nearest the door. This "pecking order" was established because the bucket used for relieving bodily wastes was kept near the door. Those who had been in the cell longest insisted they had the right to sleep as far from the bucket—and its smell—as possible. The newcomer was also charged with emptying the bucket during trips to the toilet area, which occurred once a day. Prior to my arrival in Cell 74, this responsibility had been Raijko's; it was now mine.

I accepted my humble position, finding that sleeping close to the door had at least one advantage: there was a bit more room near the door, and I preferred having only one neighbor. Later, when other prisoners were brought to our cell, I kept the position closest to the door and bucket, knowing that others were repulsed by it.

I Can Rest Here

On that first night in the cell, I prepared my humble bed, thinking of my wife, Tzvete, and our two children, Stefan and Nebesna. As has been my lifetime commitment, I knelt to say a brief prayer, asking for God's blessing and protection over them and me.

Reflecting upon my situation, in spite of the obvious discomfort and uncertainties ahead, I found cause to give thanks to God for positive things. As I reclined and tried to relax after a very tense day, I said aloud, more to myself than to anyone, "I've been dreaming of having time to rest. I can rest here."

My cellmates may have thought I was insane; at best they certainly must have been surprised at my statement. But it was the truth. I had been living under enormous physical and emotional pressure. My time had been spent overseeing the welfare of many churches in our fellowship throughout Bulgaria. Sometimes I would be gone from home for several days at a time, maintaining contact with the churches.

For years Dimitar and I had been committed to sharing the gospel with as many young people as possible, knowing they would carry our Christian witness into the future. Youth work is demanding. There were countless visits to the parents, encouraging them to openly acknowledge their Christian commitment so that the youth would have healthy spiritual models at home. In addition, we organized and led youth camps, retreats, and fellowship opportunities.

All of these commitments were added to my pastoral responsibilities at the church in Sofia. Through it all we endured the agents' harassment, the horrible interrogations, and the stressful conflict with the government about who was going to lead the church.

My family and I had lived for years with the uncertainty about if and when my arrest might take place. I, along with some of the other church leaders, had been under twenty-four-hour surveillance for months at a time. Government agents had been staked out in a black car across the street from my home. I was followed everywhere I went.

The congregation of First Church was united in resisting the Committee's efforts to take control of the church. We had carefully planned what we had to do and had thoroughly considered the consequences. Each member knew that opposing the Committee could mean prison. Our joint commitment was to be faithful to Christ, protecting our church from outside control. When it became known that the unprincipled Pavel Ivanov was seeking to take over the pulpit, that commitment deepened.

In the winter church leaders wore two or three layers of clothing when leaving home—in case they were arrested. The warmth of the additional clothing in a freezing prison cell could mean the difference between life and death.

But now many of those uncertainties had been settled. The arrest was behind me, and I was in prison. I prayed God would give me the rest I needed. Undoubtedly there would be tests ahead, but I knew God was with me and had a purpose for my being here. With those thoughts offered up as a prayer to God, I fell asleep in spite of the alien noises of the prison around me.

A Piece of Blue Sky

In the morning I awoke and looked around the cell more carefully. Having worked in construction to support myself in ministry for many years, I was interested in how the cell was constructed. Since it was an old prison, no artificial materials had been used. One advantage was the use of wooden floorboards, which provided excellent insulation from the cold concrete floor. My experienced eye told me that our cell was approximately six feet wide by twelve feet long, just enough space for three small mattresses on the floor. In the middle of the short wall was the doorway, which opened inwards, encroaching even more into our limited space when the guards swung it open.

In the corner nearest the door was the infamous bucket for our toilet needs, with only a flimsy cover on it. Across the room in another corner, we stored our shoes, a container of warm drinking water, and usually some bread hoarded to give us something to eat between sparse meals.

Regulations permitted us to arrange the cell as we wished, but options were limited with no furniture and so few basic necessities. We did have one window opposite the door, approximately thirty-two inches wide and twenty-four inches high, but of course there was a heavy steel grate on the outside to prevent escape.

The window in our cell was not cracked or broken, so our cell was not as cold as some were. We occasionally braved the freezing air outside and opened the window a crack, trying to catch a few breaths of fresh air and escape the horrible odors permeating the prison. Through the window we could see a small patch of sky. Other prisoners considered this a luxury, since some cells had windows facing another wall or an enclosed area. The prisoners often talked about wanting to see "a piece of blue sky."

A Higher Freedom

One of my most vivid impressions upon entering the cell in Central Prison was the graffiti scratched upon the walls. One particular message, words penned by a poet named Petefi, declared, "I would give my life for love, but I would give love for freedom."

Prisoners spent a great deal of time thinking about freedom. As a Christian pastor, I spent hours in Central Prison reflecting upon the nature of freedom and what it meant to me personally. Losing my social and political freedom made me realize that the most precious kind of freedom is spiritual.

Freedom for most prisoners meant the ability to move without restrictions, to go where they liked, to eat and drink with friends and family, and to enjoy an intimate relationship with their spouses. Some defined freedom as a life without restrictions or limitations. I came to see very quickly how superficial and shallow such a definition of freedom was.

Ironically, I observed that those who had lived a lawless life were the ones who found prison the hardest. Accustomed to controlling their lives, they were now unable to control even the most personal aspects of their daily routine. Once enslaved to their sins and vices, they found it hard to be confined and unable to fulfill the desires of the flesh.

Prison taught me that there was something more precious than freedom of movement: spiritual liberty. Because I had freedom of spirit, I could rejoice in the thought that God was present even in the ugly bowels of a dank prison. I enjoyed a feeling of well-being, of *shalom,* or inner peace. Neither the wardens nor my fellow inmates could understand this inner peace, for, as Paul wrote, it flows from "the deep things of God" (1 Corinthians 2:10). It is not from "the wisdom of this age or of the rulers of this age, who are coming to nothing" (1 Corinthians 2:6).

Retaining that inner peace became my primary objective, and I knew it required remaining faithful to God. From the beginning, I immersed myself in God's grace, allowing the thought of His nearness to fill my heart with the peace that passes all understanding. I would need that peace, for there were severe tests ahead.

We Must Obey God Rather Than Men

The members of the First Evanglical Church of Sofia stood firmly behind Dimitar and me in our activities of evangelizing, teaching young people, and visiting the churches. The government did everything it could to block such activities, understanding that without evangelism and fellowship the churches would soon die.

Courageously, members of First Church supported these ministries even in the face of threats made against them and their families. Government agents had done everything they could to coerce the congregation into turning against us and embracing Pavel Ivanov. Obligated to the Committee, Ivanov would help them control the church. If they could control First Church, a leading evangelical congregation, they could control many smaller churches as well.

In the end their strategies of intimidating and discrediting us failed, and the Committee was reduced to physically breaking down the doors of the church building and arresting Dimitar and me.

The freedom of religion advocated by the Communist regime was a false freedom. While they insisted that Christians were free to worship and believe as they wished, they were actually protecting only the right to hold silent beliefs. As many Christians discovered, no protection was offered for those who chose to practice the Christian faith. Christians were free to believe anything they wished as long as they didn't *act* upon their beliefs. Any attempts to witness or do good works in the name of Christ were met immediately with repressive measures.

In one sense Penkov and the other government agents were theologically perceptive. They recognized that religious beliefs were a threat only when they influenced everyday behavior. As long as belief in God didn't lead to obeying God, there was no conflict with the state. But when a person's conduct became shaped by God's authority, the authority of the government was threatened. It was when Peter and the apostles said "We must obey God rather than men!" (Acts

5:29) that they met persecution. In the same way, our obedience to God's Word brought my brother Dimitar and me into conflict with the Communist authorities.

Once our captors had us in prison, they did their best to brand us as guilty of criminal offenses. Their propaganda machine helped spread the word that we were "enemies of the state." This helped obscure the fact that we were Christians suffering persecution.

We were often accused by our interrogators of being unpatriotic, but that was not true. Both Dimitar and I loved our country very much. Bulgaria was the land of our birth, a beautiful land with great potential. Our family had always had great appreciation for the Slavic language and culture. We appreciated the struggle that had brought Bulgaria its own national identity. Like all of the Christians in Bulgaria, we strove to be good citizens. But our love for Christ and his kingdom was far greater than any earthly love. We believed that living by the principles of Christ's kingdom was best for us, for our families, and for our beloved country as well. We prayed regularly for our country and for the people of Bulgaria, but we could not comply with a government that denied the existence of God.

State officials, our interrogators reminded us, had declared that by the year 2000 there would be no more Christian churches in Communist Bulgaria. They hoped the pronouncement would discourage us so that we would stop resisting. To the contrary, we were willing, if necessary, to put our lives on the line to demonstrate our faith in an omnipotent God who promised his church that "all the powers of hell will not conquer it" (Matthew 16:18, NLT).

Prisons and Palaces

My two cellmates provided an interesting study in contrasting personalities. Mitko was thin and wiry, a restless young man, almost hyperactive at times. He had been in prison longest—almost four months now. His impulsive behavior would bring harsh discipline upon all of us from time to time, but Mitko had a good heart, and I could not help but feel compassion for him. He had been in the military at the time of his arrest. In an act typical of his impulsive behavior, he had attempted to shoplift some liquor to use in celebrating the New Year while he was on furlough.

Raijko, on the other hand, had a rather cool, stoic personality. He was older than Mitko and quieter; he was married with four children and seemed more mature. He had been in prison for three months at the time of my arrest. Raijko had been arrested when a small amount of silver disappeared from the manufacturing plant where he was employed. He was harshly treated by his interrogators, who promised that Raijko would be released if only he would give the name of the person to whom he had given the silver. Exhausted and desperate, Raijko gave the agents a name, thinking it would get him out of the spotlight. When the person Raijko had named didn't lead the police to the silver, they insisted upon holding Raijko. Since they had gotten a confession out of him, this put Raijko in an impossible situation. "What I told them wasn't true," he said repeatedly, "because I didn't take any silver. I just wanted them to leave me alone!" He seemed deeply distraught by it all, and he often broke down when he spoke of his wife and four daughters.

The walls of our cell were rough in texture. Undoubtedly they had been built this way in a largely unsuccessful attempt to prevent prisoners from writing upon them. They had been painted long ago with some yellowish color that now seemed to be melting under the light of the forty-watt bulb. The light was on twenty-four hours a day, which became irritating both to the eyes and the nervous system. While lying down, I always kept my eyes closed to provide a respite from the glare of the bare bulb in our little confined space.

As I lay in that small cell, one of my favorite disciplines was to mentally work my way through the songbook of our church, recalling as many hymns as I could. Music has a way of getting down into the crevices of my soul, touching the tender spots. It had a healing effect during the long days in prison. Faintly humming the familiar tunes, I found that in some instances I could recall several verses. For some favorites, I could even recall the page number. For instance, hymn 182 was especially meaningful and comforting. It goes like this:

> The one whose hope is in the Lord,
>   will be solid as Mount Zion.
> Just as the Holy City
>   is surrounded with woods,
> so are we surrounded with grace when we believe
>   in God.

Another of the songs that often came to mind has a refrain that says:

> Without his grace, palaces lose their beauty,
>   but when I'm with Christ, even a prison becomes
>   a palace.

I tried daily to put into practice the truths and spiritual principles contained in these and other precious songs. More than anything else, I knew it was essential to maintain my spiritual principles. Scripture and inspiring music were needed to bolster my will if I was going to withstand the onslaught of abuse from the guards and interrogators who were determined to break me down. The abuse brought most prisoners to agree with anything the agents demanded, as Raijko had done.

The Broad and Narrow Paths

Some Christians tried to work with the atheistic government, only to find themselves confused and then defeated. One compromise inevitably led to another until no principle was sacred. Those who racked their brains trying to strike a compromise with the world or who drained themselves emotionally trying to maintain a secret Christian identity, chose a very difficult path and soon found themselves trapped. Seeking the broad path, they soon discovered it wasn't as easy as some people promised. The trap they had walked into led inevitably to the destruction of both personal identity and true Christian principles.

Evangelical leaders in Bulgaria learned early in 1949 that life was more fulfilling, and faith more meaningful, when lived solely by the principles of God's Word. There could be no compromise on basic truths such as the lordship of Christ and the commission to be his witnesses. It was far healthier, even when persecuted, to simply trust God's promises, channeling intellect and energy toward maintaining one's fidelity to Christ. They learned that living for God's glory is always better than living for one's own convenience.

Dimitar and I had decided as young men that we would obey God rather than men. We would not abandon young people searching for truth just because giving religious instruction to youths was against the government's wishes. Though the government told us that Christians could not minister to physical needs, we couldn't ignore those in poverty and still call ourselves true Christians. Forbidden to speak of Christ outside of the walls of our meetinghouse, we knew that compliance would lead to lives of hypocrisy.

With unjust policies such as these, the government sought to divorce faith from action and beliefs from life. Anyone who puts Christian living ahead of the government's wishes was persecuted. Communist leaders used a list of forbidden activities to separate active believers from nominal Christians, branding the former as criminals. Nevertheless, we knew it was our duty to "act justly and to love mercy and to walk humbly with [our] God" (Micah 6:8), even if the system made us suffer for it.

Coded Messages

Though the walls of the prison cells were mostly very rough, the surface had been worn smooth in some places. I quickly discovered that this smoothness was caused by inmates tapping out messages in code to one another. Though it was a violation of the strict prison rules, the code established a fragile line of communication with other human beings. Besides, it was an interesting way to alleviate the oppressive boredom that quickly became a major factor for any prisoner. At first, a prisoner would knock a few times to get the attention of an inmate in the adjoining cell. An answering knock indicated a willingness to communicate.

The code was not terribly sophisticated; it was simply one knock for each letter in the alphabet. For example, to spell out the word *me,* a prisoner would rap thirteen times on the wall for the letter *M,* pause for a moment, then rap five more times for the letter *E.*

Some prisoners became so adept at interpreting the code that they could count and interpret the number of knocks without consciously thinking about it. When I listened, I usually just recited the letters of the alphabet along with the knocks, waiting to see which letter would be the last when the sound stopped. It was surprising how rapidly news could spread through the prison population using this very primitive communication system.

The War of Wills

After only a few days of confinement, I realized that my case was going to proceed very slowly. The interrogators considered time to be their ally. One of their favorite strategies was to simply let a prisoner "rot" in the cell, leaving him to wonder day after day what was happening with family and loved ones, speculating day after day about his future. Mounting anxiety, I soon observed, caused most inmates to begin asking about their case or even requesting to see their interrogators. This was an obvious sign to the prosecutors that a prisoner was "ripe" and perhaps ready to cooperate.

As the days passed, I suspected that this strategy was being used on me. My initial interview with Chavdar Penkov had not gone well from his perspective, and he very likely was looking for a way to make me more compliant. There were times, I must admit, when I wondered whether Penkov intended ever to meet with me again. There certainly was no indication that my case would ever be allowed to come to trial. After several days of waiting and wondering, I understood why some prisoners felt abandoned and depressed.

Prisoners at Central Prison learned quickly that the obvious intent of those operating the prison was to strip away all personal worth and identity in an attempt to gain the prisoners' cooperation. Everything from the squalid conditions to the sounds of torture routinely carried out on the dreaded second floor was designed to induce fear and break the will. Using this strategy, the wardens, interrogators, and guards hoped to gain total control over each prisoner for their own purposes.

This systematic attack on one's personal worth, combined with the feelings of abandonment and helplessness, could shatter a person's emotional balance. If it were not for my faith—knowing that God was with me and had a purpose for my life—I think I would have lost all hope.

Days went by, and still there was no word from Penkov about my case. He apparently hoped that after enough time, I would become desperate and ask to see him. That kind of uncertainty was almost impossible to live with, and it destroyed many prisoners' resolve. Sometimes I caught my thoughts wandering to when I might be called or worrying about what might happen if I was interrogated. Each time this happened, I forced myself to think of something else, resolving with God's help to remain calm and not to crumble under such tactics.

The mind games the agents played with prisoners were nothing short of psychological assault. Most prisoners in Central Prison, I learned, anticipated the physical mistreatment common in Bulgarian prisons. Just as destructive, I felt, was the psychological pressure that could shatter a person's psyche just as effectively as the beatings shattered bones. Physical abuse and torture was intermittent, but mental and spiritual stress was constant. Torture could force a victim to tell the truth or to lie in an attempt to avoid further pain, but when a prisoner's inner world crumbled under the emotional strain, he lost the ability to discern lies from the truth, to distinguish reality from unreality. I warned other prisoners to protect their personal honor and human dignity at all costs.

The days passed painfully slowly. Penkov never called for me, and no one gave any indication of what was going to happen. All I could do was wait, pray, and prepare myself. The test of wills had begun.

You Must Be the Object of Their Interest

Time lost all meaning in prison. Any fragment of news or communication with another human being became very significant. Knocking on the walls, as I have said, was strictly prohibited under threat of severe punishment, but it was hard to catch someone in the act. Mitko, especially, couldn't resist trying to communicate with other prisoners. Fortunately, the acoustics of the prison were such that it was difficult to tell where the sounds came from as the guards stood in the hallway.

Whistling and singing were also severely punished, not only because they could be used to convey information or conceal illegal activities, but simply because they alleviated the boredom. Even boredom was used by the agents since it could quickly lead to a sense of abandonment which, in turn, escalated into mounting anxiety about one's family and fate. Interrogators used this anxiety as a tool in their efforts to try to break a prisoner's will and make him compliant.

The guards were instructed to enforce absolute silence in the prison. One guard told me that when he worked in the prison at Plovdiv, one of the prisoners whistled repeatedly. "He got what he deserved," the guard said in a threatening way, implying that the prisoner was beaten or tortured. We knew from experience that it was no idle threat. The same guard told me we were fortunate to have a window in our cell, since the new prison in Plovdiv had no windows for admitting fresh air or sunlight. He described only a small opening above the door, allowing a minimum of air to circulate, and a sole light bulb surrounded by wire netting in each cell.

The walls of our cells were thick, almost two feet, I estimated. The steel door had a small peephole in the upper portion of the door covered by a sliding metal cover that could only be opened or closed from the outside. The security guards used these peepholes to observe the prisoners and their behavior. One night I did not sleep but used the quiet hours of the night to think and pray silently. This evidently did not go unnoticed, since the guard asked me the next morning, "Why didn't you sleep?"

Every movement was dictated. It was forbidden to stand to the side of the door since we would then be partially out of the guard's sight. We always had to be within full view of the peephole and could not turn our backs to the guards, since we might be doing something illegal and screening it from their view.

One day Raijko and Mitko were taken away, apparently for interrogation. It was not uncommon for prisoners to be taken away suddenly and without explanation, but it always sent a ripple of suspense among the prisoners held in that area of the prison.

While I was alone in the cell for several hours, the metal cover over the peephole scraped open and shut time after time. I thought this was strange and mentioned it to my cellmates when they returned. Raijko and Mitko said that they had been held in another part of the building but hadn't been interrogated.

The fact that I was closely observed while my cellmates were gone made it clear that someone was interested in me or perhaps trying to make me nervous about what was happening. Raising his eyebrows, Raijko said, "They've never checked on our cell so often before. You must be the object of their interest."

Strategies for Survival

Once a day we were taken to the toilet area. Even there our movements were strictly limited, and we were forbidden any form of communication that might relieve the boredom. The guards kicked or beat prisoners who took more than a minute or two in the toilet area. Prisoners tried to organize so as to take advantage of the minimal toilet break since it provided the only relief from confinement in the small cells.

Sometimes the prisoners played a game during the toilet break. While most of the prisoners moved as deliberately as they dared, using the toilet, cleaning out the bucket, and filling up the container of water, one prisoner would rush back to his cell. While the guards shouted and beat the slower prisoners in the toilet area, the other prisoner would quickly open the metal cover over the peephole while his cell door was open. When the other prisoners were back in their cells and the door was closed, they had a few seconds to look out of the peephole, observing the prisoners and guards in the corridor. It was such a simple thing, yet it was often the only form of entertainment we could manage in a day. The guards were always quick to lock our door and abruptly close the metal cover, plunging us back into the cramped, dreary world of the cell.

Strange as it may seem, we never completely lost our sense of humor in that dismal setting. At least there were little things that seemed to be funny to us at the time they happened. My cellmate Mitko, always impulsive, tried constantly to open the metal cover of the peephole in our cell's door, hoping to enlarge our world a little bit. Usually there was nothing of consequence to see, but it provided a diversion. One day Mitko was peering out just as the guard came to look in at us. Even a little incident such as that gave us occasion to laugh and joke about a guard finally "seeing eye to eye" with us.

Eventually the guard on duty became angry at Mitko for tampering with the cover, so he took a hammer and put on a heavier cover that couldn't be opened from the inside. Thus our only form of diversion abruptly ended.

Looking back, it is astonishing that humor of any kind existed in such a depressing place. Granted, there was little to laugh about in Central Prison, but when humor did surface, even for a few seconds, it signaled the survival of the human spirit. Prisoners found little things to joke about, such as red tomatoes being the favorite Communist food. Thus, humor was a psychological weapon that helped us in our fight for self-preservation. Humor helped us to rise above our situation briefly, to see things from a different perspective. The smallest chuckle or briefest smile helped make life bearable.

A true story circulated about a man imprisoned for telling jokes that put the party in a bad light. The poor man was finally released after a year in prison just for telling jokes. Prisoners put a humorous twist on the story, saying that when the man went to his dentist to have his teeth checked, the dentist leaned over him and said, "Open your mouth, please." The man's response: "Not on your life!"

It's Important for a Man to Be Patient

Food was passed through an opening in the middle of each cell's door. The opening was closed at all times except when food was being delivered. When it became damaged by overuse and could not be opened at all, as had happened in our case, the guards were forced to open the door to hand us our small share of food for the day.

When opening our cell door, the guards always stepped aside, quickly handing us the food tray from a position to one side of the doorway. It was painfully obvious that they didn't want to breathe the foul air that came from our overpopulated cell. We had no choice but to live with the offensive odors day and night. Sometimes the stench became so bad that the guards would bark at us, "Open that window!"

We did try to keep the window open as much as possible. Much of the time, however, the air outside was so cold that we were forced to close the window after a brief time and endure the offensive prison odors. In such a confined space, sometimes occupied by three, four, or even five men, these polluted conditions were unavoidable.

The window in our small cell gave us more than just a look at "a piece of blue sky"; it was also used, whenever possible, for communication with the prisoners on either side of us. The window was set above our heads, and the thickness of the wall formed a space just large enough for a small person to perch precariously, clinging to the grating outside the window.

Mitko was obsessed with jumping onto the windowsill to whisper to the inmates in the next cell. This was dangerous because if the guards caught a prisoner communicating with the occupants of another cell, the guards would make the offender pay dearly. It wasn't uncommon for them to administer beatings or to put prisoners into solitary confinement for such an offense. But the problem the guards faced was tracing the conversations and catching the culprits in the act.

Mitko even developed a creative technique for exchanging items with prisoners in the adjacent cell. This wasn't easy because it involved working through a section of the steel grating outside the window. Mitko had gathered enough thread from various materials, such as clothing and mattresses, that he had been able to braid a sort of crude rope. With this rope he was soon exchanging bread, ballpoint pens, and even larger items such as the pages of books or newspapers. Cigarettes and matches were by far the most desirable commodities, but they were hard to acquire. With such deprivation, these small items accrued great value among prisoners who lacked the smallest of things taken for granted by most people.

When we heard footsteps in the corridor, we would motion hurriedly to Mitko, and he would jump down from the windowsill as quickly and quietly as possible. With silence strictly imposed upon us, even the sound of his feet hitting the floor could be heard some distance away.

One night Mitko managed to grasp some matches and cigarettes just as the footsteps approached. He jumped down from the sill just as the guard opened the metal cover to the observation port. Mitko wasn't caught in the act, but it was obvious the guard had become suspicious; for several minutes he came back repeatedly to look through the hole.

Mitko had succeeded in concealing the rope in his clothing before the guard arrived but hadn't had time to wind it up and hide it with the cigarettes and matches. Raijko and I tried to convince him to wait until the guard's suspicions were allayed, but Mitko was too impatient.

Between visits from the guard, Mitko frantically tried to wind up the crude rope and hide it. Although he did it with his back to the door, the guard knew something was happening and began to open the door. By the time the door was open, Mitko had somehow managed to conceal the rope, but the guard was all over him.

At first Mitko tried to convince the guard that there was nothing hidden in our cell, but before long he realized how foolish he had been. When the guard insisted that "the thing" be turned over, Mitko realized it would be better to lose his precious rope than to risk having our cell searched. He had already hidden other contraband, and the guards probably would remove the parcels of food we were saving if they conducted a search.

With so little room and even less psychological space in our small cell, emotions ran high at moments of risk such as this. It would do no good to get angry at the young man, even for his obvious stupidity. Exercising restraint, I indulged myself in one brief comment, saying, "It's very important for a man to learn to be patient."

In this particular instance, all of us were very fortunate. The guard didn't become abusive or pull Mitko out of the cell for disciplinary action. He only confiscated the rope along with Mitko's precious cigarettes and matches. Perhaps the guard was preoccupied with other concerns at the time. Or, with cigarettes at such a premium, perhaps he felt confiscating them was punishment enough. It could have been much worse for all of us.

Don't Give In to the Fear!

A week passed, and I continued to adjust to the horrible prison conditions. Without a doubt my family would have tried to arrange for bail after my arrest, but after a week it was obvious that bail had been denied.

The denial of bail revealed how seriously the government was taking my case. With the prisons of Bulgaria already overcrowded, bail was almost routinely granted, sometimes allowing dangerous criminals to walk the streets until their case came to court. Criminals were sometimes even granted bail after being convicted and sentenced until space opened up in a prison.

While it was apparent that the agents had denied my bail, there was still no word about my case. I couldn't help but wonder if and when I was going to be called. It was obvious that Chavdar Penkov was playing games with me. But while many prisoners eventually succumbed to the pressure and agreed to whatever their agent suggested, I resolved, with God's help, never to crumble under their tactics. I prayed daily that God would help me remain calm.

My relationships with Raijko and Mitko continued to develop. In spite of the strain put upon relationships in such a small cell, there was a strong sense of solidarity that developed between the three of us.

One evening a guard heard Mitko whispering in his window perch and came to investigate. Mitko jumped down and assumed an innocent posture. The guard wasn't fooled. He demanded to know the identity of the guilty party. When we refused to tell him, he tried to intimidate us by saying, "It's minus eighteen degrees outside, you know." When we still wouldn't talk, he ordered us to open the window and leave it open through the night.

The cold air swirled through the small cell, seeming to come at us from all sides. We jogged briskly in place and did calisthenics to keep from freezing to death. After a couple of hours, we were exhausted and huddled in a corner to one side of the window, hoping to get away from the deadly draft. It was no use.

It was undoubtedly the coldest night of my entire life. At one point during the night, Mitko said, "I can't go on! I'll report myself to the guard and take my punishment. It would be better than having all of us freeze to death because of what I did."

In spite of Mitko's risky behavior, my heart went out to him. "You'll do nothing of the kind," I replied. "If we don't break under the pressure, the guard can't keep it up forever. Confess, and he'll take you out of the cell; it's hard to tell what he'll do when you're alone. Don't give up! We'll survive."

Mitko didn't report himself, but the worst was yet to come. When we thought the guard wasn't looking, we tried wrapping ourselves in the threadbare blankets and shielding ourselves from the cold wind with the mattresses. But the guard returned in just a few seconds and commanded us to pile the blankets and mattresses in one corner and go across the cell to the opposite corner.

"Wow, we're sure to freeze now, brothers," said Raijko.

"Don't give in to the fear!" I answered. "It's not that easy to die. And don't groan! It just makes the guard happy."

"Let me give myself up!" Mitko said again.

"You will not give up, and neither will we!" I insisted. "Keep moving!"

"How long have we been standing?" asked Raijko.

"I have no idea," I told him. "But as you can see, we're not dead yet. We will survive!"

Christo, Your God Did Help Us!

I was doing my best to encourage Mitko and Raijko, to keep our solidarity intact, but I realized the situation was becoming worse. The cold wind could strip the hide off an ox. We paced back and forth, and while urging my cellmates to not give up, I was also silently praying that God would help us endure the torture. I prayed that God would give us patience and peace, and that he would somehow work in the hardened heart of the guard who was doing this to us.

After what seemed like an eternity, I realized the guard was watching us through the peephole. Finally we heard him say, "All right. Close that window and go to sleep. And remember, the next time it could be worse."

As we closed the window, I couldn't help saying a grateful thank you to the guard before the metal cover rasped to a close. The three of us huddled together, trying to bring warmth to our frozen bodies in the last hour before dawn. Both Mitko and Raijko managed to smile at me.

There's a kind of negative happiness one experiences at such times. It's not at all the positive joy that comes when something good happens, but a kind of euphoria that comes when extreme suffering has finally stopped. It's the happiness of relief that comes after facing frozen death squarely in the face and then beginning to feel warmth creep back into tissue and muscles. As we were warming ourselves, Mitko said, "Well, Christo, your God did help us!"

Those Who Will Not Work Shall Not Eat

There was a heightened concern for health in the squalid and over-crowded conditions of Bulgarian prisons. Vital to one's health was the food, which in the Central Prison of Sofia was barely enough to sustain life.

While being processed in the induction area, I had overheard a comment that gave me an idea of what I would be facing as far as diet was concerned. A prisoner next to me was complaining that the prison trousers were too small at the waist. "Don't worry," the guard had said. "In a few days they'll fit just fine."

Prison officials operated on the principle, often quoted in socialist cultures, that "those who do not work shall not eat." This is a perversion of the biblical principle mentioned by Paul when he wrote, "Anyone unwilling to work should not eat" (2 Thessalonians 3:10, NRSV). Since the prisoners in Central Prison were not productive, it was assumed they didn't deserve anything more than a minimal amount of food. Therefore, we were given just enough food to sustain life.

Each day we were given half a loaf of black bread, usually at lunchtime. It had to last not only through lunch and dinner but also through breakfast the next day. Breakfast usually consisted of a piece of cheese three inches long by two inches wide and half an inch thick. On some days we were given a piece of pressed marmalade the same size instead. Occasionally we might be given a small piece of butter or perhaps two boiled eggs or a spoonful of jam to put on the bread from the night before. Lunch almost always was a small serving of rice and chicken, and once a week we might be given two meatballs. There were times when we were given fried fish or cucumbers, but the latter were usually so salty they were impossible to eat. Dinner was usually a small serving of pasta or some bland soup. If the soup tasted like bean soup, we knew that we would never find a bean in it. Occasionally, there was a stew I looked forward to eating, and once each week we were given yogurt, which was like a feast for me.

The food was always of inferior quality. The marmalade was especially bad and was rumored to have come from Vietnam. In an attempt to strengthen the economy in the Soviet bloc, each nation was required to use products from other Communist countries. These imported items were of poor quality, and Bulgarians routinely used sarcasm, speaking as if these foods were considered a luxury in the country of origin. Prisoners sneered when calling the marmalade "Vietnamese chocolate."

Because of the strict vegetarian diet that I had kept over the years, it was easier for me to survive on the sparse prison fare than it was for many others. For those accustomed to eating like gluttons, our diet was sheer torture. Seeing this, I was grateful that I had disciplined my eating habits so that I wasn't a slave to my appetite. Whenever we were given meat, I gave mine to Raijko and Mitko.

To make up for the meat I didn't eat, the prison had allowed me to set up an account to purchase additional food from the canteen. This account allowed me to order a small packet of cheese or butter, or perhaps small biscuits or waffles, if available. Whatever I ordered would be delivered to the cell by a guard and had to last me a full week. Even though the food from the canteen was intended to replace the meat I gave to Mitko and Raijko, I shared the canteen supplies with them as well. They were younger and had bigger appetites, and my heart went out to them. Even though I was generous with them, I noticed they occasionally couldn't resist sneaking some of my biscuits when I was out of the cell. To keep the peace, I didn't complain but often thought to myself, "The sinner cannot hide his nature."

Poignant Messages

One of the ways prisoners communicated with one another was using the tinfoil covering the yogurt containers. Prisoners quickly discovered that when rolled tightly, the tinfoil formed a slender instrument that was excellent for writing on the ceramic tiles in the toilet area.

Some of the messages were simple attempts to establish contact with other lonely humans: "My name is Stambolov, and I'm in Cell 111." Other messages were warnings: "Rakovski is frying," meaning that prisoners were attempting to ostracize someone believed to be an informer. "Ivan has started to sing" was an indication that the prisoner named was cooperating with the guards by telling all that he knew. But there were also very touching and poignant messages with addresses and telephone numbers given in hope that prisoners about to be released would pass information along to loved ones outside of the prison walls.

A Crosscutting Effect

When we went to the toilet area once each day, in addition to using the toilet and cleaning out the bucket, we were supposed to wash ourselves, fill our canister with drinking water, and wash our plates and spoons in the brief time allowed. Conditions were such that it was impossible to do all of this in the time allotted. To make things worse, we were never given toilet paper and had only one small water pipe coming out of the wall where we washed.

While struggling with these poor conditions, I realized it could be worse. At least we had water. My wife had once told me of an acquaintance who, while in prison, had hardly ever had water to wash herself. We had water in Central Prison, even though it was always ice cold.

The guards were constantly shouting in the toilet area, "Come on, there's no more time. How long do we have to wait? Move!" Prisoners who didn't jump at a command, or at least noticeably step up their pace, were threatened with a beating. More than once we were kicked or received a blow or two across the back from the guard's billy club.

With the guards constantly shouting instructions, every minute we were allowed in the toilet area was rushed. Since everyone in the cell was sent to the toilets at the same time, each person had to know what to do and when to do it. In instances where four or five people were pushed together in one cell, it was impossible for everyone to use the two toilets, wash, and clean the plates and spoons before being rushed back to the cell. Prisoners who didn't have time to use the toilet had to resort to using the stinking bucket, emptying it the next time they were allowed out of the cell. Some considered this even more degrading than abuse at the hands of the guards.

The constant abuse by the guards, when combined with the prolonged neglect of the interrogators, had a crosscutting effect that could fell the most macho of men. It resulted in a kind of institutionalization that actually seemed to change the personality of inmates. Some came into prison angry and fighting but a few days later fell into such a sullen state that they hardly lifted their gaze from the floor. Others arrived strong and determined to defend their rights, only to be transformed a week later into a shell of a human being, broken and depressed.

Prisoners who insisted at first that they were innocent usually reached a point in a few days where they were willing to confess anything if offered hope of a sentence at one of the minimum-security labor camps. Anything was better than staying at Central Prison.

The Mold of the Mighty Institution

Central Prison required all of the spiritual strength and resolve at my disposal. It was only by God's grace that I was kept from being pressed into the mold of the mighty institution around me.

I still heard nothing from Penkov or prison officials about my case, but with God's help I refused to become desperate and ask to see them. I was determined not to yield to their tactics, since they would view this as a sign of weakness.

The psychological abuse took its toll on many inmates. In spite of precautions taken to prevent suicide, there still were men desperate enough to attempt taking their own lives in any way possible. Some tried harming themselves with the plastic spoons and plates. Others broke off small pieces of ceramic tiles and swallowed them.

Deprived of the right to read, write, sing, whistle, or even to know what time it was, the only thing allowed in Central Prison was to lie quietly in the cell. There was an expression in Sofia, "He was lying in prison" or "When I was lying in prison," and that was exactly what we did. In most other prisons in Bulgaria, prisoners were put to work and didn't have to lie around their cells all day. Any form of work was preferable to inactivity; our confinement was a particularly cruel form of punishment. In the Central Prison of Sofia, waiting for interrogation, lying down became a way of life.

The only right they couldn't take away was the right to think. I determined quickly that I would do everything to prevent them from depriving me of that very precious gift. My persecutors could control my body and the surrounding environment, but I vowed they would not control my mental posture. Throughout the long days and endless nights when I did not feel like sleeping, I gave myself to the disciplines of prayer and patterning my thoughts. Thinking a concept through logically and in detail helped me maintain my mental acuity rather than lapse into inactivity that could lead to a numbing depression.

My disciplined thought life was also an important part of maintaining my spiritual resolve. Rather than just killing time, I used every precious moment for thinking, praying, or meditating upon Scripture passages I had memorized. I always tried to focus upon praising the Lord.

A Protective Wall

I knew it was unlikely that Penkov had forgotten about me—more likely than not he was playing the waiting game—but I knew with certainty that God had not forgotten about me. That important realization helped give me emotional and mental stability during the long wait.

In addition to my spiritual buoyancy, there were little things that reminded me that God was present throughout everything I faced in prison. For instance, my sinuses had given me trouble in winter for many years. There had been many a winter night that I could hardly sleep because my breathing was so restricted. Miraculously, I didn't catch a cold that entire winter in Central Prison, not even when we were forced to open the window in sub-zero temperatures. It was just one small sign assuring me that God was indeed present with me in that cell.

It was as if God's grace had formed a protective wall around me those first days in Central Prison, keeping me from being overwhelmed by the harsh circumstances. Never before had I so fully understood what it meant to rely only upon the Lord. It was as if I were swimming in God's grace.

Each night as I knelt to pray, and again each morning as I prayed upon rising, I gave thanks to the Lord Jesus Christ for his protective hand. I had my health and a peace of mind that was incomprehensible in light of the circumstances. Most of all, I praised God that my faith was strong. Knowing that much suffering was yet to come, I prayed that God would use that suffering to make my faith stronger.

CHAPTER THREE
A Father's Faith

*In this you greatly rejoice, though now for a little while you may
have had to suffer grief in all kinds of trials. These have come so
that your faith—of greater worth than gold, which perishes even
though refined by fire—may be proved genuine and may result
in praise, glory and honor when Jesus Christ is revealed.*

I PETER 1:6–7

*There is no Christian hope except that which is born at the
resurrection out of darkness and travail of being crucified with Christ.
Those who do not know that defeat do not know that hope.*

DIETRICH BONHOEFFER

Throughout my prison experience I thought repeatedly of my
parents and their teachings, reflecting often upon my upbring-
ing. In many ways I could see how God had worked through
my parents to prepare me for this rigorous test of my faith. Without the
nurture and love given by my mother and father, instilling the principles
of Scripture as they did, I could not have endured the prison experience.

During World War II, when I was growing up, life was extremely
difficult in Bulgaria—as in most of Europe. I recall my mother having
few of the coupons used in food rationing. We needed them to buy sta-
ples such as bread. It was a difficult time for my parents, trying to raise
growing boys during a time of shortage. Their faith, however, shone
like a diamond in that bleak setting.

Godly Examples
My brothers, Georgi and Dimitar, and I spent most of our time in
school those days, so we were allotted the smallest portions of bread.
Even though we were in class most of the day, we still came home from
school and worked long hours with our father, helping him build
houses. Of course, as growing boys, we could have eaten as much as any
adult.

As long as I live, I'll recall some days when our family of five sat
down to eat with only half a loaf of bread on the table. Our custom was
to stand while saying grace. I vividly recall my father's fervent prayers
over those scant meals, thanking the Lord for providing for our needs
and asking that he bless our food.

We didn't have much during those years, but God did provide. Inexplicable things happened that were marvelous in the eyes of a young boy, things that taught me that God would always meet my needs. I recall one day when all of us had eaten and were satisfied. Miraculously, there were still a few scraps remaining on the table.

On August 28, 1943, there was a church fair held on our street. The date sticks in my memory because the Orthodox church near our home always celebrated the ascension of the Madonna at that time. As I played in the street, I noticed an unfamiliar man driving a cart and a team of horses down the street. He stopped in front of our home. When I approached, he asked, "Where does Christo Kulichev live?" He was referring to my father, after whom I was named.

"Here, in this house," I replied, offering to go and get my father.

As I went into the house, I noticed that the man had dismounted and was beginning to unload something from his cart. When I returned with my father a minute or two later, the stranger had mounted the cart and was gone again! He had left behind some straw, which we used to heat our home, and a small sack of flour. There was no opportunity to offer payment or even to say thank you for those precious gifts.

To a young boy it seemed that Father anticipated the event, since he constantly spoke of how God cares for us. Although I look back today and see how naive I was, such incidents demonstrated the truth of what my parents had taught us about the reality of God's presence.

Other events from my childhood still stand out in my mind. For instance, there was a trolley that ran down the middle of our street in Sofia. The trolley stop was at the end of our block, near a cemetery. There was a bakery nearby, and it was always full of people either waiting for the trolley or stepping in briefly to purchase something.

Father knew the man who owned the bakery since his family had immigrated from Macedonia, as had Father with his parents. One day we had no bread in the house because of the rationing. Father decided to go to the bakery and ask for credit, hoping a fellow refugee might have compassion and allow him to take a loaf and bring a coupon later. Understandably, Father felt uneasy asking a favor, even in hard times. He was an upright man whose faith made him want to help others rather than ask for help.

Nevertheless, Father resolved to go ahead with his plan. He had just stepped through the door of the shop when the baker took some bread from the oven. Father told later of standing quietly near the door, waiting for the other people to leave so that he could speak to the baker alone. As he stood there silently, the baker, without any hesitation, looked directly at my father and said, "Come, take your bread."

When Father stepped up to the counter, the baker gave him two warm loaves of bread. Anyone looking on probably assumed that Father had given the baker coupons, but he had not. The exchange was over in an instant, and Father left, still not having said anything except a quick thank-you. Later he told us about this mysterious gift.

After work the next day, Father took what little money he and Mother could scrape together and went back to pay for the bread. When he and the baker were alone, Father asked, "Did you know when I came to your shop yesterday that I was coming to ask for bread on credit?"

"I had no idea," the baker said. "But when you came in, it was as though a voice spoke and told me to give you those two loaves. Please, whenever you're in need of bread, come, and I'll give it to you!"

More Light and Truth

Father had immigrated in 1913 with my grandparents, from the village of Gorno Brodi[3] in Macedonia. They were forced to leave Gorno Brodi because of the ongoing conflict between the Bulgarians, Greeks, and Serbs in that area. The move ended Father's formal education after a few years of elementary school, but he went on to become a self-educated man.

Father's family settled in the village of Rozovo, in the south of Bulgaria. It was there that he fell in love with Dimitra Angelova, who was to become my mother. All three of us boys were born in Rozovo.

It was also in Rozovo that a priest gave Father a Bible. Father was ill at the time, and the local priest brought an Orthodox Bible that had just been published. Father read it eagerly, and his life was profoundly changed. He always told us it was then that he began to crave for "more light and truth."

It was my parents' search for light and truth that led our family to move to Sofia. In a large city such as Sofia, it was also easier for Father to find work. More importantly, he and Mother found Christian fellowship. Looking for a church that preached the gospel and offered sound teaching for their sons, my parents finally settled upon the First Evangelical Church of Sofia. Little did I suspect as a small child that someday I would become the pastor of that church.

[3] This village is now in Greek territory and is known by the name Anu Vrondu. It is close to the city of Seres in northwestern Greece.

A Fledgling Faith

Father's exemplary Christian life touched everyone with whom he came into contact. He prayed and read his Bible daily, and it was evident in his conversation. When he spoke of his faith in Christ, there was a radiance about him that told others that his faith was real. Father always conducted himself with integrity both at home and in the community. Father was a carpenter, and my brothers and I often worked alongside him when we were on break from high school or the University. Watching him work among the other men, I saw the trust and respect they had for him. It was common knowledge that we quit work early on Wednesday to go to the prayer meeting at our church.

Evangelical Christians were a minority, persecuted in Bulgaria even then, but that didn't keep Father from speaking openly of his Christian beliefs. He was imprisoned briefly in 1938 for boldly witnessing to members of the Orthodox church, the dominant religion at that time.

Occupied by the Nazis during World War II, Sofia was attacked by Allied bombers. The bombs partially destroyed the First Evangelical Church, and Father invited the church to move into our home as necessary. The authorities, however, suspected that evangelical Christians were spies since our church had been started by American and British missionaries.

Those were difficult times. Old enough to understand that Father was being watched by the police, I once heard him say, "God will preserve my life as long as he has a purpose for me on this earth. Even if they put a gun to my head, nothing will come out of the muzzle unless he allows it."

I can't give a specific date when I accepted Christ as Lord of my life, but Father's love of the Lord certainly played a large part in my owning the Christian faith early in life. His commitment to Christ was contagious, and his sons caught it.

My fledgling faith was soon put to the test. One formative experience occurred when I was fourteen years old. Near the end of World War II, a friend of Father's brought construction materials to help rebuild the church building. He suggested to my parents that I return with him to his village of Ladzhene, where it would be safer. I recall his using the phrase "let him come have his fill of grapes," which is a Bulgarian expression describing the good country life.

That was my first separation from family. While I enjoyed playing with the children in the village, it wasn't long before I became homesick. When I asked to go back to my home in Sofia, my hosts tried to persuade me to stay longer. The war made things unpredictable and dangerous.

Determined to go home, even if I had to walk, I persisted until they agreed to send me by bus. Father's friend took me to a nearby bus station the next day, explaining that if I ran into any problems I was to return to his house. By this time Bulgaria had sided with the Allies against Germany, and the roads and railways were clogged with refugees returning to Sofia. Bus after bus came and went, each one overflowing with people and their possessions. It was clear there wouldn't be room on the public buses that day and probably not for several days.

No one paid any attention to the lonely child sitting at the side of the crowded street. Determined to find a way home, I dug down into my baggage and pulled out a small Bible my parents had given me. Clutching it, I prayed as only a child can: "Dear Lord, help me return to my family. You know I do not want to stay here. Please, Lord, show me the way to go home."

Looking up, I saw that a large truck had stopped in front of me, filled with people and their belongings. To my amazement, on top of the cargo was a man we called Uncle Miho, a close friend of the family who often visited us in Sofia! When I called out to him, Uncle Miho looked down and exclaimed, "Little Christo, what are you doing here?"

"I'm alone and trying to get back to my family in Sofia," I said desperately.

"Give me your hand, son," he said, pulling me and my baggage up and over the truck railing despite the loud protests of other passengers. That answer to my childish prayer gave me a powerful sense of God's care that has stayed with me throughout my life.

Don't Doubt in the Darkness

Powerful memories of God's presence and blessing in my life helped me to maintain my confidence in prison. Experience had taught me that God would never abandon those who trusted him. Even if I didn't fully understand a particular situation, I always knew God would use me and my circumstances for his glory. After all, Jesus said, "Don't be troubled or afraid" (John 14:27, NLT) and "I am with you always, even to the end of the age" (Matthew 28:20, NLT).

During the difficult times of imprisonment, I never doubted that God was with me every step of the way. A person of deep convictions, I had already resolved to stick to my principles regardless of the cost. I would not doubt in the darkness what God had taught in the light.

This commitment to stick to my principles raised some interesting issues: my vegetarianism, for example. Even though being a vegetarian is not a spiritual conviction for me, I felt it was psychologically important to be consistent. I would stand by all of my convictions, whether they pertained to food or to more important spiritual matters. If I began to compromise in one area, it would be easier to give in on other matters.

Survival in prison is mainly about willpower and withstanding the abuse your captors bring to bear upon body, soul, mind, and spirit. Resolving to keep a vegetarian diet was a practical way of reminding myself that my strength came from God. It also served as a constant reminder to the prison officials and my cellmates that I wouldn't be defeated by psychological tactics.

As often as possible, I told the guards and interrogators that my trust was in the Lord. "Whatever happens to me," I assured them, "even if you take my life, God will use it for his glory." This Christian worldview reminded them that their control over me was limited and temporary. God was in complete control, whether they acknowledged him or not.

When the food tray was delivered to our cell, the amount of food was always inadequate and of low quality. My prayer before eating would often go like this: "Lord, when the people in the crowd were hungry, you used just five loaves of bread and two fish to feed 5,000 people. Here I am, only one. If it is your will, you can feed me with just a few crumbs. Whatever is given, I accept it as a gift from you. Please multiply it and make it enough to nourish my body and my spirit."

It was indeed a miracle that during all of those months I was able to maintain my diet and never become sick. Prisoners around me who didn't know Christ and the security he brings complained constantly. Some actually groaned with hunger pains. It was truly by God's grace that when those around me were obsessed with food and complaining of hunger, I never felt the pain or found myself unable to concentrate because of hunger.

Consistency Is Absolutely Important

Observing the behavior of Mitko, Raijko, and other inmates, I never ceased to be amazed at the drama and tragedy one can find in human behavior. Even though silence was enforced, the drama was played out through whispered conversations and messages tapped out on the walls. For instance, one minute Mitko would be lamenting his foolishness in stealing property. A few minutes later, he was talking of a robbery he planned to pull off when he got out of prison.

The capacity the prisoners had, especially under stress, to rationalize their behavior was evident. The temptation for them was to make themselves gods, trying always to control their environment or take advantage of changing situations. Decisions were not made according to what was right or wrong, but by what might be gained. Tragically, applying this standard consistently resulted in inner chaos.

In my capacity as pastor at First Church, I saw some believers make the same mistake. They rationalized their behavior, trying to insure their own comfort or convenience. It began subtly. The pressure to distance themselves from the church was constant, since Christians were underemployed or unemployed if they expressed their beliefs. Frightened by the persecution, some believers disappeared from church and suddenly become silent about their faith. Rationalizing the compromise, they would ask "What else could I do?" or say "I had no choice!"

But they did have another choice, as was made clear by the guilt and defensiveness that inevitably followed. Once a person ceased to trust God and tried to control events by compromising with the secular world, life became more confused and unsettled. As I observed, giving in on one's personal principles usually led to the compromise of religious convictions until nothing was sacred. Eventually one's sense of identity came into question.

The alternative for me was to live by faith, putting my life under God's control and making decisions based upon the unchanging principles of his Word. This approach risked conflict with the world, but it gave purpose to my life along with inner peace and stability. I knew that once my Christian principles were abandoned, I would quickly be adrift on the sea of confused values, changing moods, and inconsistent behavior that surrounded me.

There were times in Central Prison when I was tempted to compromise on some small issue. Certainly I could compromise on some things, such as my diet, without letting it affect my religious beliefs. But what was logically true was not always practically wise. That single compromise, I realized, wouldn't improve my situation appreciably. It would, however, be noticed and would mark me as one who would succumb to pressure if faced with suffering.

Consistency was absolutely important. Daily disciplines such as praying before meals or maintaining a vegetarian diet were foundational to maintaining my integrity in that situation. These visible commitments were indicators that kept me spiritually and emotionally on course and also signaled to others around me that nothing in this world could cause me to deviate from my principles.

Only to Be Faithful

Prison also taught me that we don't always see what God is doing. It may appear in the midst of suffering as though God has abandoned us, but he is always working on our behalf.

During the early days of my imprisonment, a great deal of time was spent thinking about Joseph, who remained faithful to God during his exile and imprisonment in Egypt. Joseph could have rationalized and said, "My brothers sold me into slavery; there's nothing I can do but become like the Egyptians." He could have rationalized his unbelief in self-pity—and that would have been the end of Joseph's story!

It was because Joseph remained faithful to his beliefs that God used him to bless Potiphar's house and then all of Egypt. Rather than being changed by the surrounding culture, Joseph asked God to make him a positive influence within that culture. God then placed Joseph in a position where he could come to the rescue when his family was threatened by famine. Instead of bitterness about his exile and imprisonment, Joseph's faith made it possible for him to say to his brothers, "You intended to harm me, but God intended it for good" (Genesis 50:20).

Joseph's faithfulness should remind us that if we are faithful, even in hard times that we don't understand, God can use us. Living by faith, we can touch other people in ways we may never fully understand in this life. It's not our job to understand—only to be faithful.

Seventh Deadly Chamber

It's one thing to feel determined to stand by one's principles while in the comfort of one's home, surrounded by a supportive family. It's another thing altogether to maintain an unwavering commitment to one's convictions in a harsh prison environment, especially with the ghastly sounds that resonated through Central Prison at night.

Somewhere above my cell on the second floor of the prison, was a place commonly called the "Seventh Deadly Chamber." Its name came from the fact that it was the seventh cell on the floor. Horrible sounds constantly emanated from that chamber.

Prisoners sentenced to death were held on the second floor of the prison, and apparently every possible means of extracting information from them was used before execution. It was common to hear muffled beating and kicking accompanied by screams. We could hear cries of "Help!" and "Have mercy!" but the beatings continued.

The torture often went on for hours. When the interrogators quit, we would hear the crying and moaning of battered victims left to suffer alone, contemplating when their torturers might return to begin again. Some whispered that those put to death were the lucky ones. "At least they're no longer suffering," some would say.

Other options were open to guards who wanted to punish or torture prisoners. Another special cell for punishment was called the "Dynapren Room." Its walls were covered with a thick layer of neoprene padding called Dynapren. The padding served as an acoustical blanket to suppress sound. The guards took prisoners to this special cell for beatings or solitary confinement, sometimes for the most trivial things.

Although I would later be held in solitary confinement, I was fortunate never to see the Dynapren Room. Prisoners who did spend time there said it was as if they were cut off from the outside world. They could neither hear nor be heard by those around them, resulting in a feeling of absolute aloneness. It was a known fact that torture was conducted in this cell, but all kinds of inhumane devices and diabolical ways of inflicting pain were used in other cells as well.

The sounds of torture had a depressing psychological effect upon the prisoners, each one knowing they might be summoned next. Raijko told Mitko and me one night that he had been taken to the Dynapren Room and that the interrogators had played recordings of previous tortures. Raijko heard the heart-stopping screams of the victims. "Do you hear that?" one of the agents asked, leaning over him. "You are next if you do not tell us what we want to hear!"

Lingering Too Long at an Oasis

Life in the prison was bleak and depressing. Occasions for human contact or conversation were few and far between. Only one guard actually conversed with me in any meaningful way, and that was because he wanted to speak English and had discovered that I knew the language.

One morning the sergeant of the guard was tending to business near our cell, and for just a few minutes I could hear him whistling an aria from *Traviata*. Although his performance left much to be desired aesthetically, the aria provided a brief, refreshing reminder of another world and another culture out there, a world where beauty nourished the soul and culture ennobled life.

As the familiar tune wafted past the door of my cell, I found myself drifting into a reverie that took me back in time. Prior to my arrest my wife, Tzvete, and I had watched a TV program on the life of Verde, the composer of *Traviata*. Lengthy excerpts of Verde's compositions, including *Traviata*, had illustrated his work and life. We had enjoyed it immensely and for the next several days found ourselves humming the scores of *Traviata* and other works by Verde.

These warm and wonderful memories took my mind and spirit out of the prison for a time. But such a reverie could be indulged for only a brief time. Lingering too long at an oasis such as that was dangerous. Tempting as it was to savor such things, one could soon lose touch by drifting into a world that was only a fantasy in Central Prison.

The occasional memories of beauty and warmth were from a time long ago and far away from the realities facing me in Cell 74. My thoughts and feelings had to be brought back to face my situation so that I would be prepared when Penkov summoned me.

Why Haven't You Been Asking for Me?

Finally, after eight days of waiting, Penkov did call without warning for a second interview in the dreaded interrogation room. The days of waiting had seemed like an eternity to me. I was always careful to keep track of the date, and I remember that it was on January 17. There was no way of telling time in the prison, but I noticed it was 2:40 P.M. when I entered the interrogation room.

The written report of this interrogation, which I saw later at the time of my trial, was surprisingly short. Let me assure you, however, that the conversation itself was not.

No sooner had I entered the room than Penkov looked at me with a rather puzzled look and queried, "Why haven't you been asking for me?"

Looking him squarely in the eye, I responded calmly, "Why should I ask for you? You put me into the cell, and I didn't think you would forget where you left me. I assumed you would call when you wanted me."

The news that Penkov brought, if true, was not good. He began by telling me, "Your brother is in prison again. Your son-in-law, Toshko, and his friend Emanuel Tinev have also been sentenced to fifteen days' hard labor in a brick factory. Their charges were reduced to 'petty hooliganism,' or they would have been given longer sentences."

My feelings upon hearing the news were mixed. Toshko and Emanuel were two of the most committed young leaders in the church. Their arrest would be another blow for the people of the congregation to absorb. On the other hand, their arrest was an indication that the congregation wasn't giving in to the pressure of the Committee to accept Pavel Ivanov as their pastor.

Obviously the resistance had continued, or these arrests wouldn't have been made. Ivanov may have thought his control of the situation would be absolute with Dimitar and me in prison. He surely had learned otherwise by now.

Penkov continued by telling me about Dimitar Shishkov, a member of the church. "Shishkov refused to sign the agreement we asked him to sign, but after I left him in the waiting room awhile, he changed his mind. He came around voluntarily and told me, 'Comrade Penkov, after thinking it over, I've decided to sign the agreement and not oppose the Committee any longer.'" Chavdar Penkov paused with a look of satisfaction on his face. "Don't you see that all of your people are either being arrested or are deserting you?"

"What do you mean by 'my people?'" I responded. "My concern is not with who is committed to me or not committed to me. My only concern is for Christ and my faithfulness in serving him. I put all of my trust in Christ, not in other people. Besides, just because you intimidated Dimitar Shishkov into signing your document doesn't mean he'll actively support Pavel Ivanov."

Guilty until Proven Innocent

Penkov used every means possible in that interrogation to convince me that I was absolutely alone; he tried to persuade me that there was no one I could count on, that it was nonsense to even think of continuing my opposition to the Committee.

As in my first interrogation, I held firm, insisting that the right to preach had never been officially taken from me by the Committee and that no written accusations had ever been issued. Speaking respectfully yet firmly to Penkov, I stressed again, "Your arresting me for preaching the gospel of Jesus Christ is not right or legal, either for me or the church."

Penkov retorted, "If you're not guilty, you'll be able to prove it."

I countered with the obvious, "But how can I prove it when you are keeping me locked up and depriving me of every opportunity?"

Penkov said with finality, "You'll have the opportunity to defend yourself in court. Then you'll not be able to say that you had no opportunity." Penkov now launched into an explanation of Bulgarian legal procedures. He claimed that the court would dutifully weigh all of the facts and supporting documents in the case and then would render what he termed "a complete and carefully considered verdict."

"Since everyone can be assured of such thorough consideration of their case," he concluded, "any innocent person need not worry about the outcome of his trial. That is why I've been as busy as a beaver collecting everything related to your trial and putting it here in your file. As you can see, it's very thick." His tone was threatening.

Wanting to let him know that I accepted neither the assumption of a fair trial nor the fairness of the "evidence" he was collecting, I 'took the risk of bringing up a sensitive issue. I asked, "What about the case of Trajcho Kostov?"

Trajcho Kostov, a leader in the Communist party, had been accused of spying. After his trial and execution (some months prior to my arrest), evidence came to light proving his innocence. The government was unable to suppress the truth of this horrible miscarriage of justice, and word of it soon spread to every corner of the land. It was a terrible embarrassment to the party as well as government officials and judges involved in the case.

"That was a mistake of the court!" Penkov shot back.

"And someday you will find that what you're doing to my brother and me is another mistake of the court," I asserted.

Later, Penkov brought up the topic of my being a vegetarian. His brief mention of the fact that I wasn't eating meat would have later implications, as I would soon see.

While in prison, I realized the aim of every interrogator was not to learn the truth but to convince the prisoner of his guilt. The agent's sole desire was to bring the prisoner under his absolute control, to the point where the prisoner was willing to agree with everything the interrogator said. If an interrogator could get a prisoner to say "I admit my guilt," even partially, then he knew he had the prisoner under his control.

In Bulgarian prisons the accused were presumed guilty and looked upon as common criminals from the moment they stepped into the prison system. Interrogators felt no obligation to prove guilt. It was the responsibility of the accused to prove their innocence beyond any shadow of doubt. "Guilty until proven innocent" prevails, in spite of the fact that Bulgarian law (Article 83) states that "the task of proving the allegation lies upon the chief of justice, and upon those who conducted the original arrest and interrogation." In the same context, the law says "the one who is arrested does not need to prove his innocence."

Wrestling and Letting Go

At one point in this lengthy meeting, Penkov brought up the subject of my wife. It wasn't until later that I realized that he was trying to get to me psychologically. After mentioning the possibility of a trial in a rather offhand way, Penkov suggested that perhaps I could speak with my wife so that she could find a lawyer to defend me.

Of course I was eager to see my dear Tzvete. When he mentioned the possibility of talking to her, I assumed he would allow a visit or, at the very least, give me an opportunity to call her on the telephone. As I discovered later, Penkov had no intention of allowing a meeting with any family members.

Returning to my cell after the meeting with Penkov, I found myself thinking constantly of my wife and the hope of speaking with her. That night I dreamed of her and then suddenly awoke. My mind sorted through all the possibilities. *Will he contact her tomorrow? No, that is Friday, and she will be at work. Perhaps on Saturday, when she won't be working. Or maybe next week . . .*

After several hours of building up my hopes in regard to a possible visit with my wife, it suddenly occurred to me that this was precisely what Penkov wanted. The more I focused on my family, expending emotional energy hoping and worrying, the less strength and concentration I would have to resist Penkov's agenda. Wrestling with something I couldn't control was foolish. I had to let go.

As soon as I realized I was falling into Penkov's trap, I prayed for the Lord to strengthen me and control every thought. "Lord, save me from being preoccupied with personal things. This can only cause conflict and unrest within me. My only desire is that my life might bring honor and glory to You and not myself. I don't understand why you've allowed this test of my will. You know how easy it is for me to begin worrying about my wife and my future, but I believe in faith that you will somehow turn this trial into a blessing. Dear God, I ask only one thing for myself: please help me to be faithful to you, no matter what happens."

Penkov couldn't be allowed to destroy my inner peace. As much as I loved my wife, I wouldn't allow Penkov to use the promise of a visit with her to control me.

Once again, it became clear that my focus must be upon serving God's interests and honoring the principles of his kingdom. If I became preoccupied with my own interests, it would be tempting to barter with Penkov to get the visit I wanted. That would be foolish, since Penkov controlled the outcome, and the diversion could cause me to lose the mental focus and emotional balance essential to surviving this ordeal. Having made that decision, I knew that Penkov had lost the battle for my mind.

From that time onward, although I spent time praying for my family and thinking of them each day, I never again became consumed with worry for them or the desire to see them. I clearly felt God's Spirit leading me through that difficult emotional experience, helping me to understand the danger of what Penkov was attempting to do.

As anticipated, nothing came of Penkov's cruel suggestion that my wife might come to meet with me. He had no intention of following up on the comment, but was purely interested in how it would affect me. The next time he brought me in for one of our "conversations," I reminded Penkov that he hadn't kept his promise. His response: "When I contacted her to make the arrangements, she was not polite, so I forgot the whole thing."

By this time I was beginning to understand how Penkov operated and knew that there was no truth in what he was telling me. The entire episode had been a ruse to affect my emotional stability.

These Things Are True

One of the great truths confirmed in my prison experience was the power of prayer. Realizing that I was engaged in a spiritual battle, more of my time was spent in prayer than ever before. I knew that my brother was in prison again, and I prayed for him. I knew that the working conditions for Emanuel and Toshko, who were working outside in a brickyard, must have been horrible, so I prayed for them. I prayed that somehow, through all of this, God would help them grow stronger in their faith, just as I prayed that prayer for myself.

The people of First Church were constantly in my prayers. Those of us in prison had a heavy burden to bear, but it wasn't easy for the people in the church to stand firm either. All of us needed God's grace, wisdom, and strength so we would recognize the attacks of the evil one and resist them.

Most of all I prayed that God would keep us all strong and uncompromising in our commitment to Christ. Surely this is what it must have been like for the early Christians. The Bible tells us in Hebrews 11:36-40 that they were persecuted, imprisoned, separated from their families, burned at the stake, or torn apart by wild beasts. Yet they were faithful to the Lord, and their example has inspired Christians who have suffered and died for Christ in every century since.

Some of the pastors in Bulgaria had died after the infamous trials of

1949. Others of us might die for the Lord also. If so, I was confident that others would continue to witness for Christ and his kingdom. The promise from Matthew 16:18 kept coming to mind, that Christ's church will stand and that "all the powers of hell will not conquer it" (NLT). Our witness in Bulgaria might be restricted by Communism for a time, but Christ's church would continue throughout the ages. Our bodies might die, but our souls and God's truth would continue through eternity.

Another truth confirmed in my prison experience was the pervasive influence of evil in human society. Unfortunately, words such as *sin, evil, Satan,* and *wickedness* are seldom used in churches today. Considering ourselves to be modern, enlightened people, we associate these things with a medieval worldview. The evidence is undeniable, however, that evil is at work in every age.

The evil unleashed upon our world today is overwhelming. Ethnic cleansing, death camps, killing grounds, and the torture of prisoners in "modern" nations is just the beginning of a list of great wrongs. The massive persecution of people holding different religious and political views permeates society. These things are infinitely beyond mere human pride or selfishness. Something much larger is at work here.

The Bible tells us of "principalities" and "powers" (Ephesians 6:12, KJV) at work in our world. These evil forces seek to destroy what God has created and to corrupt what God desires to redeem. We are foolish if we take sin and evil lightly, pretending that the evil one, whom the Bible calls Satan, does not exist. Modern theologians may try to get rid of terms such as *original sin* or *demons,* but the concept of a pervasive evil force in our world will not disappear just by eliminating the terminology.

Please don't misunderstand me. The power of Satan and his fallen angels is not nearly as strong as the redeeming power of our holy God. But evil does have the power to deceive and destroy. In the bowels of Central Prison, I saw clearly that Satan was constantly using cunning and deceit to discourage Christians. At other times the evil one turns Christians against one another, seeking to destroy the church.

Christ defeated evil on the cross, but Satan hasn't yet given up. Fortunately, we know how the story will end: "The kingdom of the world has become the kingdom of our Lord and of his Christ, and he will reign for ever and ever" (Revelation 11:15). Amen.

Yet another truth confirmed during those years in prison was that God created humans with a strong and enduring will. The power of evil is real, but God has given us the strength to resist it. James 4:7 teaches, "Resist the devil, and he will flee from you." The choice is ours. We may submit to the influence of evil or, with God's help, stand fast against it. While some prisoners collapsed into a suicidal state, others gave evidence that the human spirit is amazingly resilient.

Human Ingenuity and Creativity

It was interesting to observe that human ingenuity and creativity cannot be totally suppressed, even in a prison as repressive as Central Prison. Just as I saw humor in the darkest days of my imprisonment, there were also attempts by the prisoners to express themselves through art and entertainment. Although any and every form of entertainment was forbidden, a variety of games was devised in prison, some at great sacrifice. Entire decks of cards were produced out of contraband. Intricate chess figures, checkers, and dice were sculpted by mixing bread with salt and water and forming them into game pieces.

Food was so scarce that using bread for this purpose was a sacrifice. The prisoners would rather have gone hungry, however, than been unable to create with their hands or been without entertainment to occupy their minds. Game boards were artfully drawn on scraps of newspaper or cigarette wrappers, the lines drawn with cigarette ashes mixed with water. If nothing else, prisoners would pass the time playing "Odd or Even" or trying to guess the name of a city one of the prisoners had in mind using a few hints.

Most of the time, rather than watching or playing such games, I recited Scripture I had memorized, spent time in silent prayer and praise, or just thought through various situations that I might face. This helped strengthen me spiritually, and it kept me mentally alert.

God Turned Evil into Good

When Raijko and Mitko tired of playing their games, they would ask me to tell them a story. This happened evening after evening and gave me a wonderful opportunity to whisper a Bible story. If the guards heard us, they never interrupted or disciplined us for it.

I told my cellmates the stories of Joseph, Moses, David, Jesus, and Paul many times. Usually my focus was on characters such as Joseph and Paul, who were in prison because of the evil perpetrated by their enemies. I especially emphasized how God turned evil into good. This always delighted my captive audience. Bible stories long familiar to me were new to the men who listened.

The Bible stories sometimes led to an interesting discussion. Raijko might ask, "Since God has allowed us to be thrown into prison and to suffer like this, don't we have the right to renounce our faith? If God is all powerful and loving, why has he abandoned us like this?" This was typical of the questions many prisoners had.

My answer was always the same: "No. We must continue to trust God even when he works in ways we do not understand. Some of the hardships that come upon us are a result of our own foolishness. But even if we experience suffering and trouble when we're innocent, we must understand that God can use it to strengthen our faith and show others how to live a more godly life."

One verse that gave me a great deal of strength in prison was 1 Corinthians 10:13: "God is faithful; he will not let you be tempted beyond what you can bear. But when you are tempted, he will also provide a way out so that you can stand up under it." I would often recite that verse to prisoners who questioned the suffering that we endured in prison.

Knowing the promises of God's Word and sensing his presence strengthened my faith. My confidence grew in the belief that God would help me withstand every test that came along.

As Christians, it is important to realize that God doesn't promise to protect us from testing or from everything that causes us to suffer. God may use testing to bring us to himself. Suffering for Christ actually strengthened the faith of countless Christians. Always, however, we have the assurance that God will not allow more suffering than we can bear. That promise from God's Word gave me great peace of mind, even in the darkest, most threatening days of my prison experience.

Listening for Footsteps

In a hostile prison environment, such a simple thing as the sound of approaching footsteps in the corridor has a chilling effect. It is as though a vicious animal is stalking its prey. Each prisoner waits breathlessly, wondering where the guard will pounce.

When the dreaded footsteps were heard at Central Prison, the imposed silence of the prison became even more pronounced, and an air of suspense permeated the foul environment. The rattle of keys at your door could mean hours of interrogation or torture. Or it might mean that another prisoner was being placed in the cell, making the already crowded conditions even more miserable.

Prisoners taken from their cells might be gone for a few minutes, several hours, or all night. Some prisoners disappeared altogether, with no explanation. It was very unpredictable. Usually there was no explanation or opportunity for farewell when a prisoner was taken abruptly.

Early one morning the footsteps led to our cell. Raijko, Mitko, and I waited to see who would be summoned. Rather than hearing the keys rattle in our door, the metal cover slid open suddenly. An unfamiliar face appeared in the opening and gruffly asked, "Kulichev? Is Christo Kulichev there?"

"Yes, I am Christo Kulichev," I answered, rising to my feet.

The scowling face announced, "Kulichev, I am the Chief of Interrogators. I'm here to command you to stop insisting that you've never been properly notified that your rights to preach have been revoked. I hereby inform you, you will not preach again! Do you understand?"

With little time to think, by the grace of God somehow I had the presence of mind to reply, "It's possible for anyone to tell me not to preach. But at no time have I been given an official order stating why I am denied the right to preach the gospel God has called me to preach. I only ask for my rights to be respected."

The chief interrogator responded as tersely as before, "If you demand to have a written order, you will stay here! You've been told not to preach, and you will not preach!" Abruptly the metal cover to the peephole rasped shut.

Obviously my repeated protests to Penkov had struck a raw nerve. Word of my protest had reached the chief of the division! *So this is their response,* I thought to myself. No evidence of due process. No written record of the Committee's action. No citing of specific wrongs allegedly committed. No evidence to support the charges. Just a harsh command not to preach, shouted through the observation hole. It was a crude attempt at intimidation, nothing more. It only showed how far they underestimated my commitment to preach the gospel.

Yes, Brother, We Are Eternal!

Oppressed by the boredom of prison life, it was Raijko who suggested we volunteer to be "sweepers." Sweepers were prisoners allowed out of their cell to assist with cleaning duties such as sweeping the corridors and lavatories. Part of Raijko's motivation was related to the fact that sweepers sometimes found cigarette butts to smoke.

When the captain of the guard was passing our cell one day, Raijko took a chance and spoke to him, informing him of our wish. A few days later we found ourselves outside of the cell doing all kinds of jobs. There were lightbulbs to change, windows to wash, and toilets to unclog. These were the unpleasant tasks the guards didn't want to do, but it was a delight for us to get out of our cell and feel like productive human beings again. We soon discovered that an extra amount of food was sometimes given for a job well done.

At about this same time, prison administrators changed the procedure for washing our plates and spoons. Before, each prisoner had been responsible for washing his own utensils. Later, however, the warden ordered that plates and utensils be turned in and washed by two women brought in to perform the task. This lasted only a brief time, however, ending in protests that the utensils were not washed clean.

In an attempt to resolve this problem, some of us who had been sweeping the prison were given the job of washing utensils. This job was not as easy as one might think, since we had to work with our hands in cold water for an hour or more each day.

As usual, however, I found there were blessings to be discovered in the hardship. Raijko, Mitko, and I were able to separate our own spoons and plates from those used by other prisoners, giving some assurance that we would be spared the germs passed in this way. Even so, when washing the utensils of the other prisoners, I insisted that we treat each item as if it were going into our own mouths. "God has given us a chance to minister to others by keeping their plates and spoons as clean as possible," I stressed to Raijko and Mitko. "We must do for others as we would have them do for us."

While washing plates and spoons one day, I came across a wooden spoon that had a small cross carved into it. Under the cross, someone in our prison had carved the words *I am eternal.* Tears came to my eyes, and a lump crept into my throat as I said to myself, *Yes, brother, we are eternal! And Christ's cross is proof of that. No matter where we are, and no matter what they do to us, we are eternal.* That spoon passed through my hands several times as I washed the eating utensils. Each time I placed it with the batch of spoons going to the first floor. A rumor had reached me that my brother was in cell number 4 on the first floor, and I hoped that if the rumor was true that somehow the spoon might reach him and lift his spirits as it had mine.

Songs of Zion in a Foreign Land
Washing plates and spoons gave me an opportunity to sing softly since the guards didn't like standing near the vats we used. As I sang one day, Mitko spoke to me. "Old Man Christo," he said (the younger prison-

ers called me "old man"). "Why don't you sing a little louder so we can hear the words of your song?"

Apologizing for my lack of musical training, I began to sing:

> Peace and rest, I don't expect here;
> Then why should I mourn in sorrow?
> The worst sorrow isn't too heavy for me.
> Since I'm walking toward Heaven,
> Glory, blessed peace, and
> Choirs of angels will meet me,
> Singing "Welcome to your home in Heaven."
> Who called me into Heaven to rest.

It was silent when I finished singing. After a pause I said, "That's my faith, Mitko. It gives me peace and strength." Mitko and Raijko said nothing for quite some time as the water sloshed and the utensils clicked softly in the silence.

Familiar hymns brought back precious memories of my family. God continued to give me a miraculous peace of mind with regard to my family during that painful separation. Daring not to even imagine what kind of threats were being made against them, I realized there was no use worrying over things I could not control. I simply committed my family and their welfare to the Lord.

I knew without a doubt that my family was worried sick. They had no idea what was happening to me. All I could do was pray that God would take care of them and give them the same comfort and peace he was giving me. This precious gift of peace, I discovered, was something God gave only when believers achieved a singleness of heart, seeking only to live a life pleasing to him.

Faith Is Nothing if It Isn't Practical

Personal hygiene was a constant problem in the prison. We were allowed to bathe only once every two weeks, with a change of underclothing given when we went to the baths. Shaving was allowed twice each week, when we were taken two by two to the lavatories and given a few minutes in front of a mirror. This became a special time for me, since those few minutes in front of the mirror were as close as I came to being alone.

The prison ran on a strict schedule. Each Saturday they gave us nail clippers to use, as well as a needle and thread to repair our clothing. Also on Saturday, we were allowed to take our blankets out of the cell to shake them out. If we wanted we were allowed a short walk in the prison yard at that time. The prison yard was only twenty-five feet square, but it gave us an opportunity to enjoy a minimal amount of exercise.

Prisoners were taken into the prison yard one cell at a time. We were forbidden to turn our backs to the guards, to crouch, or to remove our hands from behind our backs. It was difficult to exercise in that position, but we tried to stretch our muscles as much as possible while looking at the sky and breathing deeply of the fresh air.

The privilege of breathing fresh, unpolluted air has never been as important to my hygiene as it was in Central Prison. The contrast between the air outside in the yard and the putrid stench of the cells is difficult to describe. Allowed only three or four times around the perimeter of the small prison yard, our walks in the fresh air were over all too soon. I always took one last, long draught of fresh air as the guards impatiently barked, "Enough. You're dismissed!"

Mental and spiritual hygiene were just as important to me as physical hygiene. I made it a priority to put the needs of others before my own, trusting God to meet my needs and work through me to help others. When we were given extra food for our work as sweepers, I shared it with other prisoners who needed it badly.

Mitko talked obsessively about food. Having made another homemade rope to entertain himself, he worked constantly at getting games, reading material, and cigarettes to satisfy his other compulsions. Knowing that God would care for me, I shared my food with Mitko to help satisfy his physical hunger. I prayed that God would also help me show Mitko how to satisfy his inner hunger.

An important part of my spiritual hygiene was the discipline of immersing myself in passages of God's Word. Amazingly, details and the larger context often came to mind as I meditated upon a passage. My meditations moved beyond remembering the words of Scripture as I disciplined myself to also apply the truth of each passage.

This discipline of meditating upon Scripture and applying it to my life helped time pass more quickly. More importantly, I believe the practical application of God's Word gave my life a spiritual focus that kept me from the obsessions Mitko and others had. It truly was a miracle that I never craved the things they talked about constantly. This demonstrated to me the power of God's Word to alter our spirits, thoughts, attitudes, and actions. Our faith is nothing if it isn't practical, impacting our daily lives.

A God Who Suffers with Us

One of the subjects I meditated upon was what the Bible has to say about suffering. The theme of suffering is seen throughout the Bible.

Daniel has always provided a model for me of a man who maintained his purpose and dignity—even in a time of suffering. In the Old Testament, Daniel was carried away into the foreign land of Babylon and suffered as a captive of a pagan king. Determined not to compromise their principles, Daniel and his friends refused to eat the food of their captors.

Things got worse for Daniel when he was tossed into a den of lions for praying to God rather than to the king; his friends were thrown into a fiery furnace for refusing to bow to a statue of the king. In both of these instances, God spared the lives of his faithful followers. The most important lesson, I believe, is that God didn't keep Daniel and his friends from trials, but he was there with them, helping them to stay strong even in the midst of terrible suffering. What a blessing the story of Daniel was to me, clearly teaching the powerful truth that God enters into our suffering. Even if God did not spare my life as he spared Daniel's, I knew that I was never alone in tribulation.

Questions about suffering were among the most difficult to answer. I realized there must be a reason why God had not banished suffering and pain from the earth, not even from the lives of his children. That reason, it seemed to me, must be the connection between suffering and our free will. If suffering were banished, freedom would be lost with it, and the will to choose would no longer exist.

Our God-given freedom presumes there is something opposite it, otherwise it would be meaningless. It is logically impossible to know freedom without the possibility of bondage, to know love without loneliness, or righteousness without temptation. The suffering that comes with bondage, loneliness, or temptation is essential if we are to experience the joy of the opposites, which are freedom, love, and righteousness.

Scientists use Newton's third law to explain a force of nature: for every action there is an equal and opposite reaction. Similarly, in our spiritual lives we are called to live in the tension of two opposing forces. Living in this overlap, we are placed in God's workshop, where he can fashion us into the people he wants us to become—people who discern good from evil and exercise our free will to choose the good because it honors God. Unlike Newton's law, however, this principle of spiritual opposition is not a matter of "equal and opposite" forces; while we may be obliged to endure opposing forces, God's strength is infinitely greater than that of our enemies.

Most important, the Bible teaches that we're not alone in our struggle against evil. God has come into our world and enters into the depths of human suffering. Although God is all powerful, he freely chooses to share our suffering, not because he is weak and it is forced upon him, but because he loves us. In the context of suffering, God helps us discover the depth of his love.

Just as God shared the suffering of Daniel and his friends—his Spirit closing the mouths of the lions and walking through the fiery furnace—so God shared our suffering on the cross of Jesus Christ. Taking upon himself the penalty for our sins, Christ gave us the gift of new life. All we have to do to accept it is turn in faith to him. His Spirit is with us today, sharing our suffering, and he has promised never to leave us or forsake us.

What Could I Do? They Were Beating Me!

The footsteps came one day to summon Raijko. At the time, Mitko and I had no idea this would be the last time we would see this man with whom we had spent every minute of the past weeks. A new cell mate arrived in a few hours, signaling that in all likelihood we would not see Raijko again. In such a cloistered environment, where stress was required to work out a tolerable relationship, anxiety was inevitable when someone whose personality is understood is suddenly removed and replaced with someone new.

The new arrival was a young man named Anton, called Tony. With fear in his eyes, Tony told us that he had been to the dreaded Seventh Deadly Chamber, a torture cell. Frightened by the prospect of torture, he had confessed to every charge the agents had made against him. Reasoning that any amount of prison time would be preferable to torture, he foolishly agreed to the charges in the vain hope that his confession would not be checked.

The interrogators suspected Tony of stealing from a school in Plovdiv. It took only a few days for the police to check into the details of his confession. Predictably, they discovered inconsistencies and realized Tony wasn't telling the truth.

"You can be sure I got my share," Tony said to us. In spite of his efforts to avoid torture, he had been terribly abused by the frustrated agents.

"But Tony," I asked him, "didn't you realize that they might have evidence about who committed the crime? Surely you knew they would test your confession against the evidence!"

He replied, "What could I do? They were beating me!"

I spent several hours talking earnestly with Tony about his life even though he was in our cell for just a few days. He was only eighteen years of age and had once been convicted of stealing fifteen *leva* (about $1.25 US) from the purse of a lady on a train. Since that time he was constantly suspected of theft and spent a good deal of time being interrogated for this crime or that.

Tony had questions about my beliefs, and this opened the door for me to explain the basics of the Christian faith. Most importantly, I stressed that Jesus Christ died so that we might be forgiven of our sins and experience new life. The mention of sin almost always led to a long discussion in the prison. Prisoners, like most people, tend to minimize or deny their own sinfulness while putting heavy emphasis upon things they haven't done.

In talking with Tony, I explained that God knows that we all have sinned. The Bible teaches, "If we claim we have not sinned, we are calling God a liar and showing that his word has no place in our hearts" (1 John 1:10, NLT). Tony listened intently, his dark eyes flashing with surprise when I said that in God's eyes sin was sin. "My sin is no worse than yours," I told him, "for any sin separates us from God." Continuing, I suggested that it made no difference whether he stole a small or large amount; sin was sin. "All sin needs to be confessed so that God can forgive it," I told him. "And God is faithful to forgive if only we confess."

Tony listened respectfully but never gave any clear indication that he placed his faith in Christ as Savior. Most people, like Tony, never confess unless they are faced with painful consequences. As the interrogators liked to say, "Without the threat of beatings, all of you would be innocent." God calls us to freely confess so that we may experience a new way of living, not a belated confession to escape punishment.

A Grand and Eternal Purpose

The fear promulgated by the guards permeated every facet of prison life. It was my meditation upon the great themes of the Bible that helped me through many nights. It would have been easy to focus on the suffering and all-pervasive fear around me. But by focusing on God's power, wisdom, and presence, the fear and worry were driven away.

It was on a night shortly after Tony came into our cell that I found myself thinking of the apostle James, who was faithful to the Lord even though it meant death under the sword of Herod. God didn't deliver

James, but he did take him into his presence. I knew that I might have to follow in the footsteps of James because of my commitment to Christ. But that was in God's hands, and I trusted him to do what was best.

The story of James reminded me that Christians were not created for just these few years on earth. When God's eternal life flows through us, it gives life new meaning and purpose. Our purpose as God's people, both now and throughout eternity, is to exalt Christ and to serve God's kingdom. Understanding the grand and eternal purpose God has for us, it seems rather petty to put our own comfort and convenience first. The Christian's prayer, in prison or out, should be, "While we live, we live to please the Lord. And when we die, we go to be with the Lord. So in life and in death, we belong to the Lord" (Romans 14:8, NLT).

My father had possessed a faith unlike that of anyone else I have ever known. Vividly, I could recall the time when he himself had gone to prison briefly for his commitment to Christ. Also, I recalled his saying, "Your first commitment must always be to Christ, my sons. It must be an even greater commitment than your love of family. Although it would grieve me to lose any of you, if you were hanged in the village square for your faith in Jesus Christ I would be a proud father!"

Paul's writings from prison to the Philippians became extremely meaningful to me as I recalled passages such as Philippians 1:20, where Paul writes, "I eagerly expect and hope that I will in no way be ashamed, but will have sufficient courage so that now as always Christ will be exalted in my body, whether by life or by death." And in Philippians 1:29, Paul's classic summons to faith says, "It has been granted to you on behalf of Christ not only to believe on him, but also to suffer for him."

Our greatest concern as Christians shouldn't be whether we will face suffering but whether we will look back upon our lives from eternity and be ashamed that we were not willing to be faithful to Christ, who gave his life for us on the cross.

With those thoughts in mind, I finally drifted off to sleep, even with the muffled screams coming from the Seventh Deadly Chamber.

CHAPTER FOUR

His Righteousness to Their Children's Children

From everlasting to everlasting the LORD's love is with those who fear him, and his righteousness with their children's children—with those who keep his covenant and remember to obey his precepts.
PSALM 103:17-18

Some theologians claim that God cannot suffer, but I believe they are wrong. God's capacity for suffering exceeds our capacity for suffering in the same measure as his capacity for knowledge exceeds ours. Christ endured the agonies of hell itself in order to overcome sin and death, and to confer on us a life more glorious than we can imagine.
DR. ALVIN PLANTINGA

One of the miracles God performed while I was in prison was delivering me from a consuming hatred for the guards. Many of the prisoners would have killed the guards had the opportunity presented itself. In spite of their surliness and abuse, I found myself feeling compassion for the guards. The responsibility of watching over the prisoners was no easy task. We had no choice but to be confined in that horrible place with its stench and squalor, but they were there because they couldn't find another way to earn a living.

By no means could all guards be lumped together in one category. There were as many different personalities and dispositions as there were guards. The prisoners soon learned to differentiate between the guards simply struggling to make something of their lives and those who were filled with anger and hatred toward the prisoners. The angry guards were sadistic and dangerous. There was no limit to the ways they devised to make us suffer.

Some of the guards could be ingenious in thinking of ways to frustrate the prisoners. If they knew a prisoner was addicted to tobacco, they would use cigarettes to torment him. The promise of one cigarette was enough to get a desperate prisoner to do anything the guard wanted.

Most guards expressed their contempt by constantly shouting. They shouted while distributing our food, not caring if they spilled part or all of our precious ration for the day. They shouted for us to move faster in the toilets and then laughed as we scurried back to our cells while trying to button our tattered prison trousers.

Other guards, however, were quite humane, almost sensitive, at least to a few of our basic needs. One of the most important commodities in the prison was salt. One came quickly to understand how vital salt is to existence when it was in short supply. Not only was salt needed simply to sustain life, but we soon learned that a little salt sprinkled on our bread made it much tastier. We were constantly asking the guards for salt with our food, and some of the more compassionate guards would occasionally honor our request.

Sound Spiritual Stock

One day when Penkov summoned me for interrogation, he became agitated and began to shout as soon as the door closed behind me. "Christo, what's going on with that wife of yours? I can't believe the things she says when I talk with her. Now she's telling me that she's going to become a pastor?"

His frustrated demeanor, as well as the information Penkov was conveying, told me that my wife was remaining strong. I felt proud of her. She not only had supported my taking a stand against the government, but she was supporting our family while I was in prison. Her life was difficult, maintaining the home in my absence while holding down a nursing job at the medical clinic near our home in Sofia.

Pleased to hear of Tzvete's resistance and yet curious to know more, I said to Penkov, "Why are you so amazed at my wife? She's a dedicated minister's wife and shares in the ministry. Certainly she wants to see God's work continue. Now you know that I have the best wife in the whole world!"

Penkov stared at me, as though confused by my positive attitude. Finally, in exasperation, he blurted out, "And just how is it that out of all of the billions of women in the world, you happened to get the best wife?"

Smiling, I told him, "A good wife is a gift from God. Tzvete is God's gift to me!" Deeply devoted to Christ and a constant source of encouragement, Tzvete was then and still is an unusually committed woman.

Tzvete and I first met in 1954, when Dimitar and I traveled through Bulgaria encouraging the churches and challenging young people to remain firm in their commitment to Christ. I met dozens of young Christian women in our travels throughout Bulgaria, but none of them was quite like Tzvete. We met at her home church near Plovdiv while I was preaching there.

Tzvete Stephanova Marinova made a deep impression upon me

from the first. It didn't take long for me to fall in love with her. Blessed with an extremely bright mind, she was quick to discern what was at stake in any situation. She could be tender and compassionate when someone needed support, but at the same time she was resolute in pressing for what she knew to be right. These are wonderful and unusual qualities to find in any person.

Many of Tzvete's fine qualities, I discovered, were typical of her family. Tzvete's brother Marin was equally committed. He had been expelled from the University for sharing his Christian faith just six months before he was to receive his medical degree. Marin was exiled for two and a half years on the island of Belene in the Black Sea, but upon his release he was eager to serve as a pastor. One of our evangelical churches gladly received him as their minister. Marin's willingness to suffer for his faith had given him the right to preach. Bulgarian Christians view this as important.

Grandfather Marin

Tzvete's brother Marin was named after their grandfather. Grandfather Marin had once served as a tax collector in the village of Ahmetovo, an important position in that region.

The mayor of the village returned from a trip one day and, as Grandfather Marin told the story, the mayor brought back a Bible given to him by some missionaries. Curious about this book, Grandfather Marin asked to read it and later testified often that it changed his life. So moved by the power of the story of Jesus and the truth of the gospel, this proud and powerful tax collector vowed to follow in the footsteps of Matthew, the disciple of Jesus, who also collected revenue.

Grandfather Marin vowed by God's Spirit to live as the Bible taught. The change was dramatic and undeniable. Young Marin had been known to drink considerably and had a reputation for using colorful language in the village. If there was a festival anywhere nearby that offered dancing or a lewd theater, he would be there in a minute. But all of that ceased in 1884, and when people inquired as to why he had changed, Marin was quick to say, "I've given my soul to God."

The first thing Grandfather Marin did after his conversion was to approach the mayor with several reams of paper. Returning the paper to the mayor, he confessed to taking it from the city hall without permission. "Now that I have read the Bible and God has touched my heart, I can see that what I've done is wrong," he confessed. "I can't take something that belongs to someone else! Please forgive me." The mayor was so impressed with Marin's obvious change in behavior that he told him to keep the Bible!

The entire village was surprised by the change in Grandfather Marin's life and watched with interest. Problems didn't begin until the new convert began comparing what he was reading in the Bible with what he was hearing in the local Orthodox Church. Rather naively, he approached the priest and asked why there was so much talk much about loyalty to the church but never any about the importance of faith in Christ.

The priest brushed him aside, but Marin persisted, encouraging the priest to make it clear to the people that Jesus Christ was "the way and the truth and the life" (John 14:6). He was eager for others to learn what he had discovered in the Scriptures, and he wanted everyone to experience the new life he had come to know.

The priest let it be known that he viewed this brash upstart as eccentric. Because the priest was at the center of village life, it sent a ripple through the community when he began to avoid Marin. At about that time Grandfather Marin began to speak urgently with other leaders in the Orthodox church. The results were predictable. Following the priest's instructions, those on the inner circle of the church began to accuse Marin of "betraying the faith." In harsh tones they mocked him, saying, "You're a Protestant! You don't belong in our church!"

Young convert that he was, the young man who would someday be Tzvete's grandfather didn't even know what a Protestant was. Humbling himself, he went to his accusers to ask what this word meant, only to face more mockery. Someone listened long enough, however, to explain that he ought to go to Assenovgrad where he would find a group of Protestants who could explain their beliefs.

Assenovgrad was thirty kilometers from Ahmetovo, where Tzvete's grandfather lived. Rebuffed by the church in his own village, he resolved to go and meet these people who believed as he did. He was on the road to Assenovgrad long before sunrise the next Sunday. He did not own a horse, so he walked the entire distance.

Entering the village of Assenovgrad, the eager young man began asking puzzled pedestrians where he could find "the Protestants." Finally one man replied, "Oh, you mean the evangelicals. It's just a few blocks; I'll give you directions."

Slipping into the little building, young Marin hoped to sit in the back and listen for a time to see what this strange group believed. However, his plan dissolved shortly after stepping through the door of the humble church building. He was soon surrounded by Christian friends eager to hear his story and share their own.

Those next few hours of sharing from God's Word, praying together, and encouraging one another left an indelible mark on young Marin's life. He told the story often in years to come, concluding that the warmth and worship "gave wings to my heart!"

Things didn't change back in Ahmetovo, though. When he made mention of his journey to Assenovgrad and the friends he made there, he met with further ridicule. "Why did you go meet with the Protestants? Isn't your own village good enough? Are you too high and mighty to attend our Orthodox church?"

Not easily discouraged, Grandfather Marin continued to make the long journey to Assenovgrad on foot. His hunger for worship and fellowship drove him. The distance was so great, however, and the Bulgarian winters so harsh, that Grandfather Marin knew he couldn't continue walking to Assenovgrad. Something had to be done.

The Church That Faith Built

It was the prompting of the Holy Spirit that urged young Marin to begin a small church in his own home. This was entirely unheard of in a land dominated by rigid religious traditions. The people of Ahmetovo had never dreamed that there would ever be any other church than the Orthodox one that had dominated the community for centuries. The road ahead might be considerably harder than walking to Assenovgrad, but Tzvete's grandfather vowed to go ahead with the Lord's help.

The task of starting a new church in such a resistant setting wasn't easy. At first Marin and his two brothers were the only ones who gathered on Sunday mornings to pray and read the Scriptures. Most villagers doubted that the young convert's influence would ever extend beyond his own family.

Gradually, however, one or two people came to ask Marin about his strange beliefs. When two families finally attended to see for themselves what these Protestants were doing, their visit aroused the curiosity of others. In a few months, a small evangelical community, as they called themselves, was meeting weekly in Grandfather Marin's home. When asked why new members continued to join them they were quick to explain, "It's the Lord's presence that attracts them." And it was the Lord's presence that changed lives.

The mockery that Grandfather Marin had endured since he questioned the priest began to intensify. The skeptics in Ahmetovo predicted the little assembly would soon fail. Could anything of lasting consequence come of such small beginnings? Most of the people who joined the evangelical worship service were viewed as eccentrics or social outcasts.

"What happens in your meetings, Marin?" skeptics asked.

"We pray and read God's Word. We talk about how we can apply the teaching of the Bible to our lives. Why don't you come join us?"

"Does God answer your prayers?" the villagers would ask with a sneer.

"Yes, we pray for God to be with us, and he does help in many ways. We pray for the sick and discouraged. The Bible teaches that there is great power in prayer."

That'll Be the Day

Viewing this opportunity as too good to pass up, the mockers in the village began to challenge the evangelicals. "If you believe that God hears your prayers, why don't you ask him to convert Kosta Triffonov? If we could see something like that, maybe we would believe your prayers are truly being answered!"

Kosta Triffonov was the richest man in the village. He lived in an estate on a hilltop outside Ahmetovo. Most of the common people had little to do with this wealthy man. It was inconceivable that Kosta would ever be converted to these alien beliefs imported from Assenovgrad, let alone join the eccentric evangelicals in worship. The idea was laughable.

The prayer group continued to pray, often praying for various people in the village, friendly or not. They prayed for the mockers, that they might believe in Christ. They prayed for Kosta Triffonov as well. As they prayed, they did what they could to befriend Kosta, telling him of their belief in Christ and the love and forgiveness that Christ gives.

It was a shock, even to those who had prayed, when Kosta came to Marin's door one Sunday morning . There must have been some wondering looks exchanged as they invited him to join their circle for Bible study and prayer. At the conclusion of the service, Kosta knelt and prayed to receive Christ as Savior.

It didn't take long for word to reach everyone in the village that Kosta Triffonov had visited the evangelicals. When word of his conversion went out a day or two later, it was met with incredulity. But it was true, and soon there was evidence that the man's life was changed.

The mockers who had issued the challenge were hard put to ex-

plain how this turn of events had come about. Would they believe in
the power of prayer as promised? Obviously not. "Triffonov's a rich
man, insulated from the real world," they claimed. "He has no real
friends. Obviously the man's lonely. Is it any wonder that he would
respond to their overtures? He's as eccentric as they are!"

Not yet believing, the mocking crowd wouldn't be content until
they had issued another challenge. "It's one thing for a lonely rich man
to go looking for friends. It's quite another thing to change the life of
someone who's obviously warped beyond all hope. Now take Ango
Tenev, for example," the mockers said, trying to divert attention from
Kosta Triffonov.

Ango Tenev was known in the whole region to be constantly out
of control. He drank like he was trying to drown a demon inside him,
he beat his wife, and he constantly disrupted the peace of Ahmetevo.
Considering Ango to be beyond hope, the mockers chortled, "The
whole village scatters in terror when he comes down the street. Let's
see some timid prayer group touch his life. That'll be the day!"

Who Can Explain These Things?

The evangelicals had already been praying for Ango Tenev. But now
the faithful little group of believers prayed even more earnestly.

Eager to share God's love, they went out of their way to show kindness to Ango Tenev. Startled at first, Ango drew back, continuing to blus-
ter and make threats. To go near the man was to risk one's life. But the
believers knew the truth of God's Word: "God demonstrates his own
love for us in this: While we were still sinners, Christ died for us"
(Romans 5:8). No matter how despicable Ango Tenev was, God loved
him and had died for him. The evangelicals resolved not to give up.

Continuing to pray, the evangelicals spoke with compassion to
the troubled man, looking for every opportunity to help him. He obviously needed so much help that the believers wondered what would
happen. Only God could get through to someone so hostile. And so
they prayed that somehow God would work through them and perform a miracle in Ango's life.

Who can explain these things? It wasn't one act but a composite of
deeds and words that began to have an effect upon Ango's attitude.
Accustomed to seeing people flee at the sight of him, he was caught off
guard by these gentle people who drew near at his worst moments.
Only they, he noticed, spoke kindly when he spouted forth his rage.
Something about the spirit of the evangelicals touched a tender spot

deep in Ango Tenev's dark soul. Conversations with Ango finally became possible.

One day Grandfather Marin asked Ango if the evangelicals could say a prayer for him. Startled by the very idea, Ango consented. That evening a small group of believers gathered around Ango and prayed. In the middle of the prayer, the village drunk and resident bully dissolved into tears. Literally blubbering out his repentance, he pled for God's mercy, naming the people he had offended and the damage he had done. When he arose from his knees, Ango Tenev was a member of Christ's family.

Dressed in clean clothes and in his right mind, Ango made his way to worship at Grandfather Marin's house the next Sunday morning. The little village watched in disbelief. God had touched the heart of the man whom most thought had neither heart nor conscience. Would wonders never cease? Word spread with the speed of sound.

Tzvete's Grandfather Marin used to conclude the dramatic story of Ango by saying, "Tenev the terror became as meek as Moses." Only Christ could change a life so dramatically, and that's exactly what Ango Tenev began telling people.

Things got worse in some respects, however, before they got better. Ango's wife, it seems, was embarrassed by all of the talk around town about her husband. As is often the case in such strained relationships, the wife had accommodated herself to the abusive behavior of a drunken husband and didn't know how to relate to him after the dramatic change.

It was as if Mrs. Tenev was now married to a totally different man. Strangely, she wasn't sure she liked him that way! She had gotten a measure of sympathy for putting up with Ango's drinking, but now people didn't know how to deal with the changed man or his wife. Mrs. Tenev knew that anyone who didn't support the Orthodox Church was considered eccentric. Rather than sympathy, she was now faced with probing questions about Ango's religious beliefs.

Even if she was the wife of the town drunk, Mrs. Tenev wanted to cling to some semblance of normalcy, which she associated with being Orthodox. Feeling this way, she chided Ango for changing his faith. Ango's quiet reply was uncharacteristic: "My dear, I haven't changed my faith. God has changed my life!"

It wasn't long before Mrs. Tenev's life was changed also. Profoundly touched by the permanent change in her husband, she knelt gratefully with Ango in Grandfather Marin's home one Sunday morning and surrendered her life to the Savior.

Will They Find Us Faithful?

I knew that my dear wife, Tzvete, came from sound spiritual stock. She wasn't about to run from those who would threaten her for her Christian beliefs. If I had ever wavered in my own faith, Tzvete would have stood firm and encouraged me to be faithful. It was a part of her family heritage.

When Tzvete's father was born in 1896, the Orthodox priest was so incensed by Grandfather Marin's refusal to baptize his newborn son by the Eastern rite that he incited a riot. Goaded by the priest, an angry crowd overran Grandfather Marin's property, pillaging the house and the larder. The mob even plundered the food and firewood his family had stored away for the winter.

Breaking down the fence and taking wooden tools from the barn, the rioters started a bonfire on the haystack. The raging fire was allowed to spread, and it burned the nearby family home to the ground. Grandfather Marin stood on the charred door of their home and surveyed the total destruction of every material possession that he and his wife had.

We cherish Grandfather Marin's diary, in which he wrote on the date of the fire: "God has spoken to me through this disaster, reminding me of the promises of his Word. Based upon his promises, I believe that someday, on the very spot where only the charred door of our home remains, there will stand a place of worship." Seven years later an Evangelical church was built on that very site. It still stands today, shedding the light and warmth of God's love to seeking hearts.

What an inspiration my wife's family was to Tzvete and me! If those who had gone before us had stood faithfully in the face of persecution, could we give in to those who threatened us? Could we rationalize that the situation was too difficult or that we were powerless? When they threw themselves upon the Lord and found that he could change hopeless lives, could we give up? What about those who would come behind us? Would they find us faithful?

Reflecting upon this long history of faithfulness in Tzvete's family, I knew that she would never be influenced by Penkov's persuasions. She was a woman of faith and strong conscience who would rather die than compromise her faith in Christ.

Something of a smile must have flickered across my face at the thought of Penkov trying to intimidate Tzvete. He had been peering at me contemptuously during the brief silence. "Huh!" he exclaimed. "The best woman in the whole world just happens to be your wife!"

The Clash of Will and Wits

There was no one quite like Penkov, with his sharp mind and even sharper tongue, among all of my interrogators. Our "conversations" were always filled with arguments, counterarguments, and mental sparring. Like wrestlers grappling for a hold at the beginning of a match, we circled one another, looking for a weakness or some opening, each trying to gain an advantage.

My exchanges with Penkov matched not only wits and intellect but emotional strength as well. Whenever possible, I pointed to logical inconsistencies in Penkov's diatribes to show the weakness of his case. But logic was secondary in my mind because I knew his arguments provided only a cosmetic covering for a philosophical system far deeper and more diabolical.

The most basic aspect of our struggle was a contest of wills. Penkov wanted to break my will. My defense was to surround myself with the sword of the Spirit, which is God's Word (Ephesians 6:17), and prayer. If I stayed strong spiritually, Penkov would see that my will wasn't influenced by his tactics.

Throughout the interview Penkov said nothing about the possibility of my case being brought to trial, which was very much on my mind. Were they going to let me languish in prison? As much as I longed for the opportunity to speak in my own defense in court, I dared not let Penkov know how I felt. Tipping him off as to my hopes would only be used against me.

I had noticed that Penkov became agitated when I reminded him that from the first day of my imprisonment no one had ever declared formally that my rights as a pastor had been revoked. Without an official order in writing, it was not legally permissible for them to forbid me to preach.

My insistence that no written order had been issued seemed to unsettle Penkov. I maintained that if they couldn't give me the reasons for my imprisonment in writing, I should be released.

His predictable reply was, "We have no need of such an order. The Committee is a higher institution than your church, and they have the power to do as they wish."

"Would you say that if the Chief Interrogator simply came and told you, 'Penkov, you're no longer working here. You must find another place to work!'?" I rejoined. "Would you not ask for the reasons why and request a written order explaining his action?"

Once again Penkov showed his frustration by leaning across the desk and saying, "We're not talking about my employment but about your resistance to the Committee's authority!"

With that, Penkov called the guards to take me away. Ushering me out of the interrogation room, the guards placed me in a holding area so that several prisoners might be escorted to the cells at the same time.

To my amazement, as I entered the holding area, there sat my brother Dimitar! I'm sure the startled look on his face was similar to my own. It was almost too good to be true. Apparently Dimitar had been interrogated by another team of agents during the time I was with Penkov. We didn't know how long we would have but made the best of the few minutes together. Dimitar hastily told me, "They released me and arrested me again a few days later."

"Which cell are you in?" I asked.

"Cell 4, on the first floor," he replied, confirming the rumor I had heard.

"How are Tzvete and the children?" I asked hastily.

"They're doing well. The church members support both them and you. It was ten days before Pavel Ivanov could even get into the pulpit!" Dimitar informed me with a smile.

I smiled at the thought of the faithful believers standing against the intrusion of Pavel Ivanov.

"I'm writing an appeal," Dimitar whispered, "insisting that our freedom of religion is being violated."

"I'll support you," I offered, "even if there isn't much chance of it being heard. I've talked to my interrogator about it, but he laughs at the idea."

Before we could talk further, the guards ordered us to stand. "Keep praying! Be strong," I urged as we parted.

Love Is Stronger Than Hate

Thrust rudely back into my cell, I had time to reflect upon the interview and prepare myself for whatever might come. There was no guarantee that I would be given a trial, as much as I would welcome one. Many people had been arrested in Bulgaria only to disappear forever. The authorities could do anything they wished, holding me indefinitely or disposing of me for good. There were also stories in the prison of a labor camp in northern Bulgaria where prisoners were sent and never heard from again. Rumors told of human remains being fed to a herd of pigs near the so-called camp! All I could do was entrust my life to Christ and believe there was a purpose for what I was going through.

A night or two later I overheard a bone-chilling conversation between two guards as they discussed the plight of a prisoner who was desperately ill. One of the guards seemed concerned and suggested, "Don't you think we should call an ambulance? That prisoner is in pain. He's very sick!"

"Why worry?" his comrade replied. "We're responsible only for their number, not for their health!"

One guard in particular never smiled, at least not genuinely. He always had a dour look on his face. He knew I was an evangelical pastor, in prison for my religious beliefs. When he served the food, he always gave me the smallest scrap of bread, handing it to me with a sneer on his face. The same sneer would appear when he opened the door to my cell and said, "Good morning, Pastor. Well, how are you today?"

When I invariably responded, "Thank God, I am fine. Very fine!" his smile would freeze; he obviously wanted to hear me complain or give some evidence of discomfort.

The conditions in the cell were so deplorable that when the guards opened the door to allow us to step into the empty corridor, it gave us a sense of freedom. Being able to walk a few steps reminded me that I had once known a totally different life outside of prison. But that life seemed very long ago and far away from Central Prison.

Tony had been taken out of our cell after only a few days, and another inmate named Sasho had been brought in. It was always stressful when a new inmate was brought into a cell. Some of the inmates were psychopaths or sociopaths with serious mental illnesses that made them threats to others or to themselves, especially in such confined quarters.

Sasho turned out to be a fairly stable fellow and brought information that was of great interest to us. Before he had been transferred to Sofia, Sasho had spent time in two other Bulgarian prisons; one at Kremikovtzi (pronounced "Krem-ee-koff-zee") and another at Ljubo ("Lew-bow"). Mitko and I whispered our questions to him about conditions in those prisons, knowing there was a chance we might be transferred there.

Sasho told us that at these other prisons there were actually scheduled times for watching TV. Good behavior was rewarded by allowing a prisoner to use the canteen to buy cigarettes, newspapers, and drinks such as coffee and tea.

"What about using the lavatories?" we asked.

"You can use them any time you need," he told us.

"For how long are you able to use them?" we asked in disbelief.

"As long as you want. You only have to be out of the toilets before the inspection."

This was almost inconceivable after experiencing constant harassment in the toilets by the guards at Central Prison.

In one sense, the guards had a very difficult station in life. Few of the prisoners were prisoners of conscience as I was. Most were hardened criminals who would do anything possible to cheat, steal, or even assault a guard. Guarding prisoners was not an easy job, and I began to pray that God would help me love them for Christ's sake. A few words of witness to my faith in Christ could perhaps show the guards that God's love was stronger than their hatred.

Faith in Friends or God Alone?

The interrogations were beginning to increase in both frequency and intensity. Apparently Penkov had noticed that my resolve wasn't lessening and decided to apply more pressure.

Penkov called me in on January 28. Tall and angular with his black mustache neatly trimmed, Penkov met me at the door of the interrogation room. He greeted me affably as if this were a business conversation. Always well dressed, his neatly pressed black suit contrasted humorously with my tattered and smelly prison garb.

Entering the interrogation room, I was confronted with the bulky presence of Vladimir Nikolov, who had been present at my induction. Short and stocky, Nikolov sat watching me impassively with not so much as a nod when I sat down. Later I learned that Nikolov was with the SS, the state Security Service, which was an elite corps of agents delegated any power they deemed necessary to "protect the interests" of the government.

About forty years old with a bushy head of fair hair, Nikolov was also neatly dressed, as was the custom of most interrogators. The dark, well-pressed suits the agents wore gave them an air of authority that helped establish a feeling of superiority over the prisoners they dealt with daily.

As was his custom, Penkov began with one of his grand pronouncements, usually offered casually as if sharing a tidbit of news with a friend. His "news" usually indicated a theme for the day. He was in top form with Nikolov providing an audience.

"A great deal has happened since we last met," Penkov began. He went on to suggest that my "followers" had all abandoned me, and that Pavel Ivanov was already in the pulpit and doing quite well. Penkov labored through a long, well-rehearsed soliloquy designed to convince me that my stubbornness in resisting the government was in vain.

There was no trusting what Penkov said. More than likely he was twisting the truth or lying outright. I resolved to let nothing disturb my peace of mind. If my hope had been in my friends in the church, I might have become discouraged. But my faith was not in my friends; it was in God alone.

I recognized the importance of constantly focusing my faith upon God. My constant focus had to be on pleasing him, not on the approval of the congregation, the Committee, or the agents. Preoccupation with my circumstances or speculation about what was or was not happening with the church would only lead to worry.

It was my absolute trust in God that strengthened me throughout this long ordeal. Only God's Spirit could prepare me for the sudden accusations or an attack of doubt that might come. Trusting God to do what I was unable to do in taking care of my family, the church, and myself, I prayed that his Holy Spirit would work in my heart, guiding each thought, word, and deed.

This Foreign Matter

Vladimir Nikolov had sat quietly, his chestnut-colored eyes locked in a penetrating gaze. Nikolov had been in the room during my first interrogation, but he seemed to play a secondary role to Penkov. He had only spoken a word or two, always directed to Penkov.

Suddenly Nikolov showed a side of his personality I hadn't seen before. Drawing his chair up closer to the corner of the desk, he began reprimanding me for the fact that people in foreign countries were being informed about my case. He drummed his pudgy fingers on the desk as he spoke. The fact that he was well fed for doing his job was not lost on me. "You obviously know something about this," he said, concluding his harangue. "How are these foreigners being notified of your imprisonment?"

I sat in stunned silence at the news. People outside of Bulgaria asking for my release? How could it be? Somewhere, somehow, people must be asking about me or perhaps asking for my release.

What an encouragement to know that people outside of my country were concerned about my safety and well-being! All contact between our churches and Christians in Britain or the United States had been cut off long ago. Our only contact with Christians outside of Bulgaria was an occasional conversation with business representatives from Scandinavian countries. Perhaps one of them had written to the government about my imprisonment.

The news was so overwhelming that I sat silently for a time, composing myself so as to not show the elation I was feeling. Finally I responded. "Since I've been confined to my cell without visitors, it is not possible for me to even know anything of what is happening outside the walls, let alone communicate with people outside the country! How could I possibly have an opportunity to communicate?"

To my amazement Nikolov continued to press the matter, revealing how important this "foreign matter" was to him.

Knowing this foreign interest in my case could favorably influence the outcome of a trial, or even the granting of one, I decided that silence was my wisest course in these tense moments. The thought crossed my mind that with foreign interests probing for information, it would be difficult for agents to execute someone and cover it up.

Finally, when Nikolov demanded a reply, I took a chance by asking, "Isn't my case public? If so, why are you so concerned with who knows about my imprisonment?"

Lenin and the Bible

The letters from foreign countries brought about a change in Nikolov's and Penkov's attitudes. In my next interrogation with Penkov, he informed me that an exception in prison policies was being made for me. "Because your case is of international interest, you will be allowed to request reading material," he advised me with some reluctance. "This is usually allowed only after the interrogations are completed. But we don't want your foreign friends saying we're treating you inhumanely." He smiled sarcastically.

When Penkov gave me a form to request one or two titles for my family to bring, I asked, "May I have my Bible for reading? It's important to me as a Christian pastor and would allow me to continue my daily practice of reading the Scriptures."

"Sorry, but it's not allowed in our prisons. We can't have those stories of monarchies and capitalistic teachings."

"There can be no harm in reading the Bible," I persisted. "It teaches morality and ethics, including compassion for the poor and God's love for the common people. The Bible is the most widely published book in the world, and I find it strange that any government would be opposed to its moral teachings."

"If you want," Penkov replied, "I can give you the book *Lenin: For the State*." This book about Lenin was standard Communist reading fare. The government urged everyone to read it, even the prisoners.

"Thank you, but no!" I responded.

Writing my request, I asked for the titles *Time To Depart, Quo Vadis,* and *Hanging Gardens.* These were among the few pieces of classic literature the Communists allowed. What Penkov and the government censors didn't know was that the last title was a novel containing large portions of the book of Job, Psalms, and the Song of Solomon from the Bible.

My brother had also told me during our brief time together that he was reading *Quo Vadis* to the prisoners in his cell. *Quo Vadis* is an epic novel about the struggle of early Christians to survive persecution in the Roman Empire during the days of Nero. It was written by the great Polish author Henryk Sienkiewicz.

Even though I was not allowed to have a Bible, I hoped my request for reading literature would be honored. How wonderful it would be to be allowed to read books!

A Thin Skin of Reason Stuffed with a Lie

Exhausted, I lay on my mattress, giving thanks to God for protecting me thus far. This most recent interrogation had given me much to consider. The letters from foreign countries were potentially in my favor. I was gaining confidence that I was winning the war of wills. By acting strictly upon my principles, I had preserved my emotional stability. The temptation I must constantly resist was trying to influence my situation or manipulate the environment around me. If Penkov saw any sign that I was eager to improve my situation, he would know he had me.

It frustrated Penkov and Nikolov when I conceded that they controlled my environment. "I'm in your control," I had said more than once. "You can do anything with me and my family. But you should know that whatever you do, it will be done only because God allows it. Even if you take my life, God will use it for his glory! My purpose in life is to serve Christ, whether I'm in prison or free."

By refusing to negotiate for favors, I remained firm in my stance. Rather than responding to the environment, which the interrogators controlled, I spoke of the spiritual principles that guided my life. This frustrated Penkov and Nikolov to no end.

The exchanges with Penkov and Nikolov made me reflect upon the human tendency to act impulsively when under stress. Many citizens were quick to comply when faced with pressure from the government. Although they might not agree with what the government was doing, they would say, "I went along with their game. It just wasn't expedient to do anything else."

Even Christians sometimes rationalized when faced with pressure, saying, for example, "What they're doing isn't right, but I can't jeopardize my family by making an issue of it." Others said, "I can't serve Christ in prison. Besides, what would happen to the church if we all ended up in prison?" There were always excuses to be made if one was looking for the easy way out of a difficult situation. The excuses sounded reasonable, but soon those who made them ended up contradicting their principles.

It appeared far more convenient to abandon principles—giving the excuse that resistance wouldn't eliminate the problem—than to resist evil and suffer. But in prison God began to show me that excuses were merely a thin skin of reason stuffed with a lie. Excuses almost always circumvented the principle, providing an easy way to avoid suffering for Christ.

Some Christians said, "But what will happen to the church if I get arrested? If all of us are arrested, the doors of the church will be closed!" That excuse had crossed my own mind, but God reminded me that no human being or human system can close the church. The church's one true foundation is the risen Lord and Savior Jesus Christ, and nothing can destroy it. If my faith is truly in the Lord, could I so easily forget Christ's words when he said that even the gates of hell could not withstand the power of the church? Certainly not. I could look back over two thousand years of God's faithfulness in every kind of circumstance.

It seemed to me that God wanted a church that would be willing to continuously die and rise again by his power. Any theology of the church that didn't include suffering for Christ if necessary was not the kind of church God wanted. God couldn't use a church that sought only to entertain people or to make them comfortable.

Penkov and I Part Smiling

The following day Penkov summoned me again. "Your books have arrived," he announced matter-of-factly. "And here are some things from your eccentric church friends. You should be pleased that I'm allowing you to have them in light of the charges against you." Penkov handed me the volumes I'd requested, along with some literature from First Church that I never anticipated. It wasn't much—a newsletter and a page or two of devotional thoughts shared in a recent Bible study—but I welcomed any news.

"Christo, can you tell me why on earth these are of any value to anyone?" Penkov asked quizzically.

"They're gifts from my friends at the church," I explained. "They are concerned for me because I'm their pastor, and they know that my congregation is important to me. They want me to know that they care for me."

"Why don't they bring me something?" Penkov said with a twinkle in his eye.

I could not resist saying, "If they did, it would probably be *Lenin: For the State!*"

It was the only time Penkov and I parted smiling.

Mitko and Sasho were astounded when I returned with materials to read. "How did you do it, Christo?" they exclaimed. "We're starving for food and can't get enough. You ask for books, and you get them! The rest of us are at their mercy while you never give them the satisfaction of hearing you complain. And you're the one who gets them to change the policy. What's going on here?"

"God watches over me," I said.

That evening I read softly to Mitko and Sasho as they sat in rapt attention. The books provided many evenings of entertainment. When I was relocated, I was allowed to take those books with me. Wherever I went, I found they gave me wonderful opportunities to begin conversations about spiritual matters.

A Veteran of the Belene Concentration Camp

The long days in the small cell with Mitko and Sasho continued without interruption until February 6, when a guard summoned me to follow him. When I stepped into Penkov's interrogation room, to my amazement, my brother Dimitar and Pastor Bozovayski were sitting there.

Pastor Bozovayski was an elderly man who had preceded me as the pastor of First Evangelical Church of Sofia. Tall and dignified, Pastor Bozovayski greeted us, "Christo, Dimitar, my brothers in Christ. How pleased I am that they allowed me to come spend a few minutes with you!"

Lowering his voice, he said, "Chavdar Penkov called me in for an interrogation. They're curious about what I will say if I'm called to be a witness. I asked them to allow me to see you."

Dimitar and I looked at one another. The fact that Penkov was interrogating possible witnesses raised our hopes that indeed we would be given a trial.

The familiar voice of this Christian brother brought memories of the last time we spoke. Since retiring, Pastor Bozovayski had moved to the city of Pazardzhik, some two hours' drive away. I had gone to consult with him just before my arrest. When I told him I felt the Lord leading me to take a strong stand against the government, tears came to his eyes as he warned, "Christo, my brother, one cannot break a stone wall with his head!"

Pastor Bozovayski knew firsthand the dangers that faced us. He had taken a courageous stand as a young man in the Pastors' Trial of 1949. As a result, he was a veteran of the concentration camp at Belene.

When Pastor Bozovayski came out of the concentration camp, he had walked a tightrope. He maintained a tolerable relationship with the government by endorsing our secret youth camps and evangelistic activities but removing himself from any knowledge of these things. Because the agents were watching him closely, he cautiously told us he couldn't be associated with what we were doing. He asked us and the people working with us never to inform him of any secret activities.

This split-level system had worked well as Pastor Bozovayski gave his silent blessing to spiritual outreach while we protected him from any direct involvement. This arrangement also gave some comfort to his wife who lived constantly with a haunting fear that he might be arrested again as he had been in 1949. The close scrutiny continued, but Pastor Bozovayski was never again arrested.

When he retired, Pastor Bozovayski suggested that I might want to continue to work underground with someone else in the pulpit. In the end, after much discussion, the consensus was that I should become the pastor of First Evangelical Church in Sofia. Yet I knew I could never give up my underground ministries.

Even in retirement this sincere man had continued to visit Sofia once a month in his role as chairman of the Evangelical Alliance of Churches. In that role the old man had been the object of much pressure. Not even his considerable diplomatic skills could extricate him from the mounting tension.

A man by the name of Tzvetkov, Chairman of the Committee on Internal Religious Affairs, began to meet with Pastor Bozovayski regularly. Subtly at first, but more and more relentlessly, Tzvetkov put pressure upon the esteemed pastor. When Tzvetkov tried to force him to announce that Pavel Ivanov was being installed in my place, Bozovayski flatly refused.

It was a courageous stand the tall, gray-haired pastor took in resisting the government. When Tzvetkov saw that the old man was unbending, he angrily ordered Pastor Bozovayski to return to Pazardzhik. Soon after that, the announcement was made that Pastor Bozovayski had been removed as chairman of the Evangelical Alliance.

After inquiring about our health, Pastor Bozovayski briefly whispered that the church was doing well. His expression told me the opposition to Pavel Ivanov was continuing.

When Pavel Ivanov had first announced that he was coming to take over the pulpit of the church, Pastor Bozovayski, at the request of the congregation, had agreed to conduct a communion service instead. When Ivanov arrived and was informed that the esteemed former pastor was conducting the services, he stormed off in a rage, threatening to call the authorities.

We had only spoken for a few minutes when the visit was abruptly terminated. Penkov allowed us to see Pastor Bozovayski only long enough for it to be considered a visit. But it was so brief, it was frustrating to all three of us.

As the guard rudely thrust himself in front of the older man and physically turned him toward the door, Pastor Bozovayski glanced at us over his shoulder with a look of helplessness.

As Pastor Bozovayski was ushered out, I realized we had spent our time talking about our health and the church but had not had a chance to mention our families. I called out, "Please give everyone our greetings!" and breathed a prayer he would convey special greetings to our families, who were undoubtedly sick with worry about us.

CHAPTER FIVE
Enough of That Gospel of Yours!

Remember Jesus Christ, raised from the dead. . . . This is my gospel,
for which I am suffering even to the point of being chained like
a criminal. But God's word is not chained. Therefore I endure
everything for the sake of the elect, that they too may obtain the
salvation that is in Christ Jesus, with eternal glory.
2 TIMOTHY 2:8-10

We will match your capacity to inflict suffering by our capacity
to endure suffering. We will meet your physical force with soul force.
Do to us what you will and we will still love you. . . .
Bomb our homes and threaten our children, and, as difficult
as it is, we will still love you."
MARTIN LUTHER KING, JR.

My next interview with Chavdar Penkov was on a Friday. Penkov was waiting in his customary black suit. With a condescending smile he pointed to a chair across the desk from him. "Your brother will be joining us," Penkov informed me. "We want to discuss some things with both of you."

Dimitar came through the door momentarily, and we greeted one another. Our closely cropped hair and frayed prison clothing gave us an appearance that was almost humorous. We were both beginning to show the gaunt, pale look of prisoners in Central Prison, but overall Dimitar looked as if he was doing as well as could be expected.

A Psychological Ploy
Penkov began by telling us the decision had been made not to release us. "It appears you'll be staying with us awhile," he informed us.

When I requested that Penkov call my family to request additional money to purchase food at the canteen, Penkov moved to the telephone and dialed our number. Even this simple telephone call was an attempt to plant doubts and fears in my mind.

When my teenage son, Stefan, answered the phone, Penkov said, "Stefan, is that you? This is Chavdar Penkov, calling from Central Prison." For my benefit, I'm sure, he continued, "You're sick? Do you have a temperature? Are you in bed today?"

Although Penkov passed along my request for money for Dimitar and me, his primary purpose was clearly to start me worrying about the well-being of my son. But all of those thoughts I committed to God, knowing he would help me focus on nothing but remaining faithful.

It was only human to wonder what was happening to my Tzvete, our son, Stefan, and our daughter, Nebesna. Occasionally I worried for a brief time, but as soon as I became aware of it I turned to God in prayer. It was prayer and the promises of God's Word that delivered me from the torment of doubt and fear that Penkov worked so hard to plant in my mind.

The Church Extinct by 2000

As the interrogation began, Penkov tried to convince Dimitar and me that everyone in the church had turned against us. Dimitar was the treasurer of the Evangelical Union and preached only occasionally, so Penkov seemed to be focusing on me.

Penkov's goal was to elicit compliance with party orders passed down through government officials to the church, thus controlling its every activity. Obviously, he bought into the Communist belief that the church was to be tolerated only for the time being, convinced it would inevitably die out. Tzvetkov himself, Chairman of the Committee, had predicted that by the year 2000 the Christian church in Bulgaria would be extinct.

The government had warned for years that young people needed to be "protected" from people like me who would "disturb" them with antiquated ideas about God. Such archaic religious views, the people were told, no longer fit the modern Marxist view of the world, the view that was going to prevail.

Penkov's effort to paint a picture of Ivanov successfully leading the church was not as convincing as he hoped. In spite of his efforts to discourage me, God answered my prayers and kept my spirits high.

The exchange between Penkov and myself became more intense when I told him that the people had selected me as pastor because they believed, as I did, that Christ was the head of the church, not the Committee.

"What makes you think you can overrule the Committee?" Penkov shot back. "Apparently you think the church should serve you rather than obeying the authorities."

Primed to reply, I said, "You blame the church for serving the ruling classes and yet you're seeking to have it serve you. Isn't that the same thing? It isn't my desire to serve myself or any class of society but to serve God alone! If I agree to lead the church according to your terms, then I'd be serving you and not God."

Penkov laughed, "If you don't learn to obey the Committee, you won't be serving at all! I'm here to tell you the Committee is in charge!"

I responded, "What you're really seeking to do is to put yourself in God's place, and you fail to understand that as a Christian my whole life is committed to serving God and God alone. That's my only wish and desire, just as it was the desire of the apostle Paul when he wrote, 'For me, to live is Christ and to die is gain.' That's exactly how I feel. If I can honor God by standing up for the truth and going to prison, I will. If I am released, I'll go back to leading the church as God's Word instructs me."

"Yes, those are the choices," Penkov said sarcastically. "And if your attitude doesn't change, you're going to be in prison for a long, long time! When you get out in the year 2000 these little churches will have died out. Don't be stupid!"

"All of your threats that are designed to make me afraid aren't able to touch my heart," I insisted. "You know me well enough by now to know that as long as I live—even if I spend my entire life in this prison—I'll be serving God. And if I die, then I'll be with him for eternity!"

This Christ of Yours!

There was silence for a time. Changing his tone, Penkov asked quite civilly, "Is anybody disturbing either of you when you're praying?" Someone obviously had reported to Penkov that it was our custom to kneel and pray both morning and night.

"No one is disturbing me," Dimitar volunteered.

Watching Penkov's expression carefully, I told him, "It has always been my custom to pray as I do here, even in the army. I discipline myself to not let anything distract me when I am praying."

As expected, Penkov showed no emotion. Rather than warning us not to pray, he returned to the previous subject. "So, you don't mind being in prison?" he asked sarcastically.

"That's not the point," I said. "I prefer to be in prison with Jesus than to be free without him. Even if I were with my family and back in the pulpit, there would be no satisfaction if I was outside of God's will." And I reminded Penkov of our hymn that says, "The prison becomes a palace when I'm there with Christ."

"This Christ of yours! Show me what he's done for you in this miserable situation!" Penkov demanded.

"Christ has given me eternal life!"

Laughing with disbelief, Penkov shot back, "Are you serious? If you are, I'll have to send you to see a psychiatrist!"

"Certainly, I am serious," I told him. "I really mean it when I tell you that each one of us will someday face God and eternity. We have an immortal soul. It says in the gospel—"

"Enough of that gospel of yours!" Penkov shouted.

Pausing briefly, I lowered my voice and continued, "I cannot tell you anything else and be truthful. The gospel of Christ is the reason I am here. Why does it seem strange to you that there are some of us who are prepared to suffer for our Lord? Is it impossible for you to accept those who have an opinion that differs from yours?"

"Do you believe these things your brother is saying?" Penkov asked, turning to Dimitar.

"Certainly," Dimitar responded, nodding.

Penkov's patience was at an end. "We'll talk more about this later. Both of you had better think about what I've said. Maybe a few more days in a miserable cell will bring you to your senses!"

Walking the Tightrope

That exchange was my most animated and emotional encounter with Penkov to that point. Penkov was focusing on me, which seemed to indicate that Dimitar, as the treasurer, was less of a threat to the Committee. It was my hope that Dimitar's silence in our interrogations would convince Penkov to release him again so that he could return to his family and the church.

Back in my cell, I thought of other things I wished I'd said to Penkov, but overall I was pleased at the strength of my responses. With the help of the Holy Spirit, I hadn't become confused or given in to the temptation to negotiate some kind of a deal.

As I lay in the cell day after day, I carefully reviewed the situation. There were times when I thought of Pastor Bozovayski walking the tightrope. He had skillfully positioned himself as sympathetic to the underground ministry, making sure it continued without his knowledge, while at the same time presenting an image as somewhat compliant to the committee.

I asked myself, *Can I walk the same tightrope?* My personality was different from Pastor Bozovayski's. For years I had worked underground with my brother, taking risks to encourage the churches and win young people to Christ. As I saw it, to change my style now would be wrong.

Another factor to consider was that I had challenged hundreds of people to remain bold and faithful to Christ no matter what the circumstances. It would raise questions about my level of commitment if I were seen working with government officials. I knew what my friends working underground would think. The Holy Spirit clearly led me to see the importance of being constant and faithful to Christ no matter what the circumstances.

Communism Will Fall

I spent a great deal of time in my cell reflecting on the truth of Scripture. Even though I didn't have a Bible, I knew many passages by heart and could recall the details of the great stories in the Bible.

One story I recalled from the Old Testament was when the Philistines captured the ark of the covenant (1 Samuel 5–6). Discouraged because they couldn't fight the Philistines, the Israelites were powerless and thought all hope was lost.

The Philistines took the ark and placed it beside an idol of their god Dagon. Each day they arose to find that Dagon had fallen down before the ark! Plagues then began to invade the area, and the Philistines moved the ark to Gath. The plagues followed, making life miserable in Gath, so they moved the ark to Ekron.

By this time the citizens of Ekron saw what was happening and asked that the ark be taken away. The story ends with the Philistines gladly returning the ark of the covenant to Israel. The great symbol of God's glory had been recaptured without the Israelites having to lift a hand.

My situation was similar to Israel's, as I was powerless before my enemies. The lesson in the passage was clear: I could trust God to protect his glory!

Just as the Israelites learned to trust God in a difficult situation, so I learned to trust God to protect his church. The church exists neither by us nor for us. It is God's church, and its present as well as its future are in his hands. Just as the false god Dagon fell, so Communism will fall. But God's church will continue by his strength and for his glory.

A Lesson In Leadership

I thought, *It is easy for us to think that we are protecting God's glory when we are really protecting our own interests. Christian leaders, especially, must be alert to this temptation.* My thoughts went back to another Old Testament story involving Saul, the first king of Israel.

King Saul was a humble man when God called him to be the

leader of Israel. Wanting to be a godly king, Saul commanded the priests to offer up sacrifices to God before going into battle, just as God had instructed. This was done to remind the nation and its army that their strength came from the Lord.

As thousands of men began to follow Saul, however, he began to trust in his own power more than in God's. When there was a clash with the Philistines, King Saul hastily decided to go to war and called the priest Samuel to offer up sacrifices to God.

When Samuel was late in arriving and his men became impatient, King Saul egoistically usurped the role of priest. Stepping up to the altar and offering the sacrifice himself, Saul put the focus upon himself rather than upon God. When he should have been kneeling with his men, setting an example in seeking God's guidance, Saul plunged ahead, trusting in his own strength and righteousness (1 Samuel 13:1-13).

As punishment for Saul's disobedience, God caused Israel to lose the battle. Someone might ask, "What could possibly be wrong with what Saul did? A sacrifice is a sacrifice, whether offered by the priest or by the king." The problem was that Saul by his disobedience placed his own interests before God's glory. His sacrifices were motivated by ego and impatience. But the Bible says, "The sacrifice you want is a broken spirit. A broken and repentant heart, O God, you will not despise" (Psalm 51:17, NLT).

God wants our obedience more than anything else. When we're tempted to rush ahead of God—thinking we know what is best—our faith is in ourselves rather than in the God who protected Israel throughout the centuries. When we think we must compromise to protect the church, we make *ourselves* the head of the church rather than Christ, whose Spirit was with Paul and Silas in prison. Even when the circumstances are dismal, we can be sure that God is still on the throne and that he will guard his glory.

You Will Be Given the Words to Say

A few days later Penkov summoned me again. We resumed where we had left off.

"It appears the church is doing well without you," he said proudly. "Have you given some thought to what I said in our last interview? It would be very nice for both of us if you would just agree to accept the Committee's authority."

"My authority comes from God's Word and God's Spirit," I replied. "As the first disciples said in the New Testament, 'We must obey God rather than men!' (Acts 5:29). You'll remember that I told you I would rather remain in prison and be faithful to Christ than be free and faithful to your Committee!"

Penkov's sneer suggested that he thought I must be insane for allowing myself to suffer in prison rather than cooperate with the government's plan for the church. "You people are crazy," he scoffed. "We should throw all of you in prison!"

"Surely you recognize that Christians are the most decent citizens of our society. They feed the hungry and care for the poor. If you truly want a better society, why do you work with dishonest people like Pavel Ivanov who look out only for themselves? We Christians think differently because we live by biblical principles, applying the teachings of Jesus to our daily lives. Just because we think differently, you hold us in your already overcrowded prisons! Why not look at the way we live?"

"I can see that we have a long way to go in reforming you," Penkov chortled.

"How can you be blind to the overcrowding of this prison?" I asked. "This is just one piece of evidence that confirms what I'm saying. There's no reform taking place in your prisons. And you add to the problem just because we don't follow your pattern of thinking and make the government our god!"

"Christo, all we're asking is that you cooperate with us. Use some common sense and spare yourself the embarrassment of being imprisoned! If you would agree with me, you could replace Pavel Ivanov," Penkov said.

"You know the only reason I'm here is because I'm bold enough to tell you exactly what I believe," I said, looking Penkov directly in the eye. "By suggesting that I could be standing in the place of Pavel Ivanov, you hope to convince me to cater to you. That doesn't appeal to me in the least if I must accept your terms. There is nothing in the world you can offer that would tempt me to become like Pavel Ivanov, who has no principles. Force me to choose between freedom or my faith, and integrity demands that I choose my faith every time— even if it means sacrificing my freedom!"

This was one of those times when it amazed me that Penkov allowed me to continue speaking things I felt I needed to say. God's Word is true when it promises, "When they arrest you, do not worry about what to say or how to say it. At that time you will be given what to say, for it will not be you speaking, but the Spirit of your Father speaking through you" (Matthew 10:19-20).

Penkov eventually stopped me. "Enough! I'll do the talking, not you!"

Complying with Penkov's demand, I prayed silently that God would bless Chavdar Penkov. My wisdom and words could do nothing, but God's Spirit could by some miracle touch the heart of a man like Penkov. As I looked intently at him, I think Penkov realized that while he could silence me, he would never control my mind or my spirit. On that note of obvious frustration, he ended yet another interview.

God Speaks through a Dream

Back in my cell, many questions remained. My biggest question was whether or not I was going to be granted a trial. Penkov still wasn't giving any clues. In spite of the uncertainty, God gave me a sense of peace about the stand I was taking in the interrogations.

That night I had a dream in which I saw Pavel Ivanov coming out of the church building with two suitcases. Four policemen accompanied him as they proceeded toward a tram stop located on nearby Vitosha Boulevard.

Suddenly the dream changed, as they sometimes do, and in the next scene I was entering the church. The pews were packed with people, and others sat in chairs in the aisles to accommodate an overflow crowd at the worship service. As I entered, two dear brothers, Ivan Babulev and Peter Velev, were standing in front. They were delighted to see me, and we greeted one another with the traditional brotherly kiss.

As the dream continued, Brother Kozuharov came to me and led me to the front of the packed sanctuary. "Brother Christo," he said, "perhaps you're too tired to preach, but would you be so kind as to at least lead us in prayer?" It was then, as I recall, that the dream ended.

This is the only dream I can recall having in Central Prison. Although it had not been my experience to attach a great deal of spiritual importance to dreams, this particular dream was significant, assuring me that Pavel Ivanov would leave the church. It didn't portray me preaching in the pulpit again, which wasn't important; it simply demonstrated that the agents would not be successful in taking over the church. It was as if God was saying to me, "Don't link the church with persons, for people come and go, but God's Kingdom will remain forever. Seek my Kingdom and my righteousness and do not seek to please people."

The Prisoner's Advocate

There was no end to the strategies Penkov used in trying to confuse me. The next time I was called in for questioning, there was another prisoner present. I didn't know him, but Penkov introduced him as "the prisoner's advocate." He supposedly was there to lend a sympathetic ear to the complaints of prisoners, participating in the party illusion that everyone has a voice in making decisions.

In reality, the prisoner's advocate was part of a scheme to get me to talk. The scheme was nothing more than a crudely camouflaged approach to the age-old routine of alternating threats with sympathy, hoping to lull the subject into opening up. Penkov had been playing the role of the bad guy or antagonist; the prisoner's advocate presented himself as my protagonist, the good guy.

With Penkov sitting quietly at the end of the table, shuffling his papers nonchalantly, the so-called "advocate" began speaking softly. "I've always been rather interested in religion," he began. "Some members of my family are religious and have shared some literature with me."

Remaining silent, I waited for him to continue. This didn't seem likely for someone trusted by an agent of an atheistic government. Aware that he was being bribed to engage me in conversation, I was curious to see where he was going.

"Those in the government have to be careful about what they say, but some of us citizens occasionally speak quietly with one another about how unfortunate it is that religion has become so controversial." I looked at Penkov, who was pretending not to listen, as if such talk were common in a Communist prison. How gullible did he think I was?

"For instance, religion has inspired lots of art and literature, and that can't be all bad," the prisoner continued, warming to his subject. When I didn't rise to the bait, he went on. "But some of the controversies have started within the churches. For instance, I've never really understood all of the power entrusted to the pope. I would be interested in hearing your views on the subject. Don't worry, you can trust me. I'm just curious as to your feelings about the pope."

The man obviously knew I was a Protestant and had designed a not-so-subtle gambit to entice me into criticizing the pope. If successful, he could pretend we had something in common and play it for all it was worth. It was an all-too-transparent ploy to make me feel close to him.

"Personally, I've never thought it healthy to go around criticizing other Christians," I responded. "None of us are perfect, including my-self, so why should I point out the weaknesses of others such as the pope? If you want to talk about a religious leader who has power—real power—why don't we talk about Jesus?"

"Certainly, that would be fine," the so-called advocate agreed, shuffling his feet. I sensed, however, that his reply lacked genuine en-thusiasm. "Go ahead, tell me what you believe about Jesus."

"Those of us who have committed our lives to Jesus Christ are called to follow him," I began. "Not only is he the one who saves us from sin, but he is the Lord of our lives as well. There's no one else in all of history who has the power to forgive us of our sins! That is Good News, which is what the word *gospel* means. The Good News of Jesus Christ is that he died on the cross to forgive my sins and yours!"

My conversation partner, who just a moment ago had seemed open-minded, now seemed less than eager to pursue this talk of Jesus. He decided to try another tangent, saying, "Yes, but at this very mo-ment there is a famous minister who is in prison, sentenced to eight years for rape! He says the devil forced him to do it! Wouldn't you be critical of someone like that?"

In the Communist system, this was one of the favorite tactics used to discredit Christianity. If a Christian, preferably a Christian leader, could be caught in a wrong, especially a flagrant moral failure, it was used to try and embarrass and denigrate all Christians and their beliefs.

The Devil and the Torn Sandals

Disgusted with Penkov's crude tactics, I decided to take some time to respond with a lengthy story, an old one from my childhood.

"Certainly it's the devil's task to make every Christian fall into sin. I'm sure Satan is happy to have this man in prison where you can criti-cize him," I said, approaching my transition. "It reminds me of the story about the devil and his torn sandals.

"As the story goes, Satan was working hard to entice a man to commit a serious sin. Of course, he promised to help the man escape punishment for the sin. The man finally succumbed to the temptation and murdered another man.

"Time passed, and the man believed he was free. Eventually, however, the man was caught, found guilty, and sentenced to death. Satan's promise to help him escape justice turned out to be totally false!

"While being taken to the gallows in the public square, to his amazement the man saw Satan himself standing among the witnesses. The man thought surely Satan was there to fulfill his promise, but it soon became obvious the tempter had come to enjoy the man's execution!

"From the gallows, the condemned man noticed a string of sandals slung over the devil's shoulder, all of them shredded and filthy from heavy use. In fear and desperation, the man cried out, 'Please, I beg of you! Save me from this horrible death. You promised!'

"With a sneer, Satan said, 'I promised you would escape, but I am the father of lies. Everyone must die, and you will die now for your sin!' Holding up the torn sandals, he said to the prisoner, 'See how many sandals I've worn out in my efforts to deceive you. I've worked hard to bring you to the gallows!'

"The moral of the story," I concluded, "is that even when the devil's promises are kept to the letter, they are broken in spirit. God's promises, however, though they may appear for a time to be broken in letter, are ultimately fulfilled in the spirit! So I know enough not to be tempted by empty promises of pleasure or comfort but always to cling to God's promises."

A Calling Not for Sale
Penkov had grown restless and sat forward in his chair, stroking his black mustache. Clearing his throat and adjusting his chair, he tried to turn the story of Satan against me. "But here you are in prison, even though you claim you don't listen to the devil. Can you explain why you're here if you did nothing wrong?"

"Satan always attacks those who serve the Lord," I responded. "But I'm not here because I listened to the tempting promises of Satan. His promise was to keep me out of prison if I would agree to cooperate with those seeking to destroy the church. I refused, choosing to be obedient to the Lord. Even if it brings suffering, I always try to be faithful to Christ. The Bible says, 'We don't look at the troubles we can see right now; rather, we look forward to what we have not yet seen. For the troubles we see will soon be over, but the joys to come will last forever (2 Corinthians 4:18-19).'"

Scripture has a power to touch the human heart that is far beyond any human wisdom or logic. In this instance, it brought a period of silence.

Chavdar Penkov was a middle-aged man, most likely beginning to question where his life was going. Like most government agents, he appeared to be losing the passion he once had for achieving greatness. Having settled into the comfortable routine of just doing his job for the sake of security, Penkov assumed everyone would settle for the same benign comforts he sought.

Penkov's tactics, inflicting abuse and then trading comfort for co-operation, may have worked with common criminals, but my calling was from God and was not for sale. I wasn't about to barter away my Christian principles, not even if they promised to release me from prison.

The Best Defense Is a Good Offense

These interrogation sessions were grueling and strenuous. As I've said, however, I tried to use them not only to defend myself but as an opportunity to witness to my captors whenever possible. As athletes say, "the best defense is a good offense."

I had often prayed that through the Holy Spirit Penkov might be touched and changed by Christ himself. I prayed this in accordance with Luke 21:15, which promises, "I will give you words and wisdom that none of your adversaries will be able to resist or contradict."

In spite of their confident manner, I saw that both Penkov and the prisoner's advocate had a drab emptiness to their lives. Penkov's mundane pursuit of his job, earning just enough money to support a family but giving no ultimate meaning to an empty life, was a sure sign of inner unhappiness.

Risking ridicule, if not Penkov's wrath, I felt led to speak to these two men about their souls. "While I sit here in prison with these tattered clothes, my heart is filled with a joy that only God can give," I said. Looking at Penkov, I continued, "But even though you are smartly dressed, there seems to be something missing from your life. My heart goes out to you if you have no higher purpose for your life than doing your job. You surely can see the meaning that Christ brings to my life. If you would believe in Jesus Christ, too, opening your heart in faith, God would change everything for you."

They sat in astonished silence. If they were going to leave the door open, I must walk through it. Gently I continued, reminding them that each one of us will face God and eternity at the end of this life. Again they were silent. "I don't want to see you spend eternity in hell, separated from a God who loves you and invites you to come home," I concluded.

It was only then that Penkov turned to his comrade and said, "See how subtle our friend is in his provocation?" Penkov was attempting to bring a little levity to a serious moment. He had often sworn at me, but I took note that he didn't feel blasphemy appropriate on this occasion.

With those thoughts on judgment and Penkov's subdued reply, another interrogation came to an end.

A pattern had developed in our exchanges, with Penkov usually trying to leave me with something to think about at the end of each interview. Deciding that two could play at the game, I began emphasizing some point at the end of each interview, hoping to give Penkov something to ponder. Mention of my vegetarian principles and my emphasis on the lack of a written order to cease preaching had both left an impact in earlier meetings. These words on judgment surely would have a sobering impact as well. Perhaps Chavdar Penkov, like some of his prisoners, would be thinking far into the night.

Penkov Opens the Files

The following Friday, Dimitar and I met again in the interrogation unit for what would prove to be our last meeting with Chavdar Penkov. Penkov sat waiting with two thick files on the desk before him. Pushing the bulky folders across the desk, he explained, "These files contain the facts I've accumulated in regard to your case. As you can see, I've been busy."

It was soon apparent that this interrogation was the end of Penkov's investigation into the "facts." Penkov paused to gauge our responses. I waited to see if he mentioned anything about our going on trial. When he remained silent, Dimitar and I reached for our files. To my surprise, Penkov allowed us to take them and read the contents rather than interpreting them for us.

With great interest, Dimitar and I read everything in the files. Surprisingly, there were indications of what was happening in the church. The names of two members who had been intimidated into cooperating with the police were given, but scores were named as opposing Pavel Ivanov.

Reading on, I could see more evidence that Pavel Ivanov's authority came from the police and not the power of the Holy Spirit. I found myself thinking, *Certainly the backing of the authorities in a corrupt state doesn't empower one to be a minister of the gospel. The Spirit of God alone gives the gifts for ministry.*

Dimitar and I read on silently. As I read of Ivanov's underhanded strategies and misguided machinations, I couldn't help but feel sorry for the man. I prayed that God might help him to realize what he was doing to faithful people and to repent before God's judgment came upon him. The strength of our Christian brothers and sisters came through clearly in the report, making me all the more determined to remain true to Christ, whom they were striving to honor as well.

Other things in the file both touched and amazed me. For

instance, I pushed one prominent paper over for Dimitar to see. It was an official report from a gentleman named Tzvetkov Petar Mladenov, Minister of Internal Affairs for the entire country. Dimitar looked at me knowingly, impressed that someone at the cabinet level in the government was involved in our case. The Chairman of the Committee on Internal Religious Affairs had gone to the very top to get approval to arrest us.

Of course, the language of the report was skewed, portraying Tzvetkov and the Committee in the most positive light. It spoke of their "great concern" for the life of the church and how they sought to be "good servants" of the people. But the facts indicated that things weren't going well for Pavel Ivanov. The long list of "troublemakers" indicated that the people certainly hadn't abandoned us.

As we both read through the files, I looked anxiously to see if we would be granted a trial. Indeed, various documents indicated that the government was preparing for a trial. The thought was elating. I eagerly looked forward to speaking openly about my faith in Christ and his lordship over the church. A trial would also signal an end to the seemingly endless interviews with Chavdar Penkov.

Penkov finally wrapped up the meeting. I shall always recall the cynical delight in his voice when he said, "Well, brothers Kulichev, will you finally accept the Committee as your god?"

Penkov surely wasn't surprised when I answered for both of us. "My brother and I will never set your Committee up as an idol to be worshiped. As you know, we worship the God and Father of our Lord Jesus Christ, whom we are committed to serve now and forever."

"If that's so," said Penkov, "then you will be taken away to serve your time in another prison. And it just may be possible that this fate will be yours before this very day is over." What this meant specifically I did not know, but one thing I sensed did turn out to be true: when we walked out of that room, we had endured our last interrogation with Chavdar Penkov.

Songs in the Night

Back in my cell that night, I rested after the exhausting exchange with Penkov. My future seemed to be coming into focus. Although my body and mind were weary, I could sense God's Spirit giving me strength beyond my natural ability.

What would the future hold? If Penkov was not toying with us, it seemed likely that Dimitar and I might get our day in court. What a privilege it would be to testify to my belief in Jesus Christ, the Lord of the church! I welcomed the opportunity, even knowing I was more likely to be sentenced than Dimitar. Dimitar shared my convictions and wouldn't waver, but he had worked behind the scenes as the treasurer of the Evangelical Union. As pastor of the church, I was more visible.

With a peace of mind and a sense of elation that seemed out of place in my squalid surroundings, I began to offer praise to God by quietly humming the tunes to various hymns. These, better than anything else, helped express my deep feelings of God's sustaining grace at that crucial time.

The songs that I had learned to sing and love from my youth were a strong influence in my spiritual life while in prison. Fortunately, I knew many of my favorite hymns by heart and could hum them softly while meditating upon the great truths of Scripture set to music. Singing was not permitted in prison, but when I was not praying or thinking about Scripture, my soul was singing constantly. God used those songs in the night to fill my heart with a peace that passes all understanding.

There were many songs from our hymnbooks that I recalled in prison, and I would choose them according to my feelings at the moment. Although I was cut off from the fellowship of the church, I knew my brothers and sisters in Christ were gathering for prayer and worship, which would include singing their favorite hymns. Familiar with each person's favorite hymn, I could enter into their fellowship in a spiritual sense, visualize them singing, and then sing that hymn as if I were with them. I also reviewed in my mind each church in our Bulgarian Evangelical Congregational Union and sang as I thought about and prayed for each one.

My brother-in-law Mitko was an elder at the church at Krichim. Years before, the brothers and sisters there had worked side by side with Mitko and me to erect a much-needed church building. They were devout people, and I knew they were praying for me. Mitko's favorite hymn was one we had sung together often:

> I have a Savior; he's pleading in glory,
> A dear, living Savior tho' earth friends be few;
> And now he is watching in tenderness o'er me,
> But oh, that my Savior were your Savior, too!
> For you I am praying, for you I am praying,
> For you I am praying, for you I am praying,
> I'm praying for you.[4]

[4] Text in English is by Samuel Cliff and music by Ira D. Sankey

I sang hymns from our hymnbook and spiritual songs such as:

> My Jesus I love Thee, I know Thou art mine;
> For Thee all the follies of sin I resign.

Some of the songs were contemporary Christian songs our young people sang around the campfire at our camp. I rejoiced in our Christian youth, for it was especially hard for a young person to remain faithful to Christ in those dark days of Communism. Yes, the Christian young people were a great comfort to me, and I often thanked God for them.

Like Paul and Silas

It was on my fortieth day in prison that the footsteps led again to the door of my cell. Summoned to follow the guard into the reception area of Sofia's Central Prison, I wondered what lay ahead. As long as I live, I'll never forget seeing Dimitar there and being allowed to speak with him alone. For some unknown reason, we were told that we would be held near the interrogation unit so that we would be available to see a special agent investigating our case who was to come the next morning.

We were placed in a cell with one small window, but the glass in it was broken, allowing the cold winter winds to penetrate the cell. If you check the records, you'll see that the winter of '85 in Sofia was a cold one, and that night was among the coldest. It made little difference to my brother and me, however. Like Paul and Silas in the prison at Philippi, we spent the night sharing and singing and praising God.

Hardly able to believe we were left together for so long, we shared as much as we could. We speculated on the possibility of going to trial and shared what was happening in our individual interrogations.

Dimitar told me of his witness among the prisoners. One of his cell mates was a man named Assen, who seemed to be searching for spiritual guidance. I promised to pray for Assen and told Dimitar of those I was witnessing to as well.

We reaffirmed our commitment to stand firm for our faith in Jesus Christ and renewed our resolve to serve him no matter what the cost. "To compromise with them," I reminded Dimitar, "would mean losing all integrity in our relationship with God, with our families, and with the congregation."

During the night of singing and praise, my brother and I also prayed together. We prayed for one another, for our families, and for the church. We also thanked God for the opportunity to witness for him in prison.

We would not sleep that night for the joy of being together again. Wrapping our scanty clothes around our cold bodies, we spent the night moving and singing to keep from freezing.

We sang an entire concert of hymns and Christian songs that cold night! The moment we finished singing a song, one of us would think of another, and we would begin singing again. We thought of our families and sang their favorite hymns. Even though our father had been with the Lord for many years, I knew his favorite hymn and suggested we sing it. As Dimitar and I sang, we thought of Father and all he had taught us. We knew he would be proud of us.

> You, in front of whom everything is visible,
> Here on earth, and up in the sky,
> I come to You; Search me,
> From sin and slavery, save me!
>
> When the darkest days come,
> When I sink under the waves of sorrow,
> Come to my rescue, Oh Lord,
> To support and encourage me.
>
> Even if this steep road is filled with thorns,
> Grant me grace, according to my needs,
> 'Till all sorrow and suffering come to an end,
> In your joyful, peaceful, and eternal heaven.

Our hearts were overflowing with thankfulness. Neither of us felt we were in the Central Prison of Sofia. It was as though we were in heaven, singing with the angels themselves!

Sometime during the night, Dimitar asked, "Do you remember that place in Anton Donchev's novel *Time of Parting* when the Christians were tortured in an attempt to force them to renounce Christ? Remember the old man, when the Turks demanded that his daughter, Yana, denounce Christ?

"The old man was tortured, yet he remained true to the faith," Dimitar reminded me. We tried to recall the old man's words, which go something like this:

> My head I'll give, Voivoda bold,
> But I'll not give Yana to the Turkish faith.[5]

"When his torturers had begun to dismember the old man, thinking he would disavow his faith," Dimitar continued the story, "he held fast. The old man still spoke bravely:

> My head I'll give—
> My faith I will not give!

"Finally, when it seemed impossible that the old man was still alive, he spoke his final words to his beloved daughter:

> Farewell, forgive me, Yana fair!
> No arms have I to put around you,
> Nor feet to walk on to see you off,
> No eyes have I to look upon you!"

"Yes, I remember the scene," I responded. Later I would read that entire story to some of the prisoners at Kremikovtzi, where I would shortly be transferred. "It's a great story of courage in a time of persecution. And we shall have to be just as strong. . . ." I said as we finally drifted into a cold, uneasy sleep.

As it turned out, the agent we were told to expect the next day never appeared, and the interview was never held. Surely God was at work in allowing Dimitar and me to spend that night in the same cell, making sure our spirits were renewed. To this day I do not know why the prison officials allowed it. It strengthened our resolve to never give in to their attempts to break us or brainwash us. By remaining true to Christ's command not to be ashamed of him (Luke 9:26), we discovered greater depths of God's grace and mercy than either of us had thought possible. And we would not trade that for anything. That night of praise and prayer reminded us that with God's help we could endure anything the evil one might throw at us.

---

[5] Donchev, Anton; *Time of Parting*; William Morrow and Company, Inc.; New York, New York, 1968: page 136. One of the few books we were allowed to read in prison, it is a love story, set in the midst of the Turkish invasion of the Rhodope mountains and their efforts to forcibly convert Bulgarian Christians to the Islamic faith.

CHAPTER SIX

Transfer to Kremikovtzi

I want to know Christ and the power of his resurrection and the fellowship of sharing in his sufferings, becoming like him in his death, and so, somehow, to attain to the resurrection from the dead.
PHILIPPIANS 3:10

Pains and suffering would be a paradise to me while I should suffer with my God, and the greatest of pleasures would be hell to me if I could relish them without him.
BROTHER LAWRENCE

Shortly after my final meeting with Penkov, I was allowed to meet with a lawyer my family had hired. His name was Ljuben Lashkov. Mr. Lashkov was the first person permitted to see me since Pastor Bozovayski had spent a few minutes with Dimitar and me.

Anticipating that our visit might be interrupted as had happened with the pastor, I was quick to ask Ljuben Lashkov to please take greetings to my family. I didn't want to make the mistake again of becoming distracted and failing to do that.

To my great satisfaction, Lashkov had met with my family and brought a substantial amount of news about Tzvete and the children. All were well and sent greetings. I was grateful that the children had not been taken out of their schools as had been threatened. Tzvete had also asked Lashkov to tell me that the people of the church were continuing their opposition to Pavel Ivanov and the Committee.

Another piece of welcome news Ljuben Lashkov brought was that my brother and I were going to be granted a trial. We would be tried at the same time, in the same courtroom, but since we had been charged with different offenses, we would need to argue our cases separately. It was also possible, Lashkov explained, that we would be given sentences of different length.

Yet another surprising news item that Lashkov shared was that I would soon be relocated to another prison, called Kremikovtzi, located on the outskirts of Sofia. The Kremikovtzi Prison was actually a division of the Central Prison. Prisoners were transferred there after they were institutionalized. My cell mate Sasho had been held at Kremikovtzi and said the conditions were better than at Central

Prison. Prisoners at Kremikovtzi, however, were usually held for longer periods of time.

It was a good thing I shared this information with Mitko and Sasho immediately after returning to my cell, for there was little time to say our farewells and hear Sasho review what Kremikovtzi was like before I was taken away. The summons came that very night, when a guard opened the door to Cell 74 and gruffly demanded, "Kulichev! Follow me!"

The Mourning Coach

The guard led me to the processing area where I had entered the prison. The prison clothes were taken, and I was allowed to put on the clothes I had been wearing at the time of my arrest. The waistline of the trousers fit more loosely because of the weight I lost on the sparse prison diet.

A part of understanding prison life is realizing the total lack of respect for the prisoners and their possessions. At the time of my admission, a prison guard had searched me and placed my personal belongings into an envelope, supposedly to be kept in safe storage. I had been promised that when I departed, what little money and personal possessions I had would be returned.

At the time of my arrest, I was carrying a beautiful pen made in Czechoslovakia. It was a gift from a dear friend from Czechoslovakia and was very special to me both for its quality and sentimental value. When my personal possessions were brought to me, the seven leva I had with me were there, but I saw immediately that the pen was missing and reported it.

Newcomers, still in a state of shock over their arrest, were especially targeted for this kind of "working over." Obviously the guard or one of the assistants had spotted my pen and decided to take it. The prison officials, of course, were blind to all of this. One of the perks of working in the prison, it was understood, was that it was fair game to take advantage of prisoners.

When I called attention to the missing pen, the guard on duty simply shrugged, looking inside the envelope as if it might be hiding there. "There's nothing like that in there," he said, officiously announcing the obvious. "You must have lost it."

My protests were to no avail. Even in the midst of this frustration, however, I was grateful, for although I had lost the pen, some had lost their honor, their integrity, and even their lives in Central Prison. At least I was leaving with those precious possessions intact.

I was shackled to another prisoner who was also being transferred, and we were escorted out of Central Prison into the winter night. It was exhilarating to breathe in the fresh, cold air of the outdoors and leave the foul stench of Central Prison behind.

Briefly, for those few steps between the prison door and the police car, I was reminded of what it had been like to be free. The deprivation I had experienced in Central Prison surpassed anything I had previously imagined possible, let alone experienced. If nothing else it had given me greater appreciation for little things such as a breath of fresh air or the sight of starlight in a winter sky.

Emotion swept through me as I looked over my shoulder and saw the rugged stone walls of Central Prison receding into the darkness. To step outside of those walls and still be alive brought me a sense of elation. The euphoria was almost as great as if I had been set free. The confinement in Central Prison was so stultifying and the dreadful routines so oppressive that any change was significant. The thought of relocation, even to the state prison at Kremikovtzi, gave me a sense of joy and hope. I doubted that any prison could be as dehumanizing as my experience in the Central Prison of Sofia. The mere hope of more privileges at Kremikovtzi buoyed my spirits.

Sitting in the police car, I was reminded that the prisoners in Central Prison called the car that transported prisoners to and from the prison "the Mourning Coach." That was because the police car had brought them to the place of mourning, where hope of life was all but extinguished. Indeed, for some prisoners the Mourning Coach had been the last ride they were given in this life.

It was late on the night of February 20 when the police car arrived at the gate of the prison in Kremikovtzi. Once again we were hustled through the cold night air into the prison itself. Twenty years before, I had been at this prison visiting a young Christian brother who was imprisoned because of his pacifist refusal to participate in military training. He had not been as fortunate, as I had been, to find a position doing work that was not combat-related. The prison had been a new facility at that time, considered to be one of the nicer prisons in Bulgaria.

As we waited inside the door of the prison for another barred gate to be opened, I hardly recognized the place. The building looked lonely and sad, as if it had absorbed the pain of the prisoners held within it. There was evidence of a few patchwork repairs, but the interior had not been improved in all of that time. Obviously, Kremikovtzi prison had been poorly maintained.

Most noticeable was the fact that the prison was much larger than it had been twenty years before. The prison business in Bulgaria was growing. I hoped I might be fortunate enough to be placed in one of the new cell blocks, where there might be a chance of better conditions.

Rare Civility and a Clean Sheet

The induction area was covered with ceramic tiles that were cracked and shattered. Plaster and water fell from the ceiling; the lack of repairs allowed heat to escape, melting the snow on the roof.

There were bunk beds in the cell where we were held, but the melting snow dripped on the mattresses, soaking the top beds. Several prisoners huddled together on the lower mattresses. There was no choice but to join them if I hoped to find a dry spot that was halfway comfortable.

As it turned out, I was in that miserable, wet induction cell for hours. The guards didn't care about our comfort and plodded deliberately through the admission process as if they were being paid by the hour.

Finally my name was called. Wet, weary, and wondering what was ahead of me, I followed a guard into a small cubicle, where he began methodically completing the forms. He asked, "What is your profession?"

I told him I was an evangelical pastor arrested for my religious beliefs. Without hesitation he wrote it down. I'll never forget his words: "You have my respect and admiration for that."

Such decency was unheard of in prison, to say nothing of how rare it was to find someone who respected a pastor. It made my soul rejoice to finally find, in that bleak and threatening environment, one person who seemed to respect me for my desire to serve God.

The orientation was brief, admitting me to the general prison population referred to as "the accused." This was a preliminary category that indicated that a prisoner was being held for further investigation until an indictment was declared.

A prisoner in this category had the right to receive one package of food from his family each month, not to exceed 3 kilograms. An equal amount of fresh fruits and vegetables was permitted. He was also allowed to receive a small package of clothes and personal items and might receive thirty *leva* per month from his family by mail. Those in this "accused" category were also allowed to receive visitors and mail as approved by the prosecutor investigating the case.

Although prison policies allowed me to go to the canteen, I had little money. The seven *leva* (less than seventy-five cents) returned at Central Prison wasn't much. It would be a while before I could look forward to visiting the canteen and eating a little better.

My greatest hope was that my prosecutor would allow mail and visits. It seemed like an eternity since I had seen Tzvete and the children. I would give anything to be able to speak with them and find out more about what had happened after my arrest.

It must have been close to midnight when my processing was finished. A guard led me through the darkness to my "brigade," the group with which I would be housed. Walking deeper into the prison, I could see the prisoners here were housed in larger cells, dormitory style. The door to each room was locked at night, and guards were stationed outside.

Noisily unlocking the door, the guard gestured for me to step into a long, narrow cell. In the shadows I could see that upper and lower bunks lined either side of the cell. The bunk beds were similar to the ones I had known in the army barracks, but the windows were barred. The dormitory-style cell was more crowded than expected, with perhaps fifty or sixty prisoners in it. The guard walked noisily to the opposite end and pointed to a lower bunk. Making no effort to subdue his voice, he said tersely, "That's where you'll sleep." He turned to make his exit.

To my amazement, as the guard turned to walk away he threw a clean sheet on my mattress. Its whiteness seemed to actually gleam in the dark. After sleeping for weeks on a thin mattress thrown on the floor, a clean sheet on a bunk bed was an unbelievable luxury!

The guard left, his heels clicking noisily on the cement floor. The other prisoners, already in their bunks, didn't even stir. They obviously were accustomed to intrusions such as this. I made my bed, knelt to say prayers, and lay down for the first of many nights in Kremikovtzi Prison.

When I rose the next morning, a thin young man with dark brown eyes and long hair who had slept in the bunk next to mine introduced himself. His name was Tzeko. We had only enough time to introduce ourselves while making our beds before being marched off to the dining area for breakfast.

Eating in Kremikovtzi's dining hall was very different from Central Prison. For one thing, the quantity of food at Kremikovtzi was greater than at Central Prison. Nevertheless, the prisoners at Kremikovtzi still talked incessantly about food, an obsession that seemed universal in Bulgarian prisons.

The piece of bread given me at breakfast was the largest I had received since being arrested. It actually made me feel as if I had eaten a full meal. I had more food for breakfast that morning than I had been allowed to have all day in Central Prison. I bowed my head silently after breakfast to offer my thanksgiving to God for meeting my needs.

Prisons and Reform

The prison population at Kremikovtzi, I soon discovered, was constantly complaining about overcrowding, as much a problem there as it was at Central Prison. There were sixty prisoners in our cell; the double-decker bunks were pushed within a few inches of one another.

The crush of so many prisoners bred a kind of ominous fear. Forcing so many people, especially people with social disorders and compulsive tendencies, into such a small space created an atmosphere that was on the verge of explosion. I've heard that if rats are forced into too small a space, they respond by actually turning on one another, biting and consuming one another. This almost describes the psychological environment I found at Kremikovtzi Prison.

Kremikovtzi was classified as a state prison where hardened criminals were held, including repeat offenders. The sole purpose of such a prison was to limit criminal activity by depriving criminals of their freedom. No effort was made to reform or educate prisoners. Likewise, no "reforming" took place at the TPOs, a Bulgarian acronym for labor reform camps. The TPOs were medium-security prisons where first-time offenders were sent. Apparently I was being held in Kremikovtzi rather than being sent to a TPO because I would soon be going on trial and because the prison was close to Sofia.

It's sad that most prisons in the world claim to exist to reform their inhabitants but do little to fulfill that claim. In Bulgaria very few prisoners came out of the prisons or labor reform camps with any kind of a positive outlook upon life. Like Mitko, my cell mate in Central Prison, most thieves in prison actually spent time planning future robberies and sharing trade secrets.

Human Nature Needs to Be Renewed

Restrictions at Kremikovtzi were less oppressive than Central Prison; we were allowed to move about the cell block and converse with other prisoners. As Sasho had informed me, prisoners were allowed to use the toilets as needed, except at night. After the evening roll call, the dormitory was locked. Anyone needing to relieve himself used the bucket, as we had done at Central Prison.

Conversations about sex and sexual activity were almost as widespread in the prison as the obsession with food. Homosexuality was widespread in the overcrowded Bulgarian prisons and was very apparent in the open arrangement at Kremikovtzi. I was reminded of Paul's description in Romans 1:24-27: "God gave them over in the sinful desires of their hearts to sexual impurity for the degrading of their bodies with one another."

Kremikovtzi Prison seemed to have an inordinately high number of men convicted of rape. After the lockdown each evening, when there was opportunity for conversation, it was not uncommon to hear men argue, "Wouldn't it be better if the government allowed the brothels to operate so that these men could fulfill their desires without breaking the law?"

When prisoners talked like this, I challenged them to think about the consequences: "Do you think it would be better to have a bank where you could take as much money as you wanted? Or would you propose having a public car park, where people could take a car anytime they chose? What happens when you make everything available and legal? Does it solve all society's problems, eliminating crime?

"No, of course not. If everything were legal, some people would take more money from the bank than needed, and too many cars would disappear from the car park, never to return. The same problems of greed and self-centeredness would only appear in another form. In the end our problems would be just as significant as they are now. Why? Because human nature needs to be renewed so that people will love God and their neighbors as the Bible teaches."

Hell must be something like the prison system, I found myself thinking. Hell is described in the Bible as a lake of fire where sinners are tormented forever (Revelation 20:10). The prison, filled with dangerous criminals who could inflict pain or death upon others at any moment, created an environment without any sense of security. One never dared to relax.

Gosho the Red

Just a few bunks away from me was a man who called himself "Gosho the Red." Gosho was a tall, gaunt man with long, stringy, red hair. His amber-colored eyes had a penetrating quality, and his gaze told me that Gosho was not a kind man. He had a wild look that suggested that Gosho the Red was unpredictable and capable of violence. He had already been imprisoned once prior to his current incarceration, and I sensed that Gosho the Red might well spend the remainder of his life in prison.

My heart went out to Gosho, since it seemed to me that he had some kind of mental illness. When we worked, he was in another brigade, but we would occasionally be seated close to one another at meals. At lunch one day there was enough food to give some of the prisoners seconds, and I passed the plate to Gosho. When he had taken a helping, I passed it along to the next man, which made Gosho very angry. He threatened to "break my head" with the aluminum serving tray we were passing. I didn't respond angrily or try to defend myself but only bowed my head and said calmly, "Well, here is your opportunity. I am not going to fight."

Gosho didn't hit me, and soon we had each gone our way. In the next few days, I noticed that Gosho was avoiding me. Another prisoner, Vasko, approached me a short time later and said, "Old Man Christo, Gosho told me he's ashamed of the way he acted toward you in the dining room. He wants to apologize, but he's afraid of you, even though I told him you will understand."

At the first convenient opportunity, I went to Gosho and talked to him. "Gosho, your friend Vasko tells me you feel badly about what happened in the dining hall the other day."

Fear and suspicion swept over Gosho's face.

"That made me feel good about you, Gosho," I continued. "I'm a believer in Christ, and the Bible teaches us to forgive one another. You're forgiven, Gosho, and I would like to be your friend."

The hardness in the amber eyes softened, and I sensed a relaxing of Gosho's frame. "You're different, Old Man Christo, not like the others," he said. "Sometimes I have to talk like that to others, but you're different."

"Gosho, it takes strength to confess that you've done something wrong," I said. "When Vasko told me you wanted to apologize, I knew God must be working in your heart, giving you the strength to say you're sorry."

"God?" Gosho said with astonishment.

"Yes. God works in our consciences when we hurt others, urging us to say we're sorry. I really believe God is working in your heart."

Something I took to be a slight smile gave Gosho's features an appearance I had never seen before.

After that, Gosho and I formed a relationship that might even be called a friendship. While talking about his feelings was hard for Gosho, each time we filed into the dining area, it wasn't unusual for me to see Gosho's stringy, red hair out of the corner of my eye, as he worked his way close so we could sit together.

Predictably, a few years after my release, I read in a Sofia newspaper that Gosho the Red had been arrested on charges of committing sixty robberies. One of the robbery victims had also been raped. A surge of compassion swept through me, and I breathed a brief prayer for Gosho, wondering what might have happened if we had been given more time together under different circumstances.

A Meeting with the Warden

On one occasion ominous footsteps in the hallway led to our cell. I lay on my mattress, waiting to see what would happen. The guard shouted my name and demanded that I follow him. We wound our way through a part of the prison I had not seen before. Suddenly I found that I was being ushered into the office of the warden himself. A meeting with the warden surely meant something important was about to happen.

At my most recent interrogation, Chavdar Penkov had briefly mentioned my insistence on staying with a vegetarian diet. At the time I had thought it strange that he did not pursue it, but the matter had not gone unnoticed by the authorities. Eyeing me suspiciously, the warden immediately began asking questions about my diet. "Why do you not eat all of the food we give you?" he demanded.

"Because I am a vegetarian for health reasons," I explained. "It's better for my digestive system, as I discovered when I was serving in the Bulgarian army." The mention of my experience in the Bulgarian army was intentional, showing the warden that my vegetarianism had been consistent over a long period of time.

"What do you do with the meat that we give you, if you're not eating it?" he asked.

"I give it to my cell mates, since they are always hungry," I answered.

"Don't you get hungry?" asked the warden. Obviously he was concerned about the possibility of a hunger strike.

"Of course," I replied, "but God meets my needs and gives me the strength I need from the little food I do eat." It was imperative that I maintain my principles, and I looked upon this interrogation as an opportunity to show the warden that once I made a commitment, even related to a personal principle such as my diet, it was nonnegotiable. Curious as to how the warden would respond, I waited for his reply.

He had the power to make life even more miserable if he was inclined to do so.

The warden paced the room, then stopped to drum his fingers on the back of his chair. Looking at me impatiently, he turned and began walking back and forth again. Breaking the long silence, he said, "I don't want you giving me more trouble by becoming ill. Therefore I'm giving you the right to purchase additional food from the canteen. This is an unusual privilege I've never granted to another prisoner. I hope you realize how fortunate you are. Now go. The guards will return you to your cell."

As I walked back to the cell, smiling ever so slightly to myself, I wondered if the warden recalled my comment that God cared for my needs. Very likely he didn't, but from my vantage point, God had just used the warden himself to answer my prayers!

The Work Detail

Prisoners at Kremikovtzi were placed on work details from time to time, and I found myself assigned to a group sent to a nearby factory. We were bussed from the prison to the factory entrance and back again in the evening. I was assigned to load metal ingots that were going into the furnaces of a foundry. I was never allowed to go to the other end of the factory to see what was produced from the metal.

The fear in the prison permeated work details as well. Prisoners were never to be seen conversing, except about work, and were not allowed to assemble in groups of more than three persons. We worked together with regular factory workers who lived near the prison. They supervised us, but prisoners were never to speak with these "outsiders."

One of the greatest fears for prisoners was that an undercover agent might be placed in the prison, or alongside a work detail, to win a prisoner's confidence and gather information. Prisoners themselves were known to gather information, perhaps something valuable to the authorities, and attempt to pass it along to prison officials, hoping for more favorable treatment.

After languishing in the Central Prison week after week, it felt wonderful to be able to use my hands and to feel productive again. Moving around and breathing fresh air was like therapy. After the harsh conditions of Central Prison, Kremikovtzi and the factory seemed like a first-class hotel.

I have experienced lower back pain for much of my adult life, and I was concerned that lifting the metal ingots day after day would cause me serious pain. But though the work was strenuous, it never bothered my back as I had feared it would. God was surely watching over me.

When our brigade returned to the dormitory in the evening, I was able to go to the canteen and purchase toothpaste and shaving supplies with the meager funds I brought from Central Prison. Instead of ordering items, prisoners at Kremikovtzi were allowed to go to the canteen—actually a small store—and look for some small item that might make life more tolerable. My seven *leva* were gone after one trip to the canteen, leaving me to wait for more funds to be mailed by my family.

Longing to Do Laundry

The work detail presented one major problem—that of hygiene. The faded blue prison garb of Central Prison wasn't used at Kremikovtzi. The only clothes I had were the ones I had been wearing when I was arrested. The two shirts and jacket were enough to keep me warm now that spring had come, but they had become filthy, and I had no replacements.

We were kept busy on work details that were dirty and were allowed only one shower each week. When we did have free time at night, we were locked in the cell block with no running water. My biggest concern was having only one pair of underwear.

The warmer weather made personal hygiene a greater concern. I tried to make my single set of underwear last the week until laundry could be done, but it was impossible to maintain decent hygiene over such a long period. With no opportunity to do laundry, it was impossible to keep the foul odors of my clothing from becoming noticeable.

On the weekend, prisoners were given the time and access to water to do their laundry. It was a relief to wash my clothing and hang it out to dry. On Monday my work routine would begin all over again.

I found myself working alongside Tzeko, the handsome young man who occupied a neighboring bunk. Tzeko was good-natured and talked easily. We spent many hours chatting together during my time at Kremikovtzi.

Tzeko was quick to tell me that some of the regular factory workers could be trusted to pass a letter along to prisoners' families. Eager to reestablish contact with Tzvete and the children, I began writing letters. As allowed by policy, I turned in one letter a week to the prison guards, with a hope and a prayer that the censors would let it through. Other letters I hid in my clothing and took to the factory secretly, hoping the factory workers would pass them along.

In addition to informing my family of my need of money for the canteen, in each of my letters I requested clean clothes, especially underwear. When young Tzeko saw my need, he offered me some of his underwear so that at least occasionally I could have something clean next to my skin.

Tzeko told of being arrested for petty thievery. Like so many Bulgarians, he was frustrated by the shortage of good paying jobs and had attempted to make up for it by stealing clothing and other things popular with the young crowd.

Most of the prisoners worried aloud about whether girlfriends would remain faithful, and this was the case with Tzeko. He was also anxious that his time in prison might keep him from finding employment after his release. When Tzeko was mulling these worries over, his dark brown eyes lost their sparkle, and his personality changed. As he talked about his anxieties, Tzeko's usually good mood became choleric, and his voice took on a bitter edge that concerned me.

Providence in a Prison

On my second or third day at Kremikovtzi, while I was making my bed, I overheard a conversation not far away. A swarthy man of medium size with a deep voice was speaking to another prisoner. He said, "When I was in Central Prison, they put me together with an evangelical pastor. We had some interesting conversations. That man encouraged everyone in the cell."

The man had to be speaking of my brother Dimitar! I remembered that Dimitar had told me briefly of a man named Assen who was open to learning more about the gospel.

I hastily finishing making my bed and approached the man.

"Your name must be Assen," I said. "Is that correct?"

Hearing a stranger say his name, the man was speechless. When he nodded hesitantly, I smiled and told him, "The man you spoke of—the one who was with you in Central Prison—he's my brother Dimitar! When Dimitar and I talked, he told me of his friendship with you. I've been praying for you!"

Assen had just become interested in Jesus Christ and the promises of the gospel when he had been separated from Dimitar. And just when he was becoming discouraged that he could no longer talk with Dimitar, he had now made contact with me. Assen was amazed by God's providence!

God Was Guiding, Every Step of the Way

One of the secrets to endurance and knowing God's presence in our lives is prayer. As a young man, I had resolved that when I said my morning and evening prayers, I would always kneel as a sign of reverence for my Lord. That became a lifelong habit.

Of course, when I was drafted into the Bulgarian army this practice made me the object of ridicule and criticism. Not only did I pray and observe Sunday as a day of rest and worship, but I also had strong convictions against the oath of allegiance and taking up arms. Evangelical Christians in Bulgaria had long stood against taking vows other than to God, including any oath of allegiance to the country.

It was a delicate situation, but I committed everything to the Lord, recognizing that he was the only one able to resolve these things. While in prison I took great comfort in looking back upon my army experience, remembering how God had guided me every step of the way.

Hearing of my convictions, the colonel over our battalion came to my bunk to speak with me. He had the power to punish or imprison me for insubordination, and I anticipated some harsh discipline. But instead of threatening a court martial or sending me to a military prison, he spoke very gently. As God is my witness, the colonel sat on my bunk and said, "Christo, how can you best serve our country and still live in accordance with your faith?"

Quickly I told him that I would gladly do any work assigned as long as it didn't require taking an oath or bearing arms, as both were against my religion. The colonel assigned me a job working in a storage area, keeping an inventory of supplies. When I tell people what I did in the army, most of them are envious and say, "I wish I could've had a job that easy!"

My army experience taught me to always trust God for my needs. My sole responsibility was and still is to be faithful to what God has shown me and to give him all of the glory.

A Meeting with the Commandant

It wasn't long before one of the guards at Kremikovtzi reported my morning and evening prayers to the brigade leader responsible for our cell block. One morning as I rose from my prayer time, the brigade leader approached brusquely. "Christo, the commandant of the prison has said that you shouldn't pray like this. You may pray under your blankets, but we won't have a demonstration like this."

Humbly I replied, "If he wants to talk to me about prayer, please invite him to come and speak to me. I would welcome the opportunity to discuss the matter." I continued to pray morning and evening, waiting to see what would happen. As anticipated, it wasn't many more days before the commandant sent for me.

Entering the commandant's office, I was met by a middle-aged man with graying hair. Seated behind a desk, his long sleek fingers deftly shuffled a stack of papers before him. No offer was made to have me be seated. I stood alone before him as the guard stepped back to stand beside the door.

"What is your name?" the commandant demanded.

In prison the custom was to always identify yourself with your own name and your father's name. "Christo Christov Dimitrov Kulichev."

The gray-haired man stood. Tall and energetic, he moved swiftly around the desk. "Come with me," the commandant said tersely.

To one side of his desk there was a door leading out of the building into a small courtyard. The commandant stepped through the door, motioning me to follow. A few steps outside of the commandant's office, he turned, faced me squarely with his arms crossed and demanded, "Haven't I warned you not to pray like that?"

"Your men have," I responded quietly. Looking him directly in the eye, I continued, "But I'm sure they have told you my answer."

Eager to press home his point, the commandant insisted, "What you're doing is a demonstration. It violates our rules! If we allow this to continue, others will think they can join in this kind of protest."

Calmly I pointed out, "This is not a protest, and I've not seen one person willing to join me in prayer. I am in prison not because I'm a criminal but because I'm a Christian pastor. It's my Christian duty to pray; prayer is an important part of my life and service for God. I've always prayed on my knees every morning and every evening."

Pondering my words, the commandant seemed to soften somewhat. He turned, took a few paces with his hands clasped behind his back, and began another line of questioning.

"What do you pray for?" he asked me. His voice had softened a bit.

"I thank the Lord for everything he's given me, for my health and the strength he gives. I ask God to protect and guide me, keeping me from evil. My prayer differs each day according to my circumstances. I ask the Lord to be with my family. Because we are separated, I have no way of knowing what their needs are, so I pray that God will be close to my family and friends. Also, I pray that I may be strong enough to endure the hardships of prison, and I ask his blessing upon those who need it."

This seemed to stir the commandant's curiosity. The slender fingers of one hand grasped his jaw as he asked, "How long do your prayers last?"

"It's not always the same," I explained. "The prayers in our free churches aren't written in a prayer book. When I pray, I simply share whatever is on my heart. Perhaps three or four minutes."

Looking at me intensely, his index finger tapped his chin. After a few moments, he responded, "Then we'll have to put you alone in a cell, to keep you from being a negative influence, won't we?"

"That decision is up to you," I responded. "But you should know that I prayed in this same manner in the army and even in the Central Prison of Sofia."

"Who was your interrogator in Central Prison?" he demanded.

I gave him the name of Chavdar Penkov. He ended our exchange by saying tersely, "You will write down everything you've told me. Then give it to me for my records."

Taking the piece of paper he had given me, I wrote down what I had said, noting, "When Chavdar Penkov asked if anyone was disturbing me while I prayed, I understood that to mean that freedom of conscience and religion are respected here in the prison."

Returning to the cell block, my "colleagues," as the prisoners called each other, were extremely curious. Several prisoners quickly gathered around my bunk. Assen asked, "What's going on? Why did they summon you?" They listened intently as I told them everything. They were amazed, as was I, that the matter ended there. From that day on there was no interference, and I continued to pray as usual.

I Know Christ Has a Purpose for My Life

Interrogations usually left me emotionally exhausted. The unknown future—trying to anticipate what might happen next—made life difficult. Without my faith it would have been unbearable. Holding to my principles preserved my identity and my purpose in life.

Continuing to pray on my knees twice each day, I knew I wasn't alone. God was with me, but I knew also that my family and a large number of believers were praying for my brother and me.

As I prayed, I reflected upon images of God's protecting presence. I knew that the Lord, the Great Shepherd, would lead me. Psalm 23:5 says, "You prepare a table before me even in the presence of my enemies." A gentle calm settled over my mind as I considered Jesus' promise in John 14:27: "Peace I leave with you; my peace I give you. I do not give to you as the world gives. Do not let your hearts be troubled and do not be afraid."

As Assen and I became better acquainted, we rejoiced together that God had arranged for us to be in the same brigade. Although our beds weren't close, we talked frequently.

Assen was quick to tell me that since meeting Dimitar he had given a great deal of thought to his life and the new direction he wanted to take. He told me, "I knew when I came into the prison that I had started on a downward path. If I continued on the same road, my life would soon be destroyed. As it has turned out, prison has been good for me, since it made me stop and think."

Assen had been arrested for a questionable business deal. In purchasing food for his restaurant, one of the vendors had offered to sell food at a reduced price in exchange for an illegal profit-sharing arrangement. Assen had foolishly agreed. Both the vendor and Assen were discovered and imprisoned. "If I had continued to live as I had been doing outside of prison, who knows where I would be today? But I am no longer walking on that downward path of destruction because I have met your brother and you. Now I know that Christ has a purpose for my life. My life will never be the same!"

I'll Tell Penkov, Now I'm Trusting Jesus!

As we talked one day, Assen told me that he and Dimitar had been held in Central Prison with a young man who had confessed to murder. The young man had married, only to discover that his wife and her mother were secretly working as prostitutes. When he came home early one day and caught them running their business in the apartment, he killed both of them in a fit of rage.

The young man was so distraught by what had happened and by his violent response that he paced the cell constantly. He suffered terrible nightmares. "Your brother Dimitar spoke to him of Christ and prayed with him," Assen told me. "After that, a kind of peace came over the young man, and he told us the nightmares never returned."

As Dimitar and the young man had spoken further, the man had mentioned that Chavdar Penkov was his agent. Dimitar had replied that Penkov was interrogating him as well, saying, "I've spent more hours with Penkov than I've cared to."

Assen commented, "The change in the young man's life seemed to be lasting. We laughed when he told Dimitar and me, 'If Penkov calls me in to talk again, I'll tell him that I'm trusting Jesus now!'"

Nikolov and Christian Literature

One morning shortly after I arose, a guard approached me as I was making my bed. "You'll not be going to the factory to work today," he informed me. "Your investigator wants to speak with you."

After a lengthy wait typical of the Bulgarian prison bureaucracy, the guard finally appeared and asked me to follow him. We wound our way through the bowels of the prison, working our way into an area near the admission offices. Standing in the hallway, chatting with another agent, was Vladimir Nikolov. I was ushered into a nearby room and remained standing, waiting for Nikolov to finish his conversation.

"Go ahead and be seated," Nikolov said, waving to an empty chair as he entered the room. He closed the door behind him. "So you're here at Kremikovtzi now?"

The fact that I was sitting in front of him was obvious, so I did not reply.

"Penkov tells me you've been warned about your lack of cooperation with the Committee on Internal Religious Affairs. You do understand, don't you, that the only way you're getting out of this place is by following the instructions of the Committee?"

"The Committee doesn't follow the constitution of our nation," I replied. "I would think you would be more concerned about discussing that than trying to force one humble pastor to submit to the Committee."

Nikolov leaned forward in his chair and reached for a file on the desk before him. As he did so, his lip curled into ever so slight a sneer. "You have more comforts here at Kremikovtzi than you did at Central Prison. I hope you like them, since you may be here for quite some time with that attitude."

"My church has no political agenda," I countered. "All I've done is preach God's Word to the people. God's Word says clearly that the church is the body of Christ. Christ alone is Lord and guides the church, not the Committee. I must follow my Lord."

"If you have no political agenda, why did you have foreign literature at your house?" Nikolov demanded, waving his open hand over the file before him.

"It's Christian literature," I answered. "It says nothing negative about the government or the Committee. Some of the pieces of literature are sermons, or lessons on how to study the Bible, how to pray, and how to follow our Lord Jesus Christ."

"And what do you do with this literature?" Nikolov asked. "Do you pass it out to people on the street?"

"It's for my ministry at the church," I explained. "People come each week to study the Bible. We share things with one another that help us understand the Bible better. I share some of the literature with people who want to read it."

"Where do you get this literature?" Nikolov asked suspiciously. "I'm not blind, Kulichev. I can see that it's not printed in Bulgaria!"

"Some of it is printed by people who have mimeograph machines, as is obvious," I pointed out. "It's impossible to know exactly where each piece of literature was printed. Because Christian literature isn't sold in stores, Christians pass it around and share it with one another."

Nikolov pursued the matter further. "And some of it is printed outside of Bulgaria, is it not? How does it come to be stored in your house?"

"There are people from many parts of the world who travel inside of Bulgaria, many of them on business assignments. Some are Christians and have the freedom to carry whatever literature they like! They might give it to members of our churches or to me when they come to visit the church. Foreigners are allowed to visit our churches," I explained.

"And you also had many copies of the reactionary paper *Zornitza*," Nikolov said smugly, eager to show that he had gone through everything in my home. "Of what possible use is that kind of material?"

Zornitza was a newspaper that had been published since 1876, telling of activities in various churches and running articles on theological issues of interest to Christians. It had been banned in 1949 when the pastors were put on trial, and I had stored as many past copies as I could find. I had even written a letter to the government's Committee of the Press asking to publish it again. My request was denied.

"Those are dated copies. All of them were printed before September 9, 1944. Are you trying to say that all literature printed before that date is revolutionary? What am I supposed to do, destroy it?"

Nikolov sat silently writing in a notebook for several moments after I finished. When he finished the note, Nikolov stood up. It was his way of signaling the interrogation was over.

Our God Is a Living God

One of Assen's chronic worries, as with most prisoners, was for his family. His wife came from Russia and had no relatives in Bulgaria to whom she could turn for help. Assen had been in prison for more than six months without any contact with his wife. He was constantly wondering if she was able to manage alone and if she would still be there for him when he was released.

Assen's family concerns became a part of my daily prayers. When I told Assen I was praying that God would protect our families, he was skeptical. "How can you say a prayer for our families and then just go to sleep without worrying? We have no idea what's happening to them!"

"I have faith, Assen, that God is going to use my time in prison to glorify his name. God knows I'm here, and he knows what is happening with my family. When I pray, I commit everything to God. He hears and answers my prayers—not always in the way I expect, but he answers. Wait and see."

The prisoners could never tell when mail might come. Some prisoners might receive several letters or packages on one day, but then go a week or more without receiving any mail at all.

One day when our brigade returned to the cell after the workday, several letters had been delivered. I noticed a letter lying on Assen's bed. I'll never forget Assen's joy when he received that first letter from his wife. Assen had never experienced an answer to prayer. "Your prayers worked!" he exclaimed. Then he asked incredulously, "What is it with you and your prayers?"

"Assen, it isn't me. Our God is a living God who answers prayer. He cares for us and will meet our needs if only we will trust him." Assen listened in amazement as I told him about how God had kept me healthy in spite of the horrible food in Central Prison. My meager vegetarian diet had miraculously been enough to supply all my needs. Assen had no difficulty remembering the terrible diet at Central Prison. I continued, "Other prisoners were obsessed with food and in constant pain from hunger, but God blessed what little food that was given to me so that it met my needs. And God will meet your needs also, if only you will trust him."

Service for Christ

My friend Assen truly came to believe during our time together in Kremikovtzi Prison. He told me that for the first time in his life he understood that God was a living, present reality. To see my life and faith touching others gave me renewed assurance that God had a purpose for my being in prison.

One of the truths that came home to me in a particularly meaningful way in prison was the importance of service for Christ and his kingdom. Christians who aren't careful run the risk of having their commitment to God remain solely in the realm of theory. Service is important because it forces faith to become practical; what we believe must change the way we live and act and relate to others. If we think of faith only in terms of what we believe, we miss the truth that God wants to change the way we live and, through us, touch the lives of others.

The Christian faith is a practical faith. It is a faith based upon the Incarnation, the coming of God in the flesh, and not just upon a creed. God doesn't just want to change the way we think; he wants to change the way we live.

One of the antidotes to discouragement in prison was to look for ways God could use me to serve others. In Central Prison I had done little things: sharing food with the hungry, emptying the dreaded bucket, cleaning toilets, and providing clean eating utensils. At Kremikovtzi I had more opportunities to pray and provide counsel or simply speak a kind word in the midst of the incivility.

Doing these little things took my mind off my own worries and kept me from falling into self-pity. It also became a means of witness. The prisoners around me cared little for the fact that I called myself an evangelical pastor. It was only when I shared a bite to eat, spoke an encouraging word, or prayed for them that they took notice of my faith.

Through service humbly offered in the power of the Holy Spirit, I saw God miraculously open the hearts of hardened criminals. God taught me more clearly than before that unwillingness to humble myself in service would cause me to miss God's greatest blessing in my life.

Assen's letter from his wife was a painful reminder that I had heard nothing from my family. Was the prison mail going through? Were my letters lost or being censored? There was nothing I could do but keep writing.

At about the same time that Assen received his letter, Tzeko also received a package from home. He opened the package expectantly because he had asked his mother for some items he wanted. When he found that the things he had requested were missing, he threw the package carelessly to one side. Flinging himself on his mattress, Tzeko slapped the metal frame at the head of his bunk and began shouting threats and insults toward his mother.

My relationship with Tzeko was such that I felt I could say something. "Tzeko, why are you talking like this? You know your mother is doing the best she can! She probably wasn't able to send you the things you requested for some reason or another. You never know what kind of situation she may be facing at home!"

"Oh, Christo, I know you are right," Tzeko responded. "I'm so used to thinking of myself and what I want. I didn't stop to think of what my mother must be facing. She is all alone, and who knows how she can manage with the small salary she is getting!"

Writing As Therapy

The waiting and wondering about my family was the most difficult aspect of being in prison. I had written more than twenty letters to my family. While it was frustrating to receive nothing in reply, I found that the exercise of writing became a type of therapy for me. As I wrote, I found myself getting in touch with deeper feelings and reflecting upon how my prison experience was changing me.

Most importantly, writing to my loved ones engaged me so that I actually felt a kind of fellowship with them. In encouraging them to remain faithful, I found my own spirit was strengthened. But the weeks dragged on without a reply.[6]

Finally, the long drought ended. When I returned to the prison barracks from a work detail one day, Assen approached me. "Do you remember the letter you gave me to pass along through my factory friend?"

"Yes," I replied, recalling the letter to Tzvete.

"He gave me this," Assen beamed broadly, "with your name on it!" In his hand was an envelope addressed in my wife's handwriting!

The letter meant so much to me that I couldn't resist sharing it with Assen.

The letter began:

> **My love, I received both of your letters.**

I wondered if she would ever receive the many others I had written. Tzvete continued:

> **I'm thankful to God that he has arranged everything in our lives according to his will.**
>
> **My heart is filled with thankfulness to God that he is giving us the strength to overcome the trials and temptations that are besetting us. You should know that a long list of friends from all across the country are contacting me and asking about your**

---

[6] Later I would learn that my family did receive most of the letters I sent by way of the prison underground system and kept them to share with friends. When I was released from prison, they were compiled into a pamphlet entitled "Letters from Prison," which was shared with many of the Christian brothers and sisters in Bulgaria who had prayed for me during the ordeal.

> welfare. Each one of them has asked that I send you
> their greetings, but the list is too long for me to
> include their names in this letter.

I paused as tears welled in my eyes.

> Please remember there are many people praying for
> you in prison and for us as we go about our lives
> missing you very much. Don't ever think for one
> moment that we're ashamed of you. The children and I
> are so proud to have a believing husband and father
> who has the courage to stand up for his faith in God.

The lump in my throat made it difficult to go on reading.

> Our neighbors know, of course, that you're in prison.
> They come repeatedly to the door with compassion and
> care written on their faces, asking about you and
> Dimitar. Some of them suggested I start a petition,
> collecting signatures from people in the community
> eager to testify in court about your honesty and
> goodness.

Assen listened intently. His face literally shone with joy as he absorbed the words of encouragement written by my dear wife. "Bravo!" he said. "That's some wife you have. What a lucky man you are!"

I assured him he was right.

Unanswered Questions

As encouraging as Tzvete's letter was, it left unanswered questions. My wife had said nothing about the situation in the church, probably for fear of having the letter censored or stopped altogether.[7]

Also, Tzvete had apparently not received my letters asking for clean clothes, and personal hygiene had become a major concern. The

---

[7] During the long hiatus when it seemed that my letters were not getting through to my wife, I had also been writing to many of my Christian friends in the Evangelical churches around Bulgaria. All of this was done, of course, by way of the prison underground. Each time I wrote to brothers and sisters in other churches, I asked them to please pass the letter along to my wife in Sofia in case she had not received the letters I had sent her directly. Later I was to discover that many of those letters did reach her hands, thanks to these faithful friends whose names I cannot mention here. As I look back upon my prison experience, I see more clearly what a blessing my Christian friends were to my family and to myself. What joy and encouragement they gave to us all!

situation was desperate as I was allowed only occasional showers before putting on the same clothes.

The deadening routine of prison life at Kremikovtzi continued
with only the memory of my wife's letter to encourage me. Without
money from my family, I still wasn't able to get additional food from
the canteen as other prisoners were doing. While the food at
Kremikovtzi was generally more plentiful than at Central Prison,
maintaining my vegetarian diet continued to be a challenge. Assen and
Tzeko occasionally shared tea or a piece of candy with me out of concern that I was not getting enough to eat, but God helped me be content with the little that I had.

Many prisoners around me were obsessed with food during the
day and dreamed about it at night. God miraculously delivered me
from that mental torture and taught me to appreciate a simplified life.
The words of the apostle Paul to the Philippian Christians from his cell
in Rome express it well: "I know what it is to be in need, and I know
what it is to have plenty. I have learned the secret of being content in
any and every situation, whether well fed or hungry, whether living in
plenty or in want" (Philippians 4:12).

You're Going to Change This Prison!

Tzeko and I would often talk in whispers late into the night, our bunks
just a short distance apart in the crowded cell.

Tzeko was just a few years older than my son, Stefan, and my heart
went out to him. The prison seemed to be making Tzeko bitter. I noticed that he was becoming increasingly impatient with other prisoners. He seemed to respect me, however, and would listen quietly as I
tried to give him advice.

Tzeko would often say with a sigh, "I'll have to change my life
when I get out of this place!"

"Pray that Christ will come into your heart, Tzeko," I whispered
one night. "Only he can change the whole person."

Each day I tried to bring some word of kindness, respect, and human decency to those crowded around me. Seldom did I see those
seeds of kindness bear any fruit. But one night as we were lying down
to go to sleep, a young man named Ivan, who slept two beds away,
whispered, "Old Man Christo, would you please loan me a needle and
some thread to mend my clothes?"

"Of course, Ivan," I responded as I handed them to him.

Ivan took the needle and thread and then said with gratitude in his
voice, "Thank you, Christo."

"You're welcome, Ivan."

Even in the semidarkness I could see the smiling face of Tzeko in the bed between us. "Christo, you really are going to change this prison!" he said quietly. "Everyone except you says, 'This is prison; forget politeness! Just try to survive!' No one ever says please or thank you. Now you've got Ivan doing it!"

"You're right, Tzeko. If I can help someone and make his time here easier, it will make life better for all of us."

There was a thoughtful pause in the darkness, and then I heard Tzeko say, "Nobody ever thinks about that except you, Christo."

A Calculated Risk

A few days after we had begun working in the factory, I noticed two prisoners talking with a third man who was not wearing prison clothing and was obviously from outside the prison. It was unusual to see a conversation such as this, since prisoners were forbidden to speak to outsiders.

The fear of spies dominated the atmosphere. Nevertheless, violations of the rules were bound to happen when the guards weren't around. The question in my mind was whether or not this was an innocent conversation and whether I would be taking a risk if I joined it.

Trusting that my reputation in the prison as an evangelical pastor would put the two prisoners at ease, I decided to risk approaching the group. When I introduced myself, everyone in the group seemed friendly and open to my being there. They were making casual small talk.

Sizing up the situation, I made a quick decision. My instincts told me it was safe to risk asking the young outsider for help. "It's been several months now since I've heard from my family," I began. When he appeared to be listening sympathetically, I asked, "Would you be so kind as to call them at my home in Sofia?"

He agreed and asked for the telephone number.

Since strict punishments were dealt to prisoners who were caught speaking to people from outside the prison, I had to be brief and concise. "Tell them to send underwear and some money to Kremikovtzi for me. The clothes are more important, but have them send money if they can."

The conversation lasted only a minute before I walked away, hoping that we hadn't been observed. It was a calculated risk, but I felt I needed to do everything I could to establish contact with my family.

More Than Anything I Could Ask or Imagine

Prisoners were always trying to communicate with family and friends outside of the prison in this and many other illicit ways, but I had never known it to actually work. Regardless, I had taken the chance. All I could do now was pray that somehow my family might get the message.

The following day, the same young man from outside the prison was back in the factory. Although I was surprised at this, I didn't want to press the issue with him or take another chance that the guards might accost me. Turning away, I went about my work, hoping that if he was sincerely interested in helping he would come and tell me whether or not he had contacted my family.

As I went about my work, I suddenly became aware of the fact that the other prisoners, one by one, were taking their work and moving away from me. I turned to see what was happening, and there, just two steps away from me, was the young man who had taken my telephone number. To my amazement and delight, beside him was my son, Stefan!

Stefan was dressed in the coveralls worn by factory workers, helping him blend in with the workers in the area. Somehow, the visit, including Stefan's clothing, had been secretly arranged by the young man I had approached![8]

Stunned, I could only stand and stare at Stefan for a moment before throwing my arms around him, my heart pounding with surprise and joy. It was as if someone had come back from the dead, someone I thought I would never see again. I had asked for clothes and money—mere things—but I had gotten my son! I could hardly believe how God had answered my prayers, allowing me to receive far more than anything I could have asked or imagined.

As Stefan and I embraced, I realized why the other prisoners had moved away. Callous and uncivil as many of them were, they realized what a precious and private moment this was. Stepping away and turning their backs, they had arranged themselves so that they could go about their work while providing a cover so the guards wouldn't realize what was happening.

Stefan and I moved to a private area behind some supplies and enjoyed an hour of wonderful fellowship and conversation. Stefan had brought the clothes and money I had asked for. Most important, he had

[8] I must express my deepest and most heartfelt appreciation to the young man who arranged Stefan's secret visit, for which he took a great risk. I have purposely allowed him to remain nameless for fear of reprisal. God knows his name, and that is enough. There will undoubtedly be rewards for him in eternity, for he ministered greatly to me in my hour of need.

news of our family, the church, and our friends that I had been longing to hear. He told me quickly that his mother was doing well and that she sent her love. His sister, Nebesna, and her husband, Toshko, were also well. "The grandchildren miss you too," he assured me.

They Searched the House till Noon

Stefan started from the beginning, telling me what had happened at home the day after my arrest.

"Mother got up early to pack food and clothing to take to Central Prison for you," he said. "But at 6:30 in the morning, there was a knock at the door. When Mother answered, a crowd of officials was standing there, plainclothes agents in front with uniformed police behind them. One of the agents was driving the black car we always saw parked on our street. They used it to watch our home! A man named Penkov was leading the agents."

"He was my interrogator," I responded.

Stefan went on, "I couldn't believe how Mother invited them in and spoke to them as politely as she did. We were scared. They did everything they could to frighten us more. They had a search warrant and formed two teams. One team searched our home, and the other went next door to search Dimitar's home. We didn't resist. Mother told them, 'We are Christians and have nothing to hide.' She even offered them coffee and cake, but they refused it. Mother laughed and said, 'Do you think I'm trying to poison you?'" Stefan smiled as he recalled the incident.

"Did they say anything about the charges they're bringing against me?" I asked.

"Chavdar Penkov told Mother that you would be brought to trial and that someone had told him you had already confessed."

"That's a lie," I informed Stefan. "I never confessed."

"We knew it couldn't be true, and Mother said so right to Penkov's face. The agents seemed most interested in finding foreign currency and literature. One agent named Vladimir Nikolov kept asking questions about the literature and where it was printed. He took me into a corner by myself and talked to me for over an hour, trying to get me to say something bad about you, but I just told him the truth."

"You did a good job, son. Nikolov is another of the agents who has questioned me. He says the government is getting letters from outside of the country about my case. Be sure to tell Mother about that. Did they take the literature?" I asked.

"It was a mess. They separated papers in our house and took away most of the Christian literature and tapes, including the books on the Bible that are written in English. Mother challenged them. She and I followed Penkov all through the house even though he had told us to stay in the kitchen. When Penkov scolded her, she said, 'How do I know you won't put foreign currency into one of our drawers and then report you found it?' They let us follow them after that.

"Mother also quoted the constitution about freedom of religion and freedom of speech. The agents laughed and answered her, 'We can't find one copy of the constitution in all of this literature!'"

"You and your mother were brave," I said to Stefan.

"She was stronger than ever," Stefan assured me. "Mother never showed anger toward the agents, but she began to cry when they took her Bible. She cried out, 'Please don't take my Bible! You don't understand what the Bible means to me!' The agents couldn't understand why each of us had our own Bible. They finally gave Mother her Bible back.

"They searched the house till noon!" Stefan continued. "As they left, Vladimir Nikolov told us, 'You can be sure Christo is going to be tried for having all of this foreign literature.' We also got a call from Nebesna. She said the agents searched their home, too."

"How is your school going?" I asked Stefan.

"The agents wanted to kick me out," Stefan reported, "but my teachers said, 'What has the boy done? Even if his father is in prison, why should he be expelled?' I didn't miss a day!" Stefan said proudly.

Christians Have Faced Lions

"And what about the church?" I asked.

"The night you were arrested, there was a prayer meeting at the church. Mother got off work at the clinic to attend. Uncle Dimitar came even though the agents had warned him to stay away! The people knew, as we did, that the agents wanted to arrest you, so no one was surprised when Mr. Shiskov read a letter telling of your arrest.

"Two men in the church wrote letters about Pavel Ivanov's immoral reputation in the community. Some of the church leaders decided they would stand in the pulpit to keep Pavel Ivanov from taking it. The people call him 'Saul' instead of 'Pavel,' since he hasn't been converted yet!" Stefan said smiling, referring to the apostle Paul. "The church resisted Pavel Ivanov for three weeks before he was able to get into the pulpit by force."

Stefan told me of the dramatic resistance the people had shown.

"One by one, all of the men in leadership, including Toshko, stepped into the pulpit and were arrested," Stefan remarked. Toshko was my son-in-law, who felt called to ministry. "The people decided that if they all went to prison, it would soon be full and couldn't hold everyone.

"When the men were all arrested, Mother led the women in standing in the pulpit. The police had to pull her away by force! When they pried her hands off of the pulpit, she grabbed the banister near the stairs, and the struggle started again.

"By this time," Stefan continued, "other women were standing in the pulpit. The police would remove one, and another would step up."

He went on to tell of Jordanka Kozhoucharova, a dear woman of eighty years, who came and sat on the chair behind the pulpit and refused to budge. I smiled at the thought of it!

"The police saw it was useless," Stefan continued. "They couldn't arrest everyone. One of them pulled the fuses so there was no electricity, but Mother put them back. I don't know how many police cars it took to drive everyone to the Fourth Precinct station, but Pavel Ivanov never got into the pulpit that day!"

"What happened to those who were arrested?" I asked.

"Most of the people were fined," Stefan reported. "Toshko and Emanuel Tinev were charged with petty hooliganism and sentenced to a labor camp. Nebesna worries about Toshko, but she's doing well. She's a lot like Mother."

Stefan told of how policemen with dogs had cordoned off the church the next Sunday and had escorted Pavel Ivanov into an almost empty church. When he attempted to speak, the faithful members remained outside and began singing hymns. One of the young women, Ellie, went past the dogs to reach the balcony and began playing hymns on the organ.

The story rolled on as Stefan told of the police threatening to enter the church with dogs. Hearing this, Vasil Kozuharov, one of our older men known for his sharp wit, asked, "Don't they know that Christians have faced lions? Why did they bring just a few dogs?"

When You Pray, Everything Falls into Place

We dared not talk much longer lest we be discovered. Stefan had brought me the clothes and money I had requested. After he gave them to me, we paused to pray a brief prayer of thanksgiving for this time together. Then we embraced one more time, and Stefan walked away. During this entire time, the work in the shop went on as if nothing were happening. I wasn't even missed by the guards.

The greatest gift I was given that day wasn't any material thing Stefan had brought to me. It was being reminded again that God had given me a loving and faithful family—driven home by that all-too-brief meeting with my son. God was so good to have given me a loving family and faithful Christian friends who prayed and took a stand for justice in the church. The greatest gift of all was the knowledge that my heavenly Father knew what I needed even better than I did. I was reminded that he would provide for me out of his bounty and grace in ways that I could not understand and could never anticipate.

When Stefan had gone, I realized I had a problem. The food and clothing he had brought were so conspicuous that they would certainly be discovered. If they were found, harsh discipline would be certain. Others who had helped conceal this secret visit could also be implicated. Something had to be done.

The solution for the clothing was obvious. I went about putting on all of the underwear that Stefan had brought, layer after layer. The food and money were concealed inside of the clothing, and I literally wore everything back to the prison cell that evening.

To my amazement, none of the other prisoners threatened to report Stefan's secret visit when I arrived back in the prison barracks that night. Assen was the only one who briefly mentioned it. "I am amazed," he said with a smile on his face. "How is it possible that when you pray, everything falls into place?"

CHAPTER SEVEN

The Search for Truth and Justice

Jesus answered, "I am the way and the truth and the life.
No one comes to the Father except through me."
JOHN 14:6

He cannot heal who has not suffered much,
for only Sorrow sorrow understands;
They will not come for healing at our touch,
Who have not seen the scars upon our hands.
EDWIN MCNEILL POTEAT

The day after Stefan's secret visit, when I returned from my work detail, a surprise awaited me. As I approached the cell block, a guard met me at the door and said, "Come with me, Kulichev. You're being transferred to another location. We've already moved your things."

Questions rushed through my mind. Was someone aware of my meeting with Stefan? Had the guards noticed the clothing and food he had brought? Had someone talked? Was this a disciplinary action?

As it turned out my relocation was a routine move. Placed in another part of the prison, I found all my clothes awaiting me, but the food was nowhere in sight. The guards had either overlooked it or taken it. I dared not ask about it lest it raise suspicion about Stefan's visit.

The food had served its primary purpose anyway. Its greatest value was not the physical nutrition it provided but the value it had in reminding me that God's promises are always true, most especially his promise to never leave me or forsake me.

At Kremikovtzi, as at Central Prison, every effort was made to keep prisoners in total ignorance about their fate. My relocation within the prison had come without warning, and it wasn't until my lawyer, Lashkov, visited the following day that I knew why the transfer had taken place.

Preparing for Trial

Ljuben Lashkov was about ten years my junior, of medium build, with soft brown eyes that made him look more like a poet than an attorney. My first meeting with him had been brief, and our talk about my family had left little time to assess what kind of relationship I might have with him. My primary concern was that he possessed the strength of will to make a courageous stand. The pressure on him would be great.

Prisoners at Kremikovtzi were allowed to meet attorneys privately with no security screen separating us. When I entered the room, Lashkov was waiting for me dressed in a light gray suit.

Perhaps sensing my concerns about his trustworthiness, Lashkov began on a note calculated to win my confidence. "Your wife contacted me and asked that I consider defending you. Perhaps you're aware that our fathers were close friends," he said slowly, watching my response. "As I indicated to your wife, that's one of the reasons I have agreed to consider your case."

My father had indeed spoken of the Lashkov family, and I knew some of the lawyer's relatives quite well. Without a doubt this was a positive development, and surely the family relationship was the main reason my wife had sought Lashkov's assistance.

Lashkov related to me that the reason for my relocation was a change in status. "An indictment has now been handed down, which means your case will definitely be going to trial. The indictment means you're no longer classified as 'the accused' but are now in 'the convict' classification. Privileges are the same except visits with attorneys are allowed. The court indicated that your trial should be the middle of April, a little more than one month from now. We need to begin preparing immediately."

A Telling Admission of Ivanov's Impotence

With that introduction Lashkov opened his briefcase and brought out several files, which we began to review. The contents were revealing. The details of how difficult it had been for Pavel Ivanov to enter the church building were clearly related. This coincided with what Stefan had told me—although I didn't mention the secret visit to Lashkov.

Also in the files was a statement given by a Stanoj Trendafilov Gelev, a policeman from the Fourth Precinct. The sworn statement was dated January 22, 1985, and had been given in an interview with Penkov.

Gelev's statement read, "I was ordered to go to the church on Vasil Kolarov Street at approximately nine o'clock in the morning. As I approached the address, a citizen came and introduced himself as Tzvetkov, an officer with one of the government ministries. Mr. Tzvetkov explained that it was my responsibility to gain access to the church building, using force if necessary. A locksmith had been summoned, but when he unlocked the doors, they still couldn't be opened since they had been barricaded. Only after two and a half hours of work were we finally able to gain entry."

I found the conclusion of the document of special interest: "When the entry was made, we allowed Mr. Tzvetkov into the building and gave him the telephone number of the Fourth Precinct in case he needed further help. He did call us later because the people of the church had blocked him and another gentleman from stepping into the pulpit. We went to the church and escorted him into the pulpit."

This account from the police record was corroborated in Pavel Ivanov's own report, also in the file. Ivanov had written to Penkov, stating: "When I was blocked from stepping into the pulpit, I called the Fourth Precinct police station and asked for assistance." It was a telling admission of Ivanov's impotence.

As I read these documents, I breathed a prayer of thanksgiving for the brothers and sisters in the church who had had the courage to take such a strong and courageous stand. Mr. Tzvetkov, chairman of the Committee, and Pavel Ivanov must have calculated that with the Kulichevs removed, control of the church would be assured. Nothing could have been further from the truth! The arrest of my brother and me had stung the people in our congregation deeply, bringing them together with a deep resolve to resist.

Our congregation was committed to the belief that our church was Christ's church. The people were obviously doing all they could to keep the church from being used by the government as a pawn in a power struggle. Evidence of the congregation's unity provided me with more assurance at a time when I needed it. If we continued to trust God, he would lead us forward according to his perfect will.

The sworn statements that Ljuben Lashkov had shown me made it clear that the government had acted against the will of the people. The fact they had used force to impose Pavel Ivanov upon the congregation surely wouldn't look good in court.

Ljuben Lashkov concluded our meeting by outlining the two basic points with which he hoped to buttress my defense. "It's clear the Committee enlisted the police to enforce a decision that was offensive to the people of the congregation. This isn't just a disagreement between the Kulichevs and the Committee. They didn't even consult the church council. We'll hammer away at this as being disrespectful of the will of the people.

"Secondly," Lashkov continued, "your conduct has been highly principled and consistent. You've helped yourself by always pointing out that your motive is to serve God. Your motive is religious, not political. The fact that your right to preach has never been withdrawn legally is something we must emphasize and ask them to explain. I think we can make it clear that they acted precipitously, without following due diligence. We can make a pretty good case for administrative ineptitude, perhaps even malfeasance or misuse of authority. Based on that, we can argue that your rights have been grievously violated. We will work on these things more when I return."

Back in my new brigade, I contemplated Lashkov's words. He was starting strong, but would he endure the threats and intimidation? It was clear from Lashkov's comments about the possibility of misuse of authority that he wasn't a party member. Overall, I was pleased with the way things were going. When I knelt to pray that night, I gave thanks that God had protected me in so many ways.

Breaking Down the Wall of Suspicion

Developing friends in my new brigade went slowly. I missed Tzeko and Assen, seeing them only occasionally in the factory.

My experience in witnessing and working with people such as Assen taught me a great deal. It's dramatic to see someone with no faith begin to trust God in the practical, daily aspects of life, particularly when they are facing the hardships of prison.

In such situations, one's approach to witnessing shouldn't be theoretical but practical. Intellectual debates are effective only when accompanied with the example of a life lived by faith in Jesus Christ.

A chronic problem I faced in prison was the skepticism of prisoners who doubted I was in prison because of my Christian faith. Prisoners often denied their guilt and tried to cover up their crimes. Some prisoners thought I had committed an unspeakable crime and was using my story as an elaborate cover.

The wall of suspicion could only be broken down by living a godly life and humbly serving the prisoners around me. In the dog-eat-dog prison environment, the one thing that caused inmates to sit up and take notice was when they saw my willingness to give a helping hand, share what little I possessed, or offer a word of encouragement.

God constantly reminded me that I had been called to be a servant. Christ gave himself on the cross as the Suffering Servant to redeem the poor, the lost, and the outcast. In the same way, my willingness to serve Christ by sharing his compassion with others was what brought respect and made it possible for me to witness in prison. I knew if I was faithful, God would bless me and others by taking my little deeds of compassion and using them to add to his kingdom, to his glory.

Understanding this, I began praying that God would use me to minister to others in this awkward setting. When the prisoners got to know me and recognized that I was eager to help them, their attitude began to change. Some of the prisoners in my new cell block also spoke with Assen and Tzeko, who confirmed that I consistently lived a godly life.

Classified as "Dangerous Criminals"

Slowly, attitudes changed in my new cell block, and prisoners talked more openly. Much of the conversation was about prison conditions and the court system. Anger and frustration were ready to boil over. The government claimed that prisons stopped crime and reeducated criminals. But prisoners saw prison as a place where people were held unjustly and exploited as cheap labor for the government. The resentment motivated men to do everything they could to get even with the establishment when they were released.

Overcrowding in the prisons was discussed at length. When I first arrived at the prison in Kremikovtzi, I was told that five people were admitted for every two released.

One of the reasons Bulgarian prisons were overcrowded was because the government used the penal system to silence those who were critical of the government and control people viewed as inconvenient. While political enemies were put in prison, some dangerous criminals were allowed to walk the streets.

Some weeks before my arrest, a high-ranking army officer hit and killed a woman with his car. It was a widely publicized case even though public officials did all they could to keep him out of the limelight in the hopes of avoiding a scandal. By rights he should have been stripped of his rank and given time in prison for manslaughter. He got off with only a two-year assignment in a special company where soldiers were placed for disciplinary purposes. These types of inequities were widely discussed among the people and destroyed public confidence in the government and the judicial system.

My brother and I were arrested because our religious beliefs didn't prove convenient for the Committee on Internal Religious Affairs. We expected to be granted bail since the families of most criminals—including those arrested for violent crimes—were usually able to arrange for bail until the time of the trial. Our case had to do with freedom of worship, but since we were a threat to the Committee's scheme, bail was denied. We had been arrested and accused under Article 274, which states that if convicted we would face up to twelve months of imprisonment. What was not stated was that the police were also allowed to hold us in prison during the entire time they were "investigating" the case.

Many people, including other prisoners, came to see how ironic it was that criminals who were a threat to society roamed free while Dimitar and I were classified as "dangerous criminals" simply for our religious beliefs!

The Nameless Friend

Shortly after moving to the new cell block, I was assigned to work on a construction project not far from the prison. We went to and from the project in a bus.

Early in the morning of my second day on this new assignment, we had just gotten off the bus and were awaiting instructions for the day when a voice within urged me to go to a water pipe and fill a bottle with water. This was unusual since it was early and no one had worked up a thirst. But I had heard that inner voice before and had learned to obey, so I picked up a water bottle, walked to the water pipe, and started filling it.

Suddenly, a civilian from outside the prison, who apparently was working at the site, was standing beside me. Although I couldn't recall his name, I recognized the man's face and knew he lived a few houses from us in Sofia.

There was no introduction, but with a look of surprise on his face, he said quietly, "I heard you were in prison, but I never thought I would see you here on this project!"

I explained to him that this was only my second day on the new assignment.

"Tell me what you need, and I'll see what I can do to help," the man said.

Providentially, I had tucked a letter to my family into my clothes that day. "Would you please take this letter to my family?" I asked. "If possible, ask them for food to bring me when you return. I'd be grateful." I gave the man the letter and thanked him before he quietly walked away.

Assen was working on the same project and when I told him of this nameless friend, his eyes opened wide with excitement. "How could that be possible? Christo, you have experienced some kind of a miracle today!"

"When something like this happens, you know God is watching over us," I assured Assen. "He cares for us and will meet our needs if only we will trust him. Remember, nothing is impossible for God!"

Indeed, it was something of a miracle to know that someone cared about my well-being. The man returned the next day with food and a letter from my wife. His assistance was a gift from God during those difficult days.

Sea of Troubled Humanity

Each cell block had a mix of strange and unpredictable people, and one had to be careful about forming relationships. Most of the prisoners seemed to be thieves of one sort or another.

I soon learned that there was a sort of caste system among thieves. Those who had stolen private property simply to keep body and soul together or to meet the needs of their families were the "common thieves." The thieves who had stolen from the State were considered more serious offenders and received longer sentences. The forgers and counterfeiters were almost like artists, and they formed an exclusive group. The scam artists, who talked fast and took money under false pretenses, also hung together. One scam artist had even been charged with selling his house to more than one buyer! The black marketeers and con men seemed to have a lower status.

Of course, there were some men held for violent crimes such as murder and rape. Within those walls were people who had done it all—murder, violent crimes, and illegal activities of every sort—even men who had abused their own families or simply abandoned them as though they cared nothing for their own flesh and blood.

The trials of some prisoners had been highly publicized, and I recognized them when we met in prison. Prior to my arrest I had read in the Sofia newspaper about a dentist who had hit a pedestrian with his car. Because he had been drinking, he put the injured man into the trunk of the vehicle, drove outside of the city, and burned both the car and the injured man. Thinking all evidence of his crime had been destroyed, the dentist went back into the city and, when he was sober, reported his automobile stolen. He was discovered, put on trial, and convicted. We were imprisoned together in the prison at Kremikovtzi.

Believe me when I say I felt surrounded not only by the walls of the prison but by a sea of troubled humanity who were capable of doing terrible things to anyone who crossed them. And in the midst of them was one accused of the "crime" of trying to do his best to preach the gospel of the Lord Jesus Christ.

Bring This Mistress of Mine so I Can Meet Her!

The prisoners in my new brigade were mostly younger, but one man was just a little older than me. His name was Metodi. We soon struck up a conversation, out of which an enduring relationship developed.

Metodi told me he had waited months after being admitted before he saw an interrogator. As in Central Prison, the interrogators here worked slowly and let men wait and wonder.

When the interrogator finally did summon Metodi, the agent didn't pursue the theft of 3,000 *leva* from the shop where Metodi worked. Instead, the agent began by saying, "Why don't you tell me about your mistress?"

"I have no mistress," Metodi insisted.

"Come now," the official persisted, "you can tell me. If you admit it, I won't tell your wife. But you should know that your mistress has already come clean and confessed everything you told her."

Metodi was not intimidated, and he responded, "Then bring this mistress of mine so I can meet her! Is she young and pretty? I would like to meet her sometime."

"Oh, we'll bring her," the agent promised.

"But they didn't," Metodi informed me with a smile. "They couldn't possibly—because she doesn't exist!"

Agents often used these kinds of disreputable tactics just to see what information they might glean by chance. They had no respect whatsoever for the prisoners' marriages or spouses. It was common for them to drive a wedge of suspicion between a wife and her husband while he was in prison. Stung by an insult, an angry wife might well provide incriminating information to get even with her unfaithful husband.

Some wives believed this information even if it wasn't true, and relationships were tragically destroyed. The tragedy wreaked by such devious lies was beyond measure. There was no limit to the mental cruelty agents would impose upon helpless prisoners in such ways. The prisoners fully understood the kinds of tactics being used to destroy their wives' trust, but they could do nothing about it.

Tefik the Turk

The construction job I was assigned to was just the thing I needed. The fresh air was wonderful, and I was again working with my hands, which I always enjoyed. I worked on the night shift, so there were fewer guards, giving prisoners the opportunity to talk more freely.

The government had men from the Turkish community to help as common laborers on the project. Turks could be counted on for cheap labor. I quickly became friends with the foreman of the Turks, a man named Tefik.

Tefik was curious as to why I was in prison. When I told him it was because of my religious beliefs, he tentatively asked me, "Because of the Turkish question?" I explained that I was in prison because evangelical beliefs were not accepted just as Turkish religious beliefs were not accepted.

Tefik tried explaining this to his Turkish friends. They didn't fully understand the nuances of what was happening between the government and the churches, but they knew my imprisonment had something to do with my religious beliefs. Because the Turks also suffered religious persecution, they were sympathetic to my situation.

Tefik and I became close enough that I felt I could confide in him. Because the surprise visit with my son had gone so well—and the fact that the prisoners had kept it a secret—I was eager to arrange another visit. Knowing that Stefan would be on spring break from school during the next two weeks, I decided to risk making contact. It would require effort and cooperation on the part of the Turkish workers, however. I quietly mentioned it to Tefik one day and asked him to attempt to call my family.

Once again, to my amazement, God made it possible. Tefik contacted Stefan the following night and arranged to meet him at a prearranged spot a few kilometers from the prison. The Turkish workers actually walked some distance to meet Stefan and then escorted him back to the project. With the Turks clustered around him, Stefan looked like another workman. The Turks seemed to be pleased to help, even though it was a risky thing for them to do.

God Sees the Larger Picture

When Stefan came to visit, I told him about the needs of other prisoners. He agreed to deliver secret letters for some of the prisoners, and when he returned for a third visit, he brought items we could share with them. Little things such as a bottle of aspirin, a clean pair of socks, and in one case a clean pair of trousers helped alleviate some of the suffering around me. These gifts were gratefully received and gave me an opportunity to express appreciation that my meetings with Stefan had remained secret. Several prisoners told me how impressed they were with Stefan's maturity and reliability for a teen-ager.

When I met with Stefan, I was eager to learn of news from home. Not all of the news was particularly good. One of the men in the church named Boris Delchev was being influenced by the government agents and was urging church leaders to compromise.

Boris Delchev had come to visit my wife, suggesting, "With the pastor in jail, we have to do something. We can't keep resisting Pavel Ivanov if the Committee insists he take over the pulpit. Why not ask the church board to unanimously accept Ivanov and then use that solidarity to control him so he understands he can't do whatever he likes?"

"Mother stood up to him," Stefan informed me. "She said, 'Pavel Ivanov is not a godly man. He's known to be both dishonest and unfaithful to his wife. If we compromise with Ivanov, we become accomplices in his dishonesty. Besides, once Pavel is accepted by the board, no one would be able to control him as you suggest!'"

"And what did Delchev say to that?" I eagerly inquired of Stefan.

"He just shrugged his shoulders and said, 'Pavel Ivanov is going to be imposed upon the church anyway. What can we do?' He was willing to give in."

I could predict Tzvete's answer. "And what was your mother's reply?"

"She disagreed of course. She told Mr. Delchev, 'The fact that Pavel Ivanov has the authorities on his side doesn't mean anything. They're depending on human force, but we know that God's power is far greater. God sees the larger picture, and his ways are as far above our ways as the heavens are above the earth. I say we remain faithful to what we know to be right and leave the consequences to God!' She told me to be sure to tell you exactly what she said."

"Your mother's quite a woman, Stefan, speaking up like that. I couldn't have said it better myself. And you're such an encouragement to me also, taking the risk of meeting with me like this and bringing me the news. God has blessed me with a wonderful family!"

Stefan went on to explain that Delchev had visited other leaders in the church with his plan for compromise but had found little or no interest in supporting Pavel Ivanov in any way.

The Message Is Getting Through!

Most surprising of all of the news that Stefan brought was a report that a church member told my wife that he had spoken to Christians in

Scandinavia. They reported that my name was being circulated in Western Europe and the United States on a list of prisoners being held for religious beliefs. People were being urged to pray and to send letters asking the Bulgarian government to release me and other prisoners of conscience.

"That explains something," I responded to Stefan. "Please tell Mother that Nikolov questions me all the time about contacts outside of Bulgaria. He mentioned receiving letters and is concerned that foreigners know that I am in prison. It's obvious the message is getting through! Tell Mother to thank those who have gotten the word out."

That night, I lay in my bunk contemplating the events as Stefan described them. My wife was right: all we could do was be faithful and leave the results with God. God's righteousness would prevail over evil.

How thankful I was for a wife who understood these things, who encouraged me to remain faithful even if it meant being separated by prison walls. Some wives would have insisted that their husbands support the family no matter what. That is why so many men fled the churches in Bulgaria in the face of persecution. Many husbands and wives weren't willing to make the sacrifice necessary to be faithful Christians. My ministry would not have been possible without Tzvete's full support.

Standing Strong in the Portal

There was nothing I could do about Pavel Ivanov, and little my wife could do to keep Boris Delchev from suggesting compromise with the Committee. All we could do was remain faithful and leave the rest to God.

The situation reminded me of a passage in *Time of Parting* by Anton Donchev. Donchev quoted a man named Manol who spoke of guarding righteousness as we might guard a mighty fortress. As best I recall, Donchev wrote:

> The forces of evil press in upon us from outside the fortress. . . . Each of us must guard one small portal where evil may enter.
> It's not my place to worry about the entire fortress with its countless ramparts. I defend just one small space. Perhaps some great commander knows what's happening along a wide expanse of the wall. Great men may be able to defend a hundred bulwarks.

> I'm not able to do that, for I can only protect one
> small portal in the wall. If I'm not faithful, who
> will be there to meet evil and turn it back? If I
> retreat a step or two, my portal may be just the point
> where evil gains entrance.
>
> So I must remain faithful, standing strong in the
> portal, even if it is small. Faithful and vigilant,
> at least I'll know if I lay down my very life for
> righteousness' sake, my body will still block the
> portal so that evil cannot enter.[9]

With that thought in mind, I prayed, "Dear Lord, each one of us must carry a cross, just as our Savior did. Some of us carry our cross in prison, others in the church. Each one of us needs your wisdom and strength. Protect us from the cunning of evil. You have promised, Lord, that even the gates of hell shall not withstand the faithful witness of your church. Deliver us from the temptation to compromise, so that our lives may be more comfortable. Keep us pure and faithful, for your Word promises, 'If we died with him, we will also live with him; if we endure, we will also reign with him' (2 Timothy 2:11-12). I claim your promises in faith, knowing that 'the kingdom of the world has become the kingdom of our Lord and of his Christ, and he will reign forever and ever' (Revelation 11:15). Amen."

How Can I Expect Justice?

Nikolov continued to be particularly interested in our "foreign contacts" and seemed to believe I was somehow communicating with people outside of Bulgaria. The idea was preposterous. Stefan had confirmed that contact with Christians in other countries had been made by people in the Sofia church, though of course I didn't tell Nikolov that. Nikolov didn't understand that the church of Jesus Christ was a universal body of believers, of which I was only one small member. He could imprison me, but he couldn't stop the working of God's Holy Spirit through the universal church.

Faithfulness to Christian principles and integrity in my relationships were winning friends in the new cell block. One of my new friends were Pesho, a young man in his thirties. Pesho had appealed to the Supreme Court because of the harshness of his sentence. When his case wasn't heard after many months, he requested that his wife see what was causing the delay.

[9] Donchev, Anton. *Time of Parting*. New York: William Morrow, 1968.

A view of one of the towers of Central Prison of Sofia. Much has been written about Central Prison, all of it bad. It has been said that many who enter leave their bones, but all who enter leave their health.

The entrance to the interrogation area of Central Prison. I entered here to be "interviewed" before being taken to my cell.

The door to the corridor leading to the room where I was often interrogated by Chavdar Penkov and later by Vladimir Nikolov.

The steel door to my interrogation cell.

This tiny cell is similar in size to the one in which I was held
with two other men for nearly two months.

In August 1999 my friend Michael Halcomb and I were invited to speak at a Christian conference sponsored by the Greek Evangelical Churches. This picture was taken at the conference grounds on the Aegean Sea near Leptokaria, Greece.

My dear wife, Tzvete, has been a wonderful partner in ministry and supported me throughout my prison experience. This photo was taken in 1995.

On May 21, 1994, I received an honorary doctorate from North Park University in Chicago, Illinois.

Here I am being presented with my honorary doctorate by David G. Horner, president of North Park University.

Shaking hands with Peter Stojanov, president of Bulgaria, in 1998. I met with President Stojanov to discuss the importance of religious freedom in Bulgaria.

On March 13, 1999, a memorial service was held at First
Evangelical Church in Sofia to commemorate the fiftieth anniver-
sary of the Pastors' Trial. Here Todor Kavaldjiev, vice president of
Bulgaria, joins me outside the church.

Todor Kavaldjiev, vice president
of Bulgaria, speaks from the
pulpit of First Church during the
fiftieth anniversary memorial. Vice
President Kavaldjiev had been
imprisoned by the Communists
for his political views.

Pesho's wife scheduled a hearing with the judge responsible for Pesho's case. She told Pesho that at the hearing the judge called her aside and spoken to her alone. He suggested that if she would spend a night with him in a hotel, he would make sure her husband was released from prison. Pesho's wife left the room in disgust and reported the entire episode to her husband.

Pesho's case only illustrated what many prisoners suspected: that those responsible for fairness and justice in the country couldn't be trusted. Pesho's judge wasn't the only one who didn't respect the law or the feelings of family members who came seeking justice.

This sordid episode bothered poor Pesho for the remainder of his time in prison. He would often say, "Christo, how can I expect justice from a judge like that! I don't believe in your God, because a God of justice wouldn't permit this kind of evil to exist."

Pesho's questions were difficult to answer. All I could say was, "Pesho, these are sinful human beings who know nothing of God's justice. They have rejected his plan for their lives and have set up a selfish system that serves their own purposes. God has given them a free will, and they've misused it to pervert the good things God has given us in this life."

"I believe all you say about the sinfulness of human nature," Pesho would reply. "The very hypocrite who professes to protect our rights tramples them in the dust the first time he has an opportunity to gain something for himself!"

"But there is a God," I told Pesho, "and his righteousness exceeds anything we see here on earth. In the end his love and justice will prevail. Someday, when these people stand before God, their official status won't give them any power at all, and they'll realize they turned their backs upon God's eternal love and grace for the sake of a little bit of this world's material gain."

"Perhaps you are right," Pesho once said to me. "And you, Christo, are a rare exception in this sinful world. You're one of only a few people I've met in my life who seems to truly want to do what is right. But our society doesn't recognize people like you. In fact, they put you into prison because they don't want to be reminded of what true justice is like."

A World of Pervasive Fear

As one might imagine, much of the daily conversation in prison had to do with justice. Cynicism had taken its toll in Bulgarian society, but it was nowhere more apparent than among the prisoners. I commonly overheard proverbs such as "You'll get no mercy with a meager dime, and even a million won't buy you a law."

Ideally, prisons should have been in the business of reforming people, showing them that there is a better way to live. But the prisons I found myself in did nothing that even resembled reform. No one even talked about making an effort to influence the prisoners for good or discussed implementing programs to encourage reform. Prisons were primarily places of fear and intimidation.

The warden and guards used the fear of pain and deprivation to control prisoners. The inmates lived in a world of pervasive fear. Prison made me realize that there are different kinds of fear. On one level, prisoners were afraid they might be unjustly punished. At a deeper, more personal level, prisoners were afraid they might not be able to maintain their psychological composure under such threatening circumstances. Although they didn't admit it, most prisoners were also afraid that someone might notice just how fearful they were and take advantage of them.

While there were many different kinds of fear, the results of such deep and prolonged fear were almost always the same. First, when a prisoner lived constantly in a world of fear, reforming or changing was the farthest thing from his mind. Second, when fear took root deep in the soul of a human being, it inevitably bore the fruit of defensive anger. That anger eventually led to hatred.

My battle against the fear and hatred around me was constant. It was only with the Lord's help that I was able to release the feelings of anger so they wouldn't harden into an attitude of hatred. In my times of meditation, I reflected upon passages such as 1 John 3:15, "Anyone who hates his brother is a murderer," or Jesus' words in Matthew 5, which tell us that hatred will lead to judgment since it is the spiritual equivalent of murder. I repeatedly reminded myself that hatred was one of the most dangerous sins. It could be just as destructive, to myself and others, as murder itself.

Lashkov Twists Nervously
My attorney, Ljuben Lashkov, returned as promised. I sensed something of a change in his attitude, however, and immediately became concerned.

"Your wife and I have talked," Lashkov began, "and I'm suggesting we may need another lawyer to assist with this case."

The confidence I had felt in Lashkov in our earlier meeting began to wane. "What's your thinking in that regard?" I asked.

"You surely must be aware," Lashkov began, "that there's the possibility your case may be prejudged. The Committee on Internal Religious Affairs has a lot at stake here, and I'm concerned they'll leave no stone unturned in their attempt to get a guilty verdict—possibly one with a long sentence."

"What you say is undoubtedly true," I responded, trying to understand why Lashkov had changed. "The persistence of the officials is evident not just in arresting me and my brother. They've also prosecuted others—such as Toshko, my son-in-law, and Emanuel Tinev, who were both sentenced to hard labor. This certainly sent a message that they're determined to have their own way. But you've already pointed out that the government has overstepped its authority. Pavel Ivanov sought the help of the police in breaking into the church so that he could move in forcibly. I knew that he wouldn't give up in the pursuit of his goal. But he and the Committee should answer in court for acting illegally and denying us our rights. Don't you agree?"

"It really isn't important whether I agree or not," Lashkov shrugged. "If your case is prejudged, it may be impossible to bring any serious witnesses to the stand. We're dealing with people who have ways of intimidating people so that they suddenly become silent or claim to be ill."

It seemed clear that someone must have intimidated Lashkov. Perhaps Tzvetkov, the chairman of the Committee on Internal Religious Affairs, had swayed him. I wondered what had happened since we had last talked. Could others have been arrested? Taking the direct approach, I asked Lashkov, "What has changed?"

Lashkov twisted nervously in his chair. "I'm not sure anything has changed; I'm just saying that this is a difficult case, and there's no way I can guarantee the outcome."

"It is not easy being in prison because of my faith either," I countered. "The indictments state that my brother and I are dangerous. That's true only in one respect: we're a threat to Pavel Ivanov's success in taking control of the church and its building. We're considered dangerous because the Committee knows that we could return to the church and immediately have the respect and commitment of the congregation. All I ask is that we speak the truth about that. Truth is the best defense."

"I hope you understand this case isn't going to do anything to help my career," Lashkov said, his voice rising. "Arguing against an arrest order issued by someone as powerful as Petar Mladenov, Director of the Interior, can only hurt me."

"But I believe God has put me here for a purpose," I contended. "All I ask is that we tell the truth about what has happened. I've done nothing that I'm ashamed of. If necessary I will stand in my own defense. Giving testimony to my faith in Christ before an open court is something I look forward to, if given the chance. Will you help me get that opportunity?"

"Yes, I'm sure that can be arranged. All I'm saying is that it's a difficult case and that the outlook isn't good. We need a second lawyer to help prepare the witnesses and examine the charges that will be brought by the prosecution. Besides, since you and your brother have been charged with different offenses, you will each need your own lawyer anyway. Do you agree?"

"Certainly I agree," I conceded. "All I ask is a fair opportunity to tell the truth in the courtroom. The law promises freedom of religion, and we must appeal for those laws to be honored. If someone prejudges the case and doesn't honor the laws of the country, you and I cannot do anything about it. But we can tell the truth and leave the matter in God's hands. Ultimately his justice will prevail."

"Let me work on it," Lashkov said, standing. "We only have a couple of weeks, and we need to arrange for the second lawyer soon. There won't be much time for him to prepare before the trial convenes."

Guided by Principle, Not Pressure

The meeting with Ljuben Lashkov wasn't encouraging. Rather than preparing for the trial, we were preoccupied with the obstacles in our path.

What bothered me about Lashkov's timidity was that he seemed to be hinting that I should reconsider my opposition to the Committee. That would be the easy way out for everyone, but I knew it wasn't God's way.

The disciples of Jesus were forced to choose between trusting God in suffering and trusting the selfish instinct to avoid suffering. In Matthew 16, Peter wanted to persuade Jesus not to continue down the road to Calvary. Worried about what would happen to him and the other disciples if Jesus died, Peter's counsel was to take the easy way and protect God's work. Jesus rebuked Peter, saying, "If anyone would come after me, he must deny himself and take up his cross and follow me. For whoever wants to save his life will lose it, but whoever loses his life for me will find it" (Matthew 16:24-25).

With Lashkov's troubling words and the increased pressure of the impending trial in mind, I knew I needed to be careful. The constant pressure of prison and the psychological influence of the interrogators could push a person beyond normal human limits. I didn't want to say and do things I would later regret. I prayed that the Holy Spirit would help me to be wise and discerning while being bold in speaking the truth.

After a few days of thinking and praying, my future course became clear. I must be guided by principle, not pressure. Regardless of what Lashkov, the Committee, or the court did, God was calling me to remain on the course I had begun. God's people must be fully committed no matter what the cost and not become guilty of weakness or vacillation. I must defend our rights to follow Christ, regardless of the consequences.

No Right to Ask about Rights

Fewer guards were used at Kremikovtzi than at Central Prison in spite of the overcrowding. Prisoners had more opportunity to converse when not within earshot of a guard, but harsh and unpredictable discipline was the rule rather than the exception.

One particular incident found me at the center of attention. We were eating breakfast in the prison dining area. Conversation was forbidden in the area while we ate, but it was not uncommon for prisoners to whisper or communicate in one fashion or another. In the overcrowded conditions, it was almost impossible to catch the offenders.

Although I was not among those talking that day, the guard in charge of our table decided to make an example of me. Singling me out, he loudly demanded I leave the dining area immediately, returning me to the cell without my breakfast.

For just a moment, I toyed with the idea of asking about my rights to have the meal but decided against it. In Bulgarian prisons one didn't even have the right to ask about one's rights. There was no recourse except to return to my cell hungry.

When the other prisoners returned from breakfast, those who had been talking came and apologized. They also brought me bread and marmalade. All that I really lost was my cup of breakfast tea! With a few coins given to me by Stefan when he made his secret visits, I went to the canteen later in the day to supplement my meager diet.

Our Neighbors as Ourselves

My friend Metodi was an interesting man. While most of the prisoners were younger than me, Metodi was fifty-two, about two years older. As we got to know each other, we appeared to share a growing affinity, perhaps because of our ages. I noticed he often sought me out for conversation. We had the kind of confidential relationship that allowed us to share easily with one another.

One wouldn't have expected to find a man like Metodi in prison. At one time he had held a responsible position in the government, often traveling outside the country with the Foreign Ministry.

When Metodi retired, he found his government pension was too small to adequately support him and his wife. In order to make more money, Metodi went to work in a small shop where he worked as the only accountant. His lack of experience at accounting cost him dearly when he was unable to account for 3,000 *leva*. Metodi insisted it was only an accounting error and not an actual loss, but his employer accused him of stealing the money. That was reason enough to put Metodi into prison.

The investigation of his case dragged on far longer than was reasonable, and the stress placed upon him by the trial was very debilitating. I watched as his hair turned completely gray in a few weeks' time. He had also become even paler than the other prisoners.

I did all I could to help Metodi. He knew of my secret meetings with Stefan, and this was very difficult for Metodi because he wasn't receiving visits from his family. His family was apparently upset and embarrassed because of his arrest. The poor man was very depressed.

At my suggestion, Metodi wrote a letter to his family, which I passed on to Stefan during his next secret visit. I asked Stefan to find the family and give them the letter. As a result Metodi's son agreed to visit his father.

When Metodi was given word his son had arrived, he began to cry and said to me, "I always knew you to be a good and reliable man, but I had no idea whether or not your son would be as trustworthy. I don't know how I will ever thank both of you."

Serving others in the name of Christ gave me a sense of purpose in prison. Increasingly I understood that Christian service was central, not supplemental, to all I stood for as a believer. My commitment as a Christian was not only to love the Lord my God with all my heart, soul, mind, and strength, but also to love my neighbor as myself. By serving others, I established credibility among the prisoners. I was also more effective in witnessing, and service kept me growing spiritually while in prison.

Some would no doubt have said, "Yes, but if you start doing that people will take advantage of you!" And that was true. There were some people who tried to take my help and use me for their own advantage. That was a constant risk of service, but with the risk also came the possibility of spiritual reward. The reward of being an instrument of God's grace was far greater than any risk. I knew God would give me the wisdom to know who to help and when to help if I was willing to set aside my pride and comfort and be used by the Holy Spirit.

God's grace isn't something intended for us to hold, clutching it to ourselves. God's grace is given so that we might share it with others. Anything short of this is a theoretical Christianity that is truncated and undeveloped.

Another Secret Visit

Stefan's next visit came while he was still on spring break from school. "You'll never believe what happened on the way here!" he exclaimed when he saw me.

From the look on his face, I knew he surely must have run into some difficulties.

"The Turks gave me work clothes and put me on a bus full of workers coming to the construction site. When we stopped at the gate, the prison security began a thorough search of the bus, checking each person's identity. I was really sweating, since I don't have an ID card like the other workers. It was a sure thing that I was about to be caught, when the workers began to protest, 'You're keeping us from our work!' and 'Come on, can't you cut through all this red tape?'

"There was such an uproar from the Turkish workers, in a good-natured way, that the guards took the easy way out. They just smiled, got off the bus, and waved us through!"

"God was at work protecting you, Stefan!" I said. "It's as clear as the nose on your face! Praise God that you got through safely!"

As we rejoiced together, Stefan said with relief, "It was a miracle. I was praying for God to do something, and I could hardly believe it when the guards stopped just a few seats in front of me, got off, and waved the bus through! For a while I thought I might be with you as a prisoner rather than making a secret visit! God answered my prayer more clearly than I've ever seen before!"

Your Faith Is Being Reported All Over the World

On this visit Stefan brought word of communication that Tzvete had received from abroad. Marcus Diviastis, a good friend of ours from the United States, had sent a postcard. All that the card contained was a simple greeting to my family, the words "Romans 1:8," and a signature.

"Do you know what Romans 1:8 says?" Stefan asked. Without

waiting for my reply, he quoted it: "I thank my God through Jesus Christ for all of you, because your faith is being reported all over the world."

Stefan and I smiled at each other knowingly. Obviously our good friend Marcus Diviastis was sending word that he knew of my imprisonment. Marcus and his Christian friends in the United States would know what to do. Their letters protesting my arrest were surely among those Nikolov continued to refer to during my interrogations.

"Mother took the card to church and read the verse for everyone to hear," Stefan said excitedly. "You should have heard the people applaud and say 'Amen.' People were saying, 'Praise God!' and 'Thank the Lord!' Everyone felt encouraged knowing that the testing we are going through is encouraging the faith of other people all over the world! I think the church people are stronger in their faith than ever before!"

"That's good news," I responded. "What's happening with Boris Delchev? Is he still trying to persuade people to compromise with Pavel Ivanov?"

"There were a few people who wanted to form a new church board and put Mr. Delchev on it, but it was overwhelmingly rejected by the people," Stefan answered. "Also, your agent Vladimir Nikolov has been calling Nick Athanasov in for questioning. They obviously know Nick is a leader in the church and are watching him carefully. So far they haven't arrested him."

"Nick is strong in the faith and strong psychologically as well. We don't need to worry about him. Do you have any news about Toshko and Emanuel Tinev?"

"They are serving their sentence in the brickworks. Nebesna worries about Toshko, but Mother got a report from another church member that they had made contact and that he is doing well. We're praying that they will be released soon. People are mostly concerned about you and Uncle Dimitar."

"It looks like we will finally be given a trial," I informed Stefan. "Ask the people to pray that we will have an opportunity to share our faith in Christ publicly."

Alongside the encouraging reports, Stefan shared some concerns. There was evidence that the Committee on Internal Religious Affairs seemed to be intent upon suppressing the worship and witness of evangelical churches, especially in the Sofia area. Stefan mentioned church members talking about the fact that now that the Kulichev brothers were in prison, the government was turning their attention towards the Baptist church on Pelovski Street.

"My hope and prayer is that some of the Baptists will take a strong stand for religious freedom," I told Stefan. "That could help break the efforts of the Committee to control the church leaders in Bulgaria. The Committee is in a sensitive position now. Having arrested Dimitar and me and forced their way into the church building, not to mention the scene they created in using the police to escort Pavel Ivanov into the pulpit, they have surely tarnished their reputation even more around Sofia."

I Watched Stefan Slowly Drift Away

With that our conversation ended. We dared not press for too much of a good thing. Before Stefan left, I knew that I must say something that would be very difficult.

Just before Stefan's third visit, Tefik had told me that his workers simply could not continue to take the risks they were taking. They had done as much as they could do. He strongly suggested that this be the last visit.

Grateful for their assistance, which was far more sacrificial than anything I had expected, I thanked Tefik and his workers from the depths of my heart for all they had done. Even though they professed another faith they were sensitive and compassionate to my situation, and God had used them to greatly encourage me at a very low point in my prison experience.

Following the Turk's recommendations, I informed Stefan that there would not be any other opportunities for him to come and see me in this way. Assuring him of my love and appreciation for all he had done, I thanked Stefan for the risks he had taken to come be with me.

We both knew that we dared not press the Turks to do more lest we or they be discovered. The punishment would be harsh for such violations. Asking Stefan to take my love and prayers back to my wife and daughter, I told him to assure everyone that my needs were being met by God's grace.

We prayed briefly and embraced one last time, and then I watched Stefan slowly drift away into the morning mist where Tefik waited to escort him past the guards and out of the construction site. We had no way of knowing under what circumstances we would be allowed to meet again.

Truth Refracted through a Prism

My friend Metodi knew I had met with Stefan again. That night in our cell I told Metodi about Toshko and Emanuel's sentence. As we discussed the church situation, Metodi confessed, "When I was in the Foreign Ministry, I had no idea our government was treating people like this." His perspective of Bulgaria had once been from above, in a government post, but his time in prison had changed Metodi's perspective, helping him see the adversities that common people lived with much of the time.

Metodi tried to reassure me, saying, "When I finally get out of this place, I'm going to make an appointment to go and talk with Ljubomir Popov, the Attorney General. I know him well, and I'll tell him about your case and how we met here in this horrible place."

It was ironic that I had to tell Metodi, "It won't do any good. Popov is one of those who signed the order condemning me to this place! These people live in a world distorted by their own selfish interests. They don't see the truth; they only see what is refracted through the prism of their self-interests. What they consider to be truth is very often in direct contradiction with reality."

Metodi picked up on the point I was making. "And of course anyone who dares to speak about the contradiction is considered to be an enemy of the State. My own experience has taught me that anyone who disagrees, even slightly, is labeled and attacked."

"Exactly," I responded. "Those of us who disagree suffer dire consequences. But my Christian brothers and sisters aren't going to be intimidated by suffering. We believe that our Lord Jesus Christ suffered for our sins on the cross so that we might live for him and reign with him eternally. The suffering is temporary, but his kingdom is eternal!"

The Purpose of Suffering
Metodi and I spent hours in conversation.

"Christo, I can see that your life is committed to serving God," he said thoughtfully one day. "But when God saves you from sin, why doesn't he protect you from suffering? God should let sinners suffer, not good people."

The question Metodi was asking was one many people wondered about. Christians as well as non-Christians often made a direct link between sin and suffering. But the Bible clearly teaches that the righteous also suffer. How could I explain that to someone such as Metodi?

"Our salvation does save us from eternal separation from God and the suffering *that* brings," I explained. "But we're not saved from suffering in this life. Following Christ in a world that is hostile to his truth brings suffering and inconvenience into our lives. God uses that suffering to make us stronger, more holy."

Metodi was listening intently, so I continued, "Paul writes about how believing and suffering go together in the Christian life. In Philippians 1:29 he says, 'It has been granted to you on behalf of Christ not only to believe on him, but also to suffer for him.' But this suffering is to purify us from sin, as fire removes impurities from gold. When we are free from sin, God can use us to share his love and grace with everyone in the world. That's what Jesus calls us to do."

"So you believe God can accomplish something good through your suffering, even here in prison?" Metodi asked.

"Yes, Metodi," I replied with a smile. "God must have me here for a purpose. Perhaps he wants me here so we can talk like this, so I can tell you of God's love for you."

"Do you really think so?" Metodi asked almost in awe. "You certainly have encouraged me."

"If I've encouraged you, the glory goes to God," I said. "He's working in my life to make me more holy, giving me strength and guiding me in what I should do."

After a thoughtful silence, Metodi spoke again. "While the rest of us are lying in prison feeling sorry for ourselves, I can see you've found a purpose for your life even here."

Conformed to His Likeness

After I knelt and said my prayers that night, I lay in my bunk, thinking about my conversation with Metodi and reflecting upon my own preaching.

I was constantly challenging people like Metodi to trust Christ for salvation, to come to him for forgiveness, to be declared righteous in Christ. But then it was all too easy to stop there and miss the other half of the gospel: God wants to make us holy, to refine our faith through our serving and struggling in the battle against evil. We want to be declared holy but find it inconvenient to let God *make* us holy by taking up the cross and following Christ until we are conformed to his likeness (Romans 8:29).

My future was filled with uncertainty as I lay in my bunk that night. Nevertheless, I resolved that if God ever allowed me to return to the pulpit in Sofia, or to any pulpit, I would emphasize even more that when our sins are removed, God wants to purify us from sin and make us holy. It is a painful process requiring sacrifice and suffering because it rubs against our old nature and against the world.

As God makes us holy, he uses us to do his work in the world. Sin is removed to make room for the gifts of the Spirit given to God's people. The gifts of God's Spirit are not to be used for our own glory. We're filled with the Spirit, made holy, and given spiritual gifts so that we might serve God and bring glory to Him. It all starts, with God's help, by becoming "conformed to his likeness." And God can do that even in prison.

CHAPTER EIGHT

Worthy of Suffering for His Name

Everyone who wants to live a godly life in Christ Jesus
will be persecuted.
2 TIMOTHY 3:12

In some way, suffering ceases to be suffering at the moment
it finds a meaning, such as the meaning of a sacrifice.
VICTOR E. FRANKL

It was Easter—April 14, 1985. The date will always stand out in my memory as the first time my family was allowed to visit me. Stefan and I had met secretly three times, but this was the first time I had seen Tzvete and our daughter, Nebesna, since my arrest.

We couldn't embrace, or even touch, with a security screen between us. A score or more prisoners on either side of me were receiving their families, creating a cacophony of voices. Nevertheless, it was wonderful to see my loved ones.

"Thank God you're here," I said with astonishment in my voice. "All of you, and not just Stefan." I looked at my son knowingly.

Stefan grinned broadly.

Turning to Nebesna, I asked about Toshko, her husband, who had been sentenced to the brickworks.

"He and Emanuel Tinev have been out for some time," she informed me. "They were only sentenced to fifteen days' hard labor." Nebesna explained that Toshko hadn't been able to join them in visiting me because he had committed to preach at a church outside of Sofia.

"And how's my little granddaughter?" I asked, smiling at Nebesna's daughter, Mimmi, as she sat on her mother's lap.

"Thank God for faithful men such as Toshko, who will continue to serve in spite of the threats they're facing. Please give him my love and greetings."

Remember, This Is Easter!
As we talked, I noticed my wife looking at me closely.

"You've lost so much weight," she said as tears began to well in her dark brown eyes. "Stefan told me you were fine, but—"

"He's fine!" Stefan interjected. "You should've seen him before!"

I winced inwardly, knowing Stefan's words wouldn't comfort Tzvete. "I didn't even catch a cold this winter," I told her, smiling. "And I've never been better spiritually."

"It's the guards, the barbed wire, the shaved heads, and talking to you over all this noise . . ." Her voice trailed off.

"Those things are externals," I said. "But I'm confident we're doing what's right and just in God's eyes. The Lord has given me a sense of freedom I never felt possible—even in this place."

"Yes, I know," Tzvete agreed. "But I didn't realize it would be so depressing. How can you live here?"

"There's no prison that can bind the power of Christ's Spirit," I said confidently. "Remember, this is Easter!"

Tzvete began to relax, and our conversation went on to other things. "How are you doing?" I asked.

"We're well," said Tzvete. "We miss you, but we know you're where God wants you."

Throughout my prison experience, I had thanked God for my wife's faith. Even prior to my imprisonment, Tzvete had consistently encouraged me to take strong stands. It was just like her, after months of managing the family alone, to quickly assure me of her support.

"We've brought food for you," Tzvete gestured, lifting a basket neatly covered with a kitchen towel. "The guards will inspect it and give it to you before we leave. Inside you'll find a special gift from Pastor Simeonov," she said, beaming through her tears. Before I could even inquire, Tzvete hastened to tell me, "We had Communion this morning, and Pastor Simeonov gave me a piece of the Communion bread he had dipped into the cup. He told me, 'Give this to Christo with the assurance of our love and prayers.' I wrapped it in a napkin and laid it on top of the food."

Now the tears came to my eyes. "Please take greetings to the brothers and sisters at the church," I requested. "Tell them I pray for them daily. And please express my gratitude to Reverend Simeonov for sending Communion. I'm pleased he's holding the faithful together during this difficult time."

Assuring me of the prayers offered by many people, Tzvete went on, "Here's some literature that friends at the church sent, knowing how you love to read." She passed a parcel to the guard nearby. He inspected it and placed it on top of the food basket. "People at the church tell me constantly that they want to come support you at your trial," she said enthusiastically.

"Pavel Ivanov knows the people support you," Nebesna added.

"He still hasn't gained control but clings to the hope your trial will change things. But don't worry—it won't!"

Tzvete quickly reviewed what had happened at the church. "Vasil Kozuharov was preaching one of the first Sundays after you were arrested. Of course, Pavel Ivanov came and sat in the rear. Vasil has such a sharp wit. He spoke from John 10:1 that Sunday, the passage that says, 'The man who does not enter the sheep pen by the gate, but climbs in by some other way, is a thief and a robber.' Everyone knew he was talking about Ivanov's unspiritual tactics, but Vasil never mentioned him by name."

"It was really very courageous for him to speak so boldly," Stefan observed, "with Toshko and Emanuel in a labor camp and the SS following Nick Athanasov everywhere."

"Now that Pavel Ivanov is in the pulpit," Nebesna said, "the congregation often begins singing spontaneously so he has little time to speak. When he does try to preach, everyone bows silently in prayer."

Eager to discuss the trial, Tzvete asked, "Has Ljuben Lashkov told you that your trial is scheduled for April 23, just ten days from now?"

"I haven't seen Lashkov recently. Our last visit wasn't encouraging. Someone must be intimidating him," I suggested.

"He was discouraged at one point," Tzvete said. "The second time I met with him, he looked like he was sorry he'd taken the case. He actually became angry and said, 'I'm not going to sacrifice my career for this case.' Things have been improving since then, though."

"Have you been able to arrange for a second attorney as he requested?" I asked.

"Thank God for Reverend Glouharov," Tzvete shared. "He recommended a man named Proinov, a Communist party member." Here she frowned slightly and said, "That concerns me a bit. But Lashkov highly recommends him, too, and we have no choice but to trust his judgment. Lashkov is arranging a meeting."

"We've no choice but to put our trust in God alone," I reminded my family. "The trial, most likely, will be for the sake of appearance only. Let's pray that Dimitar and I will be given an opportunity to speak openly of our faith in Christ."

The visit was over before I had time to tell of Assen and Metodi, and the answers to prayer I had seen. The thirty minutes we had together seemed like three. Thrusting the food basket and literature into my hands, the guards sent me trudging back toward my cell block.

Just as Tzvete had described, among the gifts my family had

brought was the gift of a small piece of Communion bread carefully wrapped in a white napkin.

Sitting alone on my bunk, I was grateful the other prisoners were quiet. Whether granted a visit or not, all were undoubtedly thinking of their families, as I was my own. Later, I would try to recall every word and engrave a picture of my family in the deepest recesses of my memory. But now I wanted to enjoy a few moments in prayer before receiving Communion.

Worthy of Christ's Name

The barren and dusty prison at Kremikovtzi is by far the strangest place I've received Communion. It was, however, one of the most deeply spiritual moments of all my years in prison, as I paused for a time of prayer and silence, sitting on the edge of my bunk.

As I focused on the suffering and death of Christ, I was reminded that the forgiveness and new life he gives was more than anything I could offer in return. The ridicule and suffering I was experiencing was nothing compared to what my Lord did for me on the cross. As Hebrews 12:3 reminds us, remembering Christ upon the cross helps us to "not grow weary and lose heart."

Offering thanksgiving for Christ's sacrifice, I knew I could never be worthy of what Christ did for me on the cross. My prayer was that my faithfulness for Christ would be such that I would be worthy of suffering for his name.

Pausing to recite the familiar words of consecration to myself, as I had so often done aloud at church, I meditated upon the words of Christ: "This do in remembrance of me." I remembered also those given in 1 Corinthians 11:26—"For whenever you eat this bread and drink this cup, you do proclaim the Lord's death until he comes."

Receiving the Communion elements my family had brought imparted new strength and hope. First, it provided a spiritual bond with my family. I had seen far too many examples of the way imprisonment could fracture marriages, and the stress of persecution had damaged many families in our evangelical churches. Only by the grace of God did our family remain both emotionally and spiritually intact.

Second, the Communion provided a bond with my brother Reverend Simeonov. Reverend Assen Simeonov was eighty-five years old and had served nobly as pastor at First Church years ago. A brilliant and deeply spiritual man, he had been educated in Switzerland and had mastered seven languages. Active in protecting Jewish people during

World War II,[10] he had once been thrown into prison and twice told that he was about to be shot. Once he was marched at gunpoint deep into the forest and forced to dig his own grave. Still he would not renounce his faith in Christ or agree to stop helping the Jews. At the last second his life was spared.

Reverend Simeonov had survived the years of Communist domination by becoming a lawyer and serving as a translator. This allowed him to support his family while preaching on weekends. His thoughtfulness in sharing this unique Communion with me was typical of the great man.

Thirdly, that unique Communion bound me together in spiritual fellowship with the believers in our church. I was deeply touched by the thought that they had received the same bread and wine just that morning! We were all members of one body, the body of Christ. The faith of the congregation of First Church was being tested as mine was, only in a different way. Hopefully the ancient tradition and words of commitment had reminded them, as it did me, of countless others who had received the Lord's Supper before us.

For millennia, believers have suffered for their faith so that the gospel would spread. People like Elias Riggs and William and Susan Mariam dedicated their lives to bringing the gospel to places such as Bulgaria—or died trying. Just as the faithful saints who had come before me had been strong in serving the Lord, so I knew Christ would strengthen me to face whatever the future might bring. I was humbled. As John the Baptist said, "He must become greater and greater, and I must become less and less" (John 3:30).

One of the most lasting impressions of that Easter Sunday was the total and absolute freedom I felt, even while behind bars. The sense of spiritual power that came from that brief Communion service helped me to better understand the liberty that is ours in Christ. That Easter was the first of three I would spend in captivity.

A Higher Power

The contrast of the believer's spiritual power in Christ compared to the futile power of the state was abundantly apparent to me that Easter Sunday. The prison, with its abusive guards and strutting interrogators, gave the appearance of being all-powerful. But that power was negative and evil and therefore temporary and weak. Satan's pretentious power is only a pale imitation of God's redeeming power. It is

---

[10] Rev. Simeonov preserved the lives of over 300 Jewish people during the Holocaust, converting many of them to Christianity.

coercive; he uses fear and intimidation to control people. He cannot, however, motivate or energize from within, as God's Spirit does the believer. Evil has no vision but is known only for what it is against. Outwardly it appears threatening, but inwardly it is hollow.

The true spiritual power that is ours in Christ is just the opposite. God's people may at times appear weak, but the inner working of God's Spirit far exceeds the negative forces of evil. Only God's supreme power can create and even resurrect that which Satan believes he has destroyed. Paul states it well in 1 Corinthians 1:27–2:7: "God chose the foolish things of the world to shame the wise; God chose the weak things of the world to shame the strong. . . . We . . . speak a message of wisdom . . . not the wisdom of this age or of the rulers of this age, who are coming to nothing. No, we speak of God's secret wisdom, a wisdom that has been hidden and that God destined for our glory before time began."

Preparing for Trial

By necessity I was giving much thought and preparation to my upcoming trial. This required that I be thoroughly familiar with the indictment, which in Bulgaria is called the "Act of Accusation."

There were some devious and untrue statements in the indictment. For instance, it stated I had "retired" as pastor of First Church, but I had no plans to resign or retire—which was why I had been arrested in the first place. It also stated that my brother had been dismissed as church treasurer, giving the impression that he had been caught misusing funds, which was untrue.

After hearing the stories of the other prisoners, I realized how fortunate I was not to be defending myself against completely fabricated charges. At least the charges made against me would allow me to talk in court about my faith in Christ and my desire to serve him in ministry. As the Bible says, "'My thoughts are completely different from yours,' says the LORD. 'And my ways are far beyond anything you could imagine. For just as the heavens are higher than the earth, so are my ways higher than your ways and my thoughts higher than your thoughts'" (Isaiah 55:8, NLT).

Brothers Reunited

As April 23 approached, things began to happen. Because the trial would be held in the district court, situated near Central Prison, I was transferred back there the day before the trial. Dimitar was already there, being held in the small holding cell used for prisoners on trial.

Delighted to see him again, I asked him about his health and told him of the visit with my family.

The conversation soon turned to the trial. "Lashkov may have been intimidated by the Prosecutor, and Tzvete tells me that Proinov is a Communist party member," I informed Dimitar. "We must go to court prepared to speak for ourselves."

"I agree," Dimitar responded. "Proinov introduced himself to me and made a good impression, but who knows what's going on behind the scenes?"

Requesting paper and pencils from the guard, Dimitar and I spent the next few hours making notes on the questions we felt were most important to ask Tzvetkov, who would testify for the Committee. Having done that, each of us wrote out our own statement so that we would be well prepared if given an opportunity to speak.

The night before our trial we knelt and prayed together. Night after night I had prayed alone, not knowing for sure what was happening to my family, to Dimitar and his family, or to the church. There was strength and encouragement in being together again and in praying together. I was reminded of Christ's promise, "Where two or three come together in my name, there am I with them" (Matthew 18:20).

Waiting for the Trial

Dimitar and I spent much of the night singing and praying together. Finally we were going on trial! To speak openly of our commitment to Christ in a repressive society was a privilege, and we wouldn't trade that for anything.

When we awoke on the morning of April 23, Dimitar and I again slipped to our knees and prayed for the strength and courage we would need.

Breakfast was as sparse as always in Central Prison, but we enjoyed a spiritual food our captors didn't understand. I asked the guard if we could have our civilian clothes, so we could be decently dressed for the trial, but he rudely informed us that we were required to wear our frayed and faded prison clothes for the trial.

Until the last moment, I clung to the hope that we would be allowed at least a brief meeting with our attorneys, but that too was disallowed. I would have to take the list of questions Dimitar and I proposed with me into the courtroom and look for an opportunity to present it to Lashkov and Proinov.

Time moved agonizingly slowly. Countless times I thought to

myself, *Surely the hour for our trial has arrived.* We waited anxiously. There was always the possibility the trial could be denied at the last moment. Dimitar and I bowed again to pray. We had just finished when footsteps approached, and the door to our cell squeaked open.

A Cloud of Witnesses

Stepping outside of the cell, we saw that the guard was accompanied by a court bailiff. The bailiff verified our identities and informed us, "You're being tried under Article 274. Your trial will last only a day or two. Look for me when court is adjourned. I'll escort you out of the courtroom each time there's a recess. You'll also wait in the cell for the verdict to be given." The bailiff was obviously experienced; he had probably recited a speech similar to this hundreds, if not thousands, of times.

Approaching the courtroom in handcuffs, both Dimitar and I were surprised to see a crowd of people assembled in the room and standing around the entrance. To my amazement people had come to our trial from churches all across Bulgaria! It took great courage for them to even appear as interested parties at our trial. Their faithful presence throughout the trial reminded me of Hebrews 12:1-2, "Since we are surrounded by such a great cloud of witnesses . . . let us run with perseverance the race marked out for us. Let us fix our eyes on Jesus."

Dimitar and I, clothed in our prison garb, heads shaved, were escorted down the central aisle to our seats alongside Lashkov and Proinov. Our attorneys were dressed in elegant dark suits, and their immaculate appearance contrasted sharply with our shabby prison clothes.

"We're praying, brothers," someone whispered as we passed. Every eye was upon us, assessing our condition.

Turning to nod a quick greeting to Tzvete and the children, I saw the familiar faces of friends from the church. All told, over 150 people from various evangelical churches from around the country had come to stand alongside us. Travel was not easy, and with the depressed economy it was a considerable financial sacrifice. Such a "cloud of witnesses" was irrefutable evidence of our innocence. My heart was deeply touched.

Proinov's Protest

Across the aisle from the defense table sat Mr. Gichev, the Prosecutor. Gichev was of medium build and was dressed in a black suit; his appearance was typical of those who were successful in the Communist bureaucracy. He did not look our way; his dark eyes busily perused the papers on the table before him.

There was no opportunity to speak to Lashkov and Proinov before the bailiff notified everyone to stand as the panel of three judges entered through a door behind the dais. The judges, like our attorneys, were dressed in dark suits.

No sooner were the judges seated than the chief judge motioned for the bailiff to approach the bar for a whispered consultation. When the one-way conversation ended, the bailiff announced that the trial would be closed to the public. A murmur rippled through the audience.

Proinov was on his feet instantly, inquiring as to the reason for this unusual action. The chief judge answered that our trial was of a sensitive nature and had to be conducted behind closed doors. Proinov replied, "Your honor, Article 262 in the Penal Code provides for excluding the public only when it protects national interests!"

The judge beckoned both Proinov and Lashkov to the bench for a private conversation. "This case is not of a sensitive nature," I heard Proinov exclaim.

Mr. Tzvetkov was there, of course, prepared to witness for the Committee on Internal Religious Affairs, responsible for all matters having to do with the Bulgarian Orthodox Church and other religious groups. He watched Proinov and Lashkov with a knowing smile.

Tension rose as the people sat in absolute silence. Some stood in the doorway craning their necks to hear each word. Some had come great distances to witness the trial. If they decided they didn't want to leave voluntarily it could become awkward for the judges.

Let Us Hear about Their Robberies!

The judges continued to confer.

Flustered by the delay, Tzvetkov stood and in an officious voice began speaking, "Let me inform the court that my office has received over 2,000 letters of protest from outside of Bulgaria." He was out of order, and as a witness for the Prosecutor had not been recognized to speak. The judges, however, listened curiously as if they had given permission for him to speak. "It's obvious this case has serious implications for the foreign affairs of Bulgaria!" Tzvetkov concluded.

Tzvetkov could have left the matter at that, but, since he had the floor, he couldn't resist the opportunity to throw out a challenge to the partisan audience. Turning in a stiff-necked manner to acknowledge the people's presence, he continued, "And if anyone in the courtroom wants to join our list of people attempting to block the government in this case, they'll have to deal with me and my office!"

There was a pause, the judges listening with furrowed brows as if Tzvetkov had spoken some great intellectual truth that they must ponder. Tzvetkov had obviously overextended himself, first by speaking without being recognized and then by issuing a threat that presumed his control of the Secret Service.

Heady with power and confident that his stentorian words were stirring the emotions of others as much as his own, Tzvetkov offered his clinching assessment. "After all, the essence of this case has nothing to do with religion, since we will be dealing with evidence that they are thieves."

At that, the tension in the courtroom broke as the audience laughed. Dimitar and I looked at one another and smiled. Someone shouted, "If this is a trial of thieves, then we should be able to remain in the courtroom to hear about all of their robberies!" Laughter resonated throughout the courtroom at an even higher level as Tzvetkov sat down, red-faced and flustered.

Tzvetkov's charge of theft was based upon an unfounded allegation that we had illegally used foreign currency. It was a blanket accusation brought against religious groups thought to have foreign connections, but it was totally unfounded. Churches had received money from abroad prior to the Communist rule, but the charge was easily refuted since our foreign ties had been severed by the party years ago.

It took several minutes for the chief judge to restore order and render a decision. While the judge's language was more tactful than Tzvetkov's, the panel of judges asked that the courtroom be cleared. The people from the churches were obviously disappointed but understood that these things happen in a totalitarian state. They left peacefully, casting sympathetic glances in our direction. The trial would now begin.

The Trial

As the crowd was ushered out of the courtroom, Proinov leaned over to Dimitar and myself. "We did the best we could," he offered.

Lashkov leaned into the huddle. "Since you're being tried under the little-known Act 274, we'll make it clear that this law applies specifically to religious activities. The theft charge is easily dismissed."

I whispered back, "As you know, Dimitar and I have prepared

statements in our own defense. It's important that we be allowed to speak."

"Yes, we know," Lashkov replied. "But not until the end of the trial."

I gave the list of questions Dimitar and I had prepared to Lashkov. "Please consider using these if you would like." He took the questions and placed them where both he and Proinov could read them.

Lashkov whispered again, "We've carefully read over all of the materials confiscated from your homes. They're required by law to share them with us.[11] You should also know that we've spoken with some of the believers in your churches. They've made helpful suggestions as to how we can approach the case.[12] Rest assured; we'll do the best we can."

Opening Statements

Bulgarian custom allows the prosecution to go first, with the defense having the last word. Gichev, the Prosecutor, called Tzvetkov to the witness stand to give the opening statement and describe the charges being brought against us. Mr. Tzvetkov began by vociferously claiming that my brother and I had actively obstructed him and the Committee. "I work with the Committee on Internal Religious Affairs," he said, "and the disrespect these men have shown for the Committee's authority is most serious. These men obstructed the Committee when we appointed the person best qualified to serve as pastor and chief operating officer of First Evangelical Church of Sofia."[13]

That person, of course, was Pavel Ivanov.

Tzvetkov labored on in his officious manner, "These men obstructed the work of Pavel Ivanov and made it difficult for him to exercise his rightful claim to the pulpit of the church. It should also be noted that these charges of subversion and obstruction have been

[11] At the time of our arrest, the police had searched every inch of our homes, confiscating box after box of files, books, literature, and records. While our attorneys were given copies of documents to be introduced as evidence, these confiscated materials were never returned. Much of it was personal correspondence and items of a sentimental nature, such as my ordination certificate and the letter of call issued by First Church.

[12] We later learned that a dear Christian brother, Mr. Vekso Ignatov, who was trained as a lawyer, had taken the risk of approaching Lashkov. Vekso Ignatov gave generously of his time in researching our case and in making valuable suggestions as to how it could best be presented. Ignatov himself had suffered discrimination as a believer in Christ, having been demoted and placed in a position where he would not have access to the general public in his law practice.

[13] The transcriptions of the trial, together with notes that Dimitar and I took during the trial, give a detailed record of everything that transpired during the entire litigation. Neither time nor space permits reviewing each and every aspect of the proceedings, but the highlights are presented more-or-less word for word to give the reader an understanding of the events.

made in writing with copies going to the President of the Committee and to the Minister of Internal Affairs for Bulgaria."

As Tzvetkov continued, he took care to emphasize that from his point of view, the government had not taken the initiative in forcibly entering the church. "Our agents were only responding to the dutiful request of the offended Pavel Ivanov after he had attempted to carry out the duties he was called by the Committee to do."

Concluding his opening statement with a rhetorical flourish, pointing a chubby finger of blame directly at my brother and me, Tzvetkov said menacingly, "It's the Kulichev brothers who are guilty of causing these problems. They are the ones who object to Pavel Ivanov. They are the ones who changed the locks and reinforced the doors of the church. They are the ones who caused the damage and thereby obstructed justice. They continue, even in prison, to make matters worse by making provocative statements that disturb the peace of the people. They are the ones who must stand trial for these matters and answer for all they have done."

There seemed to be little concern on Tzvetkov's part that his accusations contradicted the written indictment. His written statement complained that he and the Committee had not been informed as to who changed the locks. This assumed that the Committee had the right to take possession of any church they wished. Now he was charging us with changing the locks, which was not true. They had been changed by the church board.

That Church Is Full of Troublemakers

It was now time for the defense to make an opening statement. Then our attorneys would direct questions to the prosecution. Lashkov began as he had promised, stressing that our trial had to do with our religious convictions. He went on to explain that First Church had always been a part of the free church tradition, which allowed each congregation to choose its own minister. Lashkov emphasized, "We are here today to raise the question as to whether or not an arm of the government has the right to interfere in the life of a congregation by attempting to take control of the church when the people themselves are supportive of the minister they have chosen."

With that, Lashkov began the cross examination.

"Mr. Tzvetkov," he asked, "can you inform us as to what Article 274 says specifically about the internal organization of a church?" The point Lashkov was driving at was that no provisions in the article allowed government officials to meddle in the internal affairs of churches.

Tzvetkov responded, "You should understand that we don't interfere in the internal affairs of cults such as this."

"Perhaps, then, you can tell us," Lashkov continued, "what information you have that would make anyone think these men are disloyal citizens or misbehaving in some way?"

Tzvetkov replied eagerly, "First of all, they visit churches. Second, they preach without Committee approval. All of this adds up to the fact that they disobey our laws!"

Lashkov stayed on course. "That's an allegation, but I'm asking for evidence. We're talking now about whether these men exercised authority not given to them by the church. You have given no evidence of that. The church appointed them to serve as leaders, and they've done what was asked of them! Is that not true?"

"That church is full of troublemakers," Tzvetkov puffed.

"Let's see where the trouble started," Lashkov continued, "by looking at the Committee's involvement in internal church matters. Are you aware of precisely how a pastor is elected in a church?"

"There has to be a mutual agreement between the church and the Committee," Tzvetkov said, shrugging his shoulders.

"And specifically where is this made clear in the law?" Lashkov asked.

"It is found in Articles 9 and 16, the laws on religious matters," Tzvetkov said confidently.

Lashkov looked at the judges as he spoke. "But these articles apply only to churches that have denominational links outside of Bulgaria. It's only when churches have links outside of our country that they must come to your Committee for approval in choosing a minister. The First Evangelical Church of Sofia does not have foreign ties."

Somewhat flustered, Tzvetkov answered hastily, "But they still must have our approval if we require it."

Do You Have Documentation to Verify That?

Facing Tzvetkov again, Lashkov persisted, "Are you aware that Christo Kulichev has been duly registered as a pastor?"

"I have never seen any proof of his registration," Tzvetkov insisted.

"Are you aware that Christo Kulichev has served honorably as the pastor of the church in Krichim and that he has been properly registered with the Committee since that time?"

"It may be true that he preached for three or four years in Krichim, but that doesn't prove he's a pastor," Tzvetkov insisted.

"That does not mean that he's been registered with the Committee. How could that be?"

"Let me assure you, Mr. Tzvetkov, that he does have a document showing that he is registered. Here, you may look at it." Lashkov picked up the document and offered it to Tzvetkov.

Tzvetkov refused to even look at the document. "I know nothing about any registration he might have with the city council in Krichim." He was trying to imply that the document Lashkov was entering as evidence was a certificate from some local government and not from the Committee on Internal Religious Affairs.

Lashkov placed the document before the judges and continued undeterred. "Mr. Tzvetkov, could you please tell the court what, if anything, happened to create a vacancy at First Church? When Pavel Ivanov was appointed by you, had you received any documentation showing positively that Christo Kulichev had been dismissed?"

Tzvetkov responded tersely, "It was my understanding that his registration had been taken from him."

"But do you have the documentation to verify that?" Lashkov inquired.

Tzvetkov drew himself up haughtily, "You may not have such a document, but I do!"

With a curious tone in his voice, Lashkov inquired, "And when did you receive this document that you claim to have? Did you duly notify both of the Kulichev brothers that their registrations had been revoked? Did you do all of this before assigning Pavel Ivanov?"

Tzvetkov could see where Lashkov was heading. "Yes, I told them in prison! I told them they weren't registered to preach."

"Oh, you did this after they had been arrested and put in prison! Assuming you did notify them as you claim, would that not mean they were legally registered as pastors until they were properly notified of their change in status? Your notice was given after they had been imprisoned? They were then legally registered at the time of their arrest!"

"No, I wouldn't say that," Tzvetkov said, squirming.

Smiling ever so slightly, Lashkov continued. "So, help me understand this, Mr. Tzvetkov. When you finally spoke to them, after they were in prison, what was it you told them you were taking from them?"

"Their registration to preach!" Tzvetkov snorted.

"So they had every reason to assume they were properly registered to preach until that very moment?"

"No, they did not!" Tzvetkov was clearly irritated and beginning to perspire.

Lashkov leaned forward. "Please stop, Mr. Tzvetkov, and think carefully about your testimony. You've clearly contradicted yourself! No matter how much you twist the words, it's clear that my clients were registered to preach at the time you arrested them for preaching without being registered. There's been no violation of the law here!" Having said that, Lashkov turned and looked at the judges, allowing a few moments of poignant silence in which his point could be driven home.

When Lashkov had taken his seat, the judges conferred before announcing there would be a recess. As the gavel tapped out the order, two bailiffs advanced across the room. Lashkov had only a moment to inform us, "Proinov will take over the cross-examination this afternoon."

Solidarity

As the bailiff opened the door of the courtroom, I was startled to see the crowd awaiting us in the corridor! I had assumed that they returned to their homes. It had been a lengthy session, but they had waited over two hours to again signal their support. The judge had said nothing about clearing the corridor, and they had remained there to pray and wait in hope of a favorable outcome.

Seeing Dimitar and me, the believers immediately stood and faced us. No one spoke a word, and there was no attempt to communicate with us. They simply stood to acknowledge our presence, silently squeezing together to make a pathway for us as we passed.

The bailiff appeared even more surprised than we were as he ushered us through the crowd. Walking down the hallway, the bailiff turned to ask, "Why are these people standing here like this?"

"It's because we're passing by," I told him.

Still confused, he said, "So? I've escorted a thousand people down this corridor, but I've never seen anything like this! What's going on?"

"It's because we serve their churches," I briefly explained. "I'm their pastor, and they're here to support us. It's their way of showing their solidarity with us as Christian brothers and sisters."

Back in our cell, eating our sparse prison meal, Dimitar and I discussed the events of the morning. We were encouraged by the presence of so many brothers and sisters in Christ, and we compared notes as to whom we had seen. We reviewed Tzvetkov's opening statement and laughed at his charge that we were thieves. "Lashkov pressed home the point that our registration to preach was valid at the time of our arrest," I said. "Tzvete and I once thought someone had intimidated him. Apparently it wasn't Tzvetkov."

When we were summoned back to the courtroom, again the believers stood as we passed. We had eaten the poor prison food, but they had apparently gone without food altogether.

Proinov Presses Home the Point

As the trial reconvened in the afternoon, Proinov took the lead. Hired late in the process, Proinov had had only four days to prepare for the trial. This was a concern since we were being tried under a little-known article of law, and the sequence of events surrounding our arrest was confusing. Dimitar had met only once, very briefly, with Proinov. We were nervous about having him represent us. As it turned out, our concerns were unfounded.

I would like to point out here that throughout the trial and preceding events, both of our attorneys did everything they could to represent us fairly and to prove our innocence in each and every allegation. It was an uphill battle they were fighting because, as I have said, in the Communist system the accused was considered guilty until proven innocent. This point was made very clear to me both in my interrogations prior to the trial and in the trial itself. Lashkov and Proinov, however, fought courageously, and both Dimitar and I were grateful to have such skilled advocates with us in the courtroom.

Proinov's tall, angular frame made him an impressive figure. His dark hair was combed neatly into place, and his hair together with his neatly pressed suit gave the impression of a man with immaculate habits. His distinctive dress and manners were not at all typical of party members, most of whom dressed blandly to blend in with the crowd.

As the trial resumed, Tzvetkov moved again to the witness stand. Tzvetkov's brown suit was somewhat rumpled, contrasting noticeably with Proinov's striking appearance.

"Mr. Tzvetkov," Proinov began gently, "do you know with certainty who barricaded the pastor's apartment with the beams mentioned in your report?"

Tzvetkov immediately pointed at us. "I assume they did!"

"But we're not interested in assumptions in a court of law, Mr. Tzvetkov." Proinov waited a few seconds, then turned and addressed Tzvetkov again. "Did you actually see the defendants putting those beams into place?"

"Well, no, I didn't," Tzvetkov began. Then turning rather surly, he suggested, "I didn't follow them around watching their every step!"

Ignoring Tzvetkov's offensive tone, Proinov spoke as evenly as before. "And to whom would you say the pastor's apartment belongs?"

"To the church, I suppose," said Tzvetkov

Proinov was moving casually back and forth in front of our table. Without notes, it was obvious he was well prepared. "Do you think the church could opt to leave the apartment empty if they desired?" he asked.

"What do you mean 'empty'?" Tzvetkov asked incredulously. Even the chief judge had to suppress a smile at such a foolish reply to such a simple question.

"Could it be," Proinov explained, "that perhaps the pastor could decide not to live in the apartment, or the church could decide that they wanted their pastor to live somewhere else?" Proinov's dark eyes flashed with intelligence. I was beginning to feel confident in him.

Tzvetkov scoffed, "It would be foolish for them not to use it! Leave an apartment empty in the center of the city?"

Proinov stopped and looked directly at the witness. "Please remember, Mr. Tzvetkov, I'm asking you a question. My question, very clearly, is this: Is the church free to use their apartment as they please?"

There was a long embarrassing silence as Tzvetkov looked off into space and didn't answer. He didn't like the point Proinov was pressing home. Scratching his paunch, Tzvetkov seemed to suppress a belch, or maybe it was a laugh. It came out, barely audible, as a subdued "hrumph." It might have conveyed contempt for the question, but the actual words never came out.

Proinov patiently pursued his question. "For example, Mr. Tzvetkov, if the church decided they wanted to use the apartment as a warehouse, are they free under this law to do that if they want?"

Finally, Tzvetkov spoke. "Well—yes. I suppose they could, but—"

"Thank you very much, Comrade," Proinov concluded.

As Proinov turned, a trace of a smile flickered in his features. This would have been a crucial turning point in any fair trial, since Tzvetkov had finally admitted that the Church was free to administer its own internal affairs.

One thing was clear, and that was Proinov's fearless confidence. It was evident he possessed a conviction that the charges against us were fabricated. Whatever his position in the party was, it clearly didn't deter him from challenging Tzvetkov and the Committee.

Lashkov also seemed to have gained confidence in the presence of a strong personality such as Proinov's. There was no sign of Lashkov's previous discomfort in taking our case.

Pavel Ivanov to the Stand

When the cross-examination of Tzvetkov concluded, Gichev was ready to call other witnesses. Standing stiffly and stroking his straight black hair to make sure his appearance was perfect, he spoke in a low voice, asking permission to call the first witness for the prosecution. Gichev's nondescript personality, with even the modulation of his voice carefully controlled, made him appear to be the ultimate party loyalist. His primary witness, of course, was Pavel Ivanov.

Ivanov was a short, stout man with dark, chestnut-colored eyes. In trying to dress for this somber occasion, he had very likely borrowed his dark suit. It was a trifle long in the sleeves and tight around his stout waistline.

Witnesses were allowed by Bulgarian law to make an opening statement if they wished. Pavel turned to the judges and somewhat nervously asked to speak.

"Proceed," the chief judge said, nodding.

Pavel Ivanov was not a well-educated man, but he was nevertheless a gifted speaker. He was at his best when speaking extemporaneously and seemed to feed on the emotion of the moment, gaining confidence as he went along. With his personal interests heavily invested in the outcome of the trial, however, he had apparently decided to come prepared with a written statement. Fumbling for a moment or two, he finally got it out of his breast pocket.

Clearing his throat and wiping his upper lip, Ivanov began. "Thank you for allowing me to speak, Comrades," he began deferentially, glancing quickly at the judges. "I would like to make it clear at this time that I'm not elected by the First Evangelical Church of Sofia but by the Committee on Internal Religious Affairs. That committee is chaired by Mr. Tzvetkov and is charged with full responsibility for overseeing all of the churches in our country. When I spoke with Mr. Tzvetkov, he told me to take over the pulpit of First Church. I then wrote to the Committee, requesting my position be confirmed. That was done."

With nervous starts and stops, mispronouncing words here and there, Pavel Ivanov droned on. None of his natural flare for oratory came through. He was clearly nervous and insecure.

Ivanov was apparently trying to present himself as having authority derived from the Committee. He made no mention of the church and its interests, nothing of feeling called by God, just the Committee this and the Committee that. It seemed to me that he came across not as a dynamic leader but as a groveling pawn of the Committee. But perhaps that would ingratiate him to the court. We would see.

After concluding his lengthy statement, Ivanov mopped the perspiration from his lip again. He carefully folded the statement and put it back into his breast pocket. Finally, unable to find anything else to do with his hands, Ivanov glanced nervously at the attorneys sitting at our table, knowing full well they were allowed to question him.

Gichev rose to indicate his approval of the statement. His bland and emotionless style was carefully crafted to evoke neither affection nor hatred. "I've no questions for this witness," he said officiously, resuming his seat at the Prosecutor's table without even a glance in our direction.

Lashkov took his turn first. "Mr. Ivanov," he began. "We've heard about the exchange of information between you and the Committee. But have you actually applied to the church itself, asking them to consider you as their pastor?"

"No!" Ivanov answered tersely.

"Were you ever invited by the church leadership to submit an application for the position?" Lashkov continued.

Lashkov's light brown eyes were not at all threatening, but still Pavel Ivanov could not look at him directly. Again the answer was no.

"When you went to the church, planning to become its pastor, did you know why the previous leaders were no longer there?"

Ivanov answered eagerly this time. "They didn't coordinate their activities with the Committee. For example, both Christo and Dimitar Kulichev had been forbidden to preach and yet the leadership of the church had allowed them to continue preaching!"

Lashkov pressed on. "But on what basis did you attempt to take over the pulpit when you knew that you must first be elected by the congregation?"

"On the basis of my consultation with Mr. Tzvetkov."

At this point Lashkov became more pointed. "But you know that Mr. Tzvetkov is not the law itself. . . ."

The chief judge reached for his gavel but did not use it. Speaking to Lashkov, he said, "You're not to make a summary statement at this time, Comrade. Please pose your questions to the witness, being more specific in the answer you are seeking. Please stay away from your own generalized impressions."

Responding respectfully, Lashkov paused to consult his notes, then continued. "Mr. Ivanov, how many members are on the church committee for selecting a pastor?"

"I suppose ten or eleven."

"And how many people are on the church board, which oversees the ministry at the Church?" Lashkov asked.

"I believe there are ten people," Ivanov replied.

"So, when you combine those two groups of church leaders who oversee the process for selecting a pastor, you eliminated at least twenty people in order to fulfill your personal ambition of putting yourself in that pulpit?" Lashkov was careful to frame his point as a question.

Ivanov flinched before responding defensively, "Yes, but I did it because those people—" he nodded toward Dimitar and me, "— those people would not agree with the Committee. Christo and Dimitar Kulichev have no right to be in that pulpit. They are not even registered as pastors. I had reason to believe they didn't follow the church constitution, and besides, that constitution is only valid within the church and its internal organization. Everything else comes under the control of the Committee. I was dealing with the Committee," Ivanov asserted with an air of superiority.

Lashkov had made his point, and he moved on to point out that Pavel Ivanov had attempted to take over First Church long before our arrest in January. "Mr. Ivanov, when did you receive the letter from the Committee asking you to attempt to take over the pulpit of First Church?"

Ivanov replied, "I received the document at the beginning of January. It was in January when I went to take over the pulpit of the church. I had the document in hand when I went to the church."

"But that wasn't the first time you made such an attempt, was it, Mr. Ivanov?" Lashkov clearly avoided using the title of Reverend for Pavel Ivanov.

Pavel Ivanov shifted in his chair and cleared his throat, composing his answer carefully. "The first time I went was on September 30 at ten o'clock in the morning, when there was a worship service. But when I went into the church there were people already in the pulpit."

"Did you have the letter with you then?" Lashkov inquired.

Pavel Ivanov flushed. "No," he stammered.

"What is the date on the letter, Mr. Ivanov?" Lashkov asked, extending the letter to the witness. "Would you please tell the court?"

"The letter is dated October 6," Ivanov offered weakly.

Lashkov repeated the information Ivanov was giving. "You went to claim the pulpit on September 30, but the document from the Committee is dated October 6, and you did not receive the document until the beginning of January? By what authority then, Mr. Ivanov, did you take such an action on September 30, when you had no official documents authorizing you to do such a thing?"

"The Committee, appointed by the Ministry of Internal Affairs, had sent me," Ivanov said defensively. "Mr. Tzvetkov told me, 'Go to the church in Sofia and take over the pulpit.'"

Lashkov deftly concluded, "But you had no documentation to show that your invasive actions were legally authorized, did you? Your actions were prompted by nothing more than just a private conversation between two citizens, is that not true?"

Pavel Ivanov was silent. "Well, yes, but . . . uh . . ."

Letting Ivanov's confusion speak for itself, Lashkov said with finality, "I have no further questions."

People, Not Pews!

Proinov had been observing Pavel Ivanov closely. He now stood and moved around the defense table to face Ivanov, who was seated in the witness stand. Proinov picked up where Lashkov left off. "Were these men you're accusing in the pulpit of First Church on that day in September when you attempted to occupy the pulpit?"

"No, they were in the pews," Ivanov responded.

Proinov turned sharply, "You mean they were sitting among the believers?"

Ivanov shrugged, "That's what I said; they were in the pews."

Proinov's voice rose with an emphasis I hadn't heard before. "Let me remind you, Mr. Ivanov, we're not talking about things; we're talking about the lives of people! These men were sitting among the believers, not just 'in the pews'!"

Dimitar and I looked at one another, hardly believing we were listening to a lawyer who held a position in the party! Perhaps he was only trying to provoke Pavel Ivanov, but Proinov spoke with such conviction that he seemed almost to be identifying himself with the believers. His words expressed the outrage our congregation felt towards Pavel Ivanov and his attempts to take over the church.

Choosing his words more carefully, Pavel Ivanov tried to recover. "Well, yes, anyway, I told the people that I had been appointed by the Committee. I asked the people in the pulpit to step down, but they didn't. And so I went back to Assenovgrad, but a few days later Tzvetkov summoned me to Sofia again. I knew it was only because of the Kulichevs' objections that I wasn't being allowed to go into the pulpit!"

Proinov asked for details. "Exactly how did the Kulichevs object?"

"It wasn't outward, such as using force; it was by the influence they were exerting from the pulpit," Ivanov offered rather limply.

Proinov jumped at the opportunity. "It was just a feeling you had about them, wasn't it? You have no evidence that the Kulichevs were behind the objections raised by the congregation, do you?"

Ivanov looked rather helplessly toward Gichev. Finding no help from the passionless Prosecutor, he flicked a piece of lint off the sleeve of his suit and cleared his throat nervously. Proinov had his answer in the form of a prolonged and embarrassed silence. He continued with another question.

"Could you tell the court how you were elected as pastor for the church in Assenovgrad?

Ivanov seemed glad to move on. "I was elected in 1979, then I was inducted as pastor and approved by the government Committee."

Proinov seemed curious about the process. "Which of those three things happened first?"

Innocently, Pavel Ivanov offered the information, "The election by the church was first."

"So everything was done properly in that case?" Proinov summarized. Again he had made his point that the wishes of the congregation at First Church were completely overlooked.

"Yes, of course," Ivanov replied, as if the congregational process used at Assenovgrad was totally irrelevant to the situation at First Church.

"According to the records we've been given," Proinov said, giving his notes a rare glance, "you continued to draw your salary for being pastor in Assenovgrad through the end of December. Why did you have ambitions for taking over the pulpit of the church in Sofia in September and October if you were still committed to the church in Assenovgrad?"

Shrugging helplessly, Ivanov tried to explain. "Mr. Tzvetkov sent me to take over the pulpit in Sofia. He had already coordinated my appointment with the Minister of the Interior."

"But you have no documentation of that either, do you?" Proinov persisted. "Once again, these were only conversations—and improper ones at that, is that not true? You failed to ask the congregation to consider your request, but did you not also act prematurely without proper written authorization from the Committee?"

Ivanov stammered, "But I . . . uh, when . . . I just assumed . . ." Once again he looked helplessly to Gichev, who only continued working his way studiously through the papers on the table before him.

Proinov pounced. "Mr. Ivanov, we're not here to talk about assumptions but documented facts! Speaking of documentation, did it ever occur to you to ask in your numerous contacts with the Committee about Christo and Dimitar Kulichev's call to the church? Did you ask to make sure their call was proper?"

"No, I didn't. I was confident they would tell me if that was relevant to the case," Pavel Ivanov replied.

"For the record, Mr. Ivanov," Proinov added, "if you had investigated, you would have found that there was never any concern expressed by the Committee about the process by which the call was made, nor was there any objection to the Kulichevs' being installed as pastors of the church. That's all, Mr. Ivanov."

A Communist Lawyer with a Sense of Humor

With Proinov's dramatic questioning of Pavel Ivanov over, the afternoon session of the trial was concluded. When the gavel announced the conclusion to the day's activities, Lashkov requested that the bailiffs wait for a few minutes while we discussed the testimony that was to be given the next day.

"We must talk briefly about our plans for tomorrow," Lashkov began. "Let me emphasize that it's always difficult to find witnesses willing to take the stand in cases such as this. As I told you earlier, certain pressures are brought to bear, and it can be risky to speak out publicly. In your case, it seems, we're fortunate. Your wife called me on the night of April 22 to report that all three witnesses were unavailable, but that has changed. Let's see, their names are . . ."

As Lashkov shuffled through his papers, I couldn't help wondering what had happened. Had my wife had problems getting witnesses? Would our Christian friends abandon us at the last moment?

After half a minute or so, Lashkov found his record of the witnesses and began again. "We have a Pastor Bozovayski. It appears that he has been ill, but our latest report indicates he will be with us tomorrow. He's a credible witness. Then there's your friend Jordan Milanov. I believe he serves on the church council, does he not?"

I nodded.

"At first he reported that he would be out of the city," Lashkov continued, "and your wife was concerned. But he made a special effort to return and will testify."

Jordan was a wonderful friend, and I knew I could rely upon him for support. The process of arranging for these witnesses must have been pure torture for my poor wife, Tzvete. It wasn't easy to ask friends to put their lives and reputations on the line, and there was always a concern that they might suddenly back out at the last minute. I knew Tzvete must have spent hours on her knees praying for God to work all of this out.

Consulting his list one more time, Lashkov went on, "And we have a Vasil Kozuharov, who I believe is also a church leader. Is that correct?"

I nodded. "Yes. He is the chair of our church council."

Lashkov's uncertainty about the witnesses surfaced again, and he shrugged. "If something doesn't interfere between now and tomorrow, it appears we'll have three witnesses."

"These are good people," I assured Lashkov and Proinov. "I know their commitment, and you can plan on their being here."

"You must understand," Lashkov continued, "we have had no opportunity to meet with these witnesses to prepare them. We must trust them to speak simply and straight to the point."

"They will do well," I repeated.

Lashkov looked at Proinov and smiled. "We will continue to do our best. I feel we made some important points evident today. Mr. Proinov has done unusually well in light of the fact that he's had only four days to prepare. I know for a fact that he worked on your case over the weekend. We're fortunate to have him on the team."

Proinov acknowledged the kind words with a nod, saying, "There was a lot to read. I wasn't familiar with the church regulations, the statutes, or the policies of the Committee." Nodding at Gichev, who was walking out of the courtroom, Proinov concluded with a smile, "Fortunately for us, the opposition doesn't seem to be familiar with them either!"

A Communist lawyer with a sense of humor! That was, indeed, an unusual combination.

Both Dimitar and I smiled and expressed our appreciation for the work both men had done. As they stood to leave, the bailiff came to handcuff us and escort us back to the holding cell.

The courtroom had emptied, but not the hallways. Our dear Christian friends had remained there all day and had refused to leave until we came out. These dear Christian friends, many of whom had left jobs and family to be with us, stood again in support as we passed by. They realized we were engaged in a spiritual battle and wanted to be there to support God's ministry.

Each time we passed through the crowd, I caught the eyes of various people I knew from visits to the evangelical churches. Some were young people who had gone with us to the clandestine camps in the mountains. There were couples I had married, and others who had brought children for baptism. They didn't speak, but the looks in their eyes spoke volumes. It was such a source of strength to see them and know they were willing to stand firm in their faith at a time such as this.

Amen, Brother, Amen

That night in our cell, Dimitar and I sang and prayed, praising God for the fact that we were allowed a trial. Our attorneys were doing a good job. I reminded Dimitar of the famous case of Trajcho Kostov, sentenced to death by the government, only to be exonerated later. "Reverend Simeonov, who is trained in law, attended the trial and said Kostov's lawyer was more of an adversary than an advocate."

"Tomorrow, hopefully, it will be our turn to speak," Dimitar said. "Perhaps we should review what we're going to say. If we just preach, we may be called to order and not allowed to say anything."

When we had reviewed our statements, we prayed, and our prayers led to singing. Walking the length and breadth of the small holding cell, we sang our favorite hymns. The cell had no windows, and the sound of our voices resonated off the walls, making it seem that an entire choir was singing. As it did so often in prison, the music entered a portal of my soul and lifted my spirits like nothing else.

Between hymns we talked about our coming opportunity to witness in court for Christ. "I have no illusions regarding the outcome," I told Dimitar. "Tzvetkov has most likely already made arrangements for a guilty verdict. I'm fully prepared to serve a sentence, but it will be worth it if only we're allowed to testify. We must make sure everyone knows that it is for our faith in Christ that we are being tried."

There was thoughtful silence for a time as we both contemplated the uncertainty of our future.

As we were settling in for the night, I said, "We must be bold, my brother. We're being given an opportunity to testify for our Lord, an opportunity to demonstrate that God's truth is more valuable to us than freedom."

We each lay in our bunks, and it was quiet for a time. Then I heard Dimitar say softly, "Amen, brother, amen."

With that we drifted into sleep. We had done all we could to prepare, and now we needed rest. I slept that night like a child waiting eagerly for the first day of school—eager to share what I had learned from my Master, eager to do my best for Christ's sake.

The Second Day

The next day, the corridor was again crowded with believers. Most had on the same clothes they had worn the day before. Very likely those who had come a long distance had slept on a sofa or the floor of a friend's apartment.

Tzvete, Nebesna, and Stefan were there as usual. Certainly they had invited some to spend the night in their homes. These believers understood this was not just a trial but an opportunity for us to give witness to our faith. It was an opportunity to let the world of militant atheism know that God had his witnesses everywhere—even in an atheistic state.

Dimitar and I walked through the crowd and into the courtroom with as much dignity as the handcuffs and bulky prison garb would allow. Lashkov and Proinov awaited us, conferring as we approached.

Lashkov spoke first. "We've got a big day ahead of us. We may be able to interview all of the witnesses in one day. If so, we'll ask that each of you be allowed to give a final statement this afternoon. Are you prepared?"

Dimitar and I nodded our agreement. Lashkov pulled our chairs away from the table while the bailiff removed the handcuffs.

Proinov said, "When we give our final appeal to the judges, I will be speaking for you, Dimitar, and Mr. Lashkov will be making the appeal for you, Christo. Let me assure you that we'll do our best. However, we can never predict how these things will go. At any rate, I doubt that the judges will be giving a verdict today."

The bailiff asked us to stand as the three judges in their dark suits entered and took their respective seats in the high-backed chairs situated behind the large desk. No sooner were they seated than the gavel cracked, announcing the beginning of the day's proceedings.

The first witnesses of the day were two policemen from the

Fourth Precinct. That was the precinct near First Church. Their names were Georgi Markov, a young man in his middle thirties, and Stanoj Gelev, who appeared to be approaching fifty.

Markov took the stand first, and Gichev began leading him through the events of January 3. That was the date when Pavel Ivanov had made an appeal to Tzvetkov, who in turn had called the police and asked them to break into both the church and the pastor's apartment next door. After establishing the date and location, Gichev asked, "When you attempted to enter the church doors, what did you find?"

Markov responded, predictably, "Someone had nailed the doors shut and had added a padlock in addition to the one for which the Committee possesses a key."

Gichev was trying to build a case of obstruction against us. The truth of the matter was that the church board had installed the second padlock because the police had already made a forced entry on December 29, but Gichev was not mentioning that at all. I whispered a reminder of this to Lashkov.

Gelev, the second policeman, reiterated what Markov had testified about the forced entry on January 3. Among other matters discussed, the Prosecutor inquired of Gelev, "Was this entry into First Church approved by the Prosecutor's office?

The young policeman dutifully answered, "Yes, we were told at the precinct station that permission had been granted. We would never have acted otherwise."

When Markov and Gelev had testified for quite some time, Lashkov requested the right to cross-examine. When permission was granted, Lashkov asked, "Can you prove that the Prosecutor's office ordered this forced entry by showing us the written order?"

Both Markov and Gelev were forced to admit there had been no written order. Our point had been made, that all of this had been handled hastily and by telephone, bypassing all of the formalities and legal requirements.

Lashkov inquired next, "Were either of you present on December 29 when the church was broken into by the police?" Neither had been. Nevertheless, Lashkov made a point of following up with the question, "Were you aware that the members of the church— not the defendants in this case, but the members of the church—barricaded the doors to prevent another such forced entry without written orders?"

The two policemen only shrugged, but Lashkov had clearly made the point he wanted to make.

Witnesses for the Defense

When we left the courtroom for the noon recess, we again saw the faithful supporters who still refused to leave the corridor. When we returned, it was time for our attorneys to begin questioning the witnesses called for our defense.

When the door through which witnesses entered the courtroom opened, I shall never forget the tall, distinguished figure of Pastor Kostadin Bozovayski standing there. He stood erect and moved with a grace uncommon for his seventy-three years. He had survived the Pastors' Trial of 1949 when he was young, and for decades he had walked the tightrope that spanned the gulf between church and state. I was confident he would not disappoint us.

Proinov stepped forward to question the esteemed pastor. After establishing the gray-haired pastor's long tenure at First Church, Proinov asked, "Pastor Bozovayski, were you ever aware of any plans that Pavel Ivanov was making to become a candidate for the pastorate at First Evangelical Church?"

Bozovayski responded emphatically, "Pavel Ivanov was never elected to be my assistant. To my knowledge, he was never a candidate for any position at our church. If he had declared his candidacy, either verbally or in writing, I think I would have known about it."

With a note of curiosity in his voice, Proinov went on, asking Pastor Bozovayski, "Can you recall any previous situations such as this in the church, where there has been confusion about who is called to be the pastor?"

"No. This is the first time that Mr. Tzvetkov has ever sent a man to our church with instructions to be our pastor."

"Would you say, then, that this is totally unprecedented in the history of the church?"

"Yes, I would say it is."

Lashkov stepped forward with his questions. "Pastor Bozovayski, do you know if the church was ever officially notified in writing that the registration of the Kulichev brothers had been declared invalid?"

"No. Neither the church nor the Evangelical Union was ever notified. Mr. Tzvetkov did tell me when he came to question me about this case. I must also say that I have never heard anyone declare that Dimitar Kulichev was being released from his post as treasurer. There was an audit of the books, and everything was found to be in order."

Dimitar permitted a slight smile of satisfaction. The accusations against him were written to make it appear as though he had been charged with malfeasance, when in fact the books had only been turned over for a routine audit.

Gichev waved aside his opportunity for the prosecution to cross-examine Pastor Bozovayski, as if his testimony was of no merit.

Vasil Kozuharov, president of the church board, testified next. A surge of gratitude swept over me as I saw my dear brother in the Lord make his way into the courtroom. He and the other witnesses knew as well as we did that the chances of our being acquitted were slim indeed. But he shared our commitment to speak out and wanted to be with us.

Short of stature and slender, with fair hair, Vasil had always amazed me. He was quiet by nature and often gave a first impression of being naive and innocent. This served him well for the many years he carried Bibles and religious literature from town to town. When questioned, his modest nature led the authorities to believe he was harmless.

Those of us in church leadership had discovered that the outward impression Vasil gave was far from the truth. In reality he was very bright and thoughtful and possessed nerves of steel. He would never comply with Pavel Ivanov, nor would he be intimidated by the Committee. These qualities made him an excellent witness. His quiet humility demonstrated that our church leaders were not acting out of personal ambition, and his ability to speak forthrightly made clear his intelligence and commitment.

Lashkov asked Vasil Kozuharov to comment upon our character.

Vasil responded, "I cannot say anything bad about the Kulichev brothers, and I've known them extremely well over the years."

A few minutes later, Vasil was asked about the process for calling a minister.

"It has always been the practice of our church to elect the pastor according to the directions given in our church constitution. The church elects the pastor. Both of these brothers you're accusing are ordained pastors, and we recognize their right to preach from the pulpit."

Lashkov asked Vasil to comment upon any notice from the Committee that our right to preach had been withdrawn.

Vasil spoke forcefully. "There's never been any document sent to our church that would prohibit them from preaching. Our board would know. No documents were ever issued prohibiting the Kulichev brothers from preaching or doing pastoral work."

Asked if we had ever criticized the Committee before the church members, Vasil answered, "Let me assure you, I've been listening to their sermons for many years, and neither of them have spoken negatively of the Committee or of the Bulgarian government. They're good citizens and feel called of God to preach the gospel. They do that faithfully and without compromise."

Nothing Less than Excellence Will Do

Jordan Milanov, vice-president of the First Church board, entered the room next to testify. Lashkov asked him to comment upon our character and reputations among the church members.

Jordan responded much as Vasil Kozuharov had. "I've never heard Christo or Dimitar Kulichev speak in a derogatory way of our government or the people's interest in our nation. At no time have they tried to organize the people of our church against the Committee."

Jordan went on to tell of working with us. "Let me also say that for the many years I've worked with them in the construction industry, they have consistently upheld the highest standards of ethics and workmanship. Their motto is, 'We will do our work as if it is being done for God, and nothing less than excellence will do.'"

In regard to our leadership in the church, Jordan said, "They have not been self-promoters, seeking power and influence, but have served only when called by the people to do so. When we were searching for a minister, I remember Christo Kulichev saying, 'If I'm not selected to be your pastor at this time, I can support my family by working in construction until God opens a door for me to preach.' Christo is not the kind of man who just looks for a position or a salary, for he truly desires to serve God!"

Jordan continued, mentioning that I had even offered to resign as pastor when Pavel Ivanov had come seeking the position the autumn before my arrest. I didn't want to see the church suffer and knew that persecution would most likely come upon us all if we resisted the wishes of the Committee. My offer to resign had been resoundingly rejected, and the people had made it clear that the time had come to take a stand.

Lashkov asked if the people of First Church respected my ministry.

Jordan emphasized, "The great majority of people in our congregation respond to Pastor Kulichev's challenging sermons. He preaches that we should practice what we profess. He challenges us to live godly lives and to be faithful in our witness for Christ. I recall only one occasion when a church member, Mr. Boris Delchev, told me he didn't like such sermons. He was afraid of what the Committee might do to the church."

When Jordan was asked by Lashkov to describe Pavel Ivanov's reputation and to tell the court how the congregation viewed his leadership, his words were graphic. "In our churches a pastor is not allowed to marry a divorced woman. I've received two letters, one from a pastor who has known Pavel Ivanov for many years and another from a sexton who served the church where Pavel Ivanov was preaching. They were both letters of warning, one telling our board that Pavel Ivanov is divorced because of his immoral behavior, the other informing us that Ivanov had been excommunicated from the Pentecostal church for the same reason."

I saw Gichev begin to squirm at the Prosecutor's table.

Milanov continued, "We had heard these things spoken of, but the written testimony of two highly respected believers made it clear. I am confident that if a vote were taken, the people of the church would reject Pavel Ivanov by an overwhelming majority."

Proinov rose and requested an opportunity to question Jordan Milanov. He began, "Did I understand you to say that the Kulichev brothers have never spoken against the Bulgarian government?"

"Yes," Milanov replied. "Not only have they never spoken critically of our government from the pulpit, but I have been a visitor in their homes and have never heard derogatory comments about the government or officials."

Proinov then inquired, "As a leader of the church board, can you tell us if there has ever been any investigation into the bookkeeping or the handling of church finances by the church treasurer?"

Milanov's reply was unequivocal, "No. We've been pleased with the way all of the financial transactions have been conducted." He then added, "I've never seen or heard discussions regarding any order to dismiss Dimitar Kulichev as the treasurer of our church."

When Jordan Milanov finished answering Proinov's questions, he turned to the panel of judges and asked, "May I make one final statement?"

When the judges nodded approval, Milanov read this statement: "Let me say in closing that both of the Kulichev brothers have served our churches honorably as pastors since they were ordained in 1975. There is no document revoking their registration as pastors. The law of our nation states that the internal organization of our church must be conducted in accordance with a church constitution. Our constitution does not need to be approved by any government committee, and neither does any committee have the right to select a pastor for our church. First Church selected the Kulichev brothers to be our ministers. All of the years I have served under the ministry of these two men of God, they have sought the very best for our church and its members. It is the desire of our congregation that they continue being our pastors, and we regret they are not being allowed to preach at this time."

Jordan Milanov's statement was courageous. From our viewpoint, the testimony of our witnesses could not have ended on a stronger note.

Where Is the Evidence?

It was now time for our attorneys to give their summations, after which we would be allowed to give brief statements in our own defense. It was the moment for which we had long prayed and prepared.

In his closing statement, Mr. Lashkov spoke as eloquently and thoughtfully as I had ever heard him speak. "Comrade Judges, you have the great responsibility of making the decision as to whether these gentlemen before you will be convicted according to the indictments or released to return to their families after these many months spent in prison. As you make that decision, please ask yourselves this question: Among the charges made against these gentlemen, have any been proven to be true and accurate?"

Lashkov spoke freely as he outlined the details of his point. "The indictment makes three basic accusations: First, that they appointed themselves as ministers at the First Evangelical Church of Sofia; second, that they insulted the will of the people who make up that church; and third, that they acted against the government of Bulgaria. As you review these accusations, it's important for you to remember the history of the evangelical churches in our country. For over one hundred years, the government has never challenged the constitution, which allows churches without foreign contacts to choose their own ministers. Where is the proof that these two pastors appointed themselves to the pulpit against the will of the congregation? There is none! And where is the evidence that their ordinations were invalid when they were arrested? Again, there is none! The church does not have foreign connections and no letter even questioning their credentials to preach was sent.

"Mr. Tzvetkov," Lashkov continued, gesturing toward the prosecution table, "has testified that he gave personal notice of the Committee's desire to remove Christo Kulichev, but that raises serious questions of legality. Where is the documentation? If Mr. Tzvetkov truly felt this was such an important matter, why did he operate in such an informal and undocumented fashion?"

Leaving his notes, Lashkov moved toward the judges and spoke with emotion. "Comrade Judges, it is both unconstitutional and morally wrong for the government to force a pastor upon a church. Does it not seem strange that Mr. Tzvetkov had go to the church himself and introduce Mr. Ivanov before the congregation, knowing that none of the church leaders was willing to do it? When we examine these strange and unprecedented actions, it appears that Mr. Tzvetkov has some kind of personal agenda that is distracting him from the tasks that should have his attention. This raises a question of the man's competence."

Lashkov continued down a list of improper actions conducted by Tzvetkov and condoned by the Committee. Why had the church constitution not been respected? Why had Pavel Ivanov been imposed when there was no vacancy? Why the forceful entry and the arrests?

"I'll tell you why," Lashkov summarized, his voice filled with conviction. "When this hostile takeover of the church did not work as he wished, Mr. Tzvetkov arranged for the pastors, Christo Kulichev and Dimitar Kulichev, to be arrested in order to provide a vacancy in the pulpit! No documentation exists showing that Christo Kulichev retired. No documentation exists proving withdrawal of registration. No documentation exists to show that funds were mismanaged. No documentation exists showing that the Committee is empowered to act without the approval of the church members."

Lashkov paused, allowing his points to sink in. "On what basis was all of this done? Will we be the kind of nation that uses the constitution only when convenient, dismissing it when it interferes with our personal wishes? This is exactly what the Committee on Internal Religious Affairs would have you do to Christo and Dimitar Kulichev!"

Lashkov was pushing the limits in what he was saying, but he went further. "Do you recall Mr. Tzvetkov confessing he was not aware that Christo Kulichev was once the pastor of the church in Krichim? Mr. Tzvetkov is the head of the Committee. He has the records—it is his job to know such things! When he comes before you and confesses his ignorance of such facts, he demonstrates his incompetency!"

As Lashkov reached his conclusion, his voice softened. "In closing my summation for the defense, let me stress that the actions of the church in voting to call Christo Kulichev to the pulpit were in accordance with the laws of the country and the constitution of the church. Likewise, only the church can remove the minister they have elected. Since the accusations made against this man are not supported by the evidence, and since the actions of the prosecution are not in accordance with the explicit meaning of Article 274, I stand before you today asking respectfully that you find Christo Kulichev not guilty and allow him to be released."

Lashkov had given his all as he turned to be seated. The anxiety Tzvete and I had felt about him early on had proven unfounded. As he had promised, he had done the best he could.

Wishing Proinov Was a Believer

It was then Proinov's turn to stand and offer his closing argument. He began, "Allow me, Comrade Judges, to ask that you find Dimitar Kulichev not guilty of the accusations that have been made against him."

Proinov was moving slowly across the front of the defense table, almost as if he wasn't sure of himself. "As I begin, I'm not sure whether I should feel sad or glad for the very eloquent exposition that has just been made by Comrade Lashkov. His is a hard act to follow.

"Some of Mr. Lashkov's points, however, also apply to Dimitar Kulichev. As we have gathered the facts related to this case, listening carefully to the testimony of everyone concerned, it has become increasingly clear that these two gentlemen cannot be found guilty of the accusations brought against them." Proinov waved the Act of Accusation in the air. "During this trial we have seen no documents or proof by which it is possible to convict Dimitar Kulichev. Certainly not by using the statues as they stand in Article 274 of our penal code."

Proinov's voice had a clear, penetrating quality that filled the courtroom. Pointing to Dimitar and me, he continued. "Neither of these gentlemen has violated either public or private interests! That is why there's no proof brought forward by the Prosecutor to show how the law applies to this case!"

Turning around, Proinov appeared to be looking for someone in the courtroom, his eyes finally settling on Gichev at the Prosecutor's table. Pointing at Gichev, Proinov asserted boldly, "On the contrary, it was Pavel Ivanov who illegally assumed the duties of pastor at First Evangelical Church! It was Pavel Ivanov who claimed the position of pastor without proper approval from the congregation. It was Pavel Ivanov who interfered in the life of the church from October through

January." Each time he mentioned the name of Pavel Ivanov, Proinov said it with emphasis, pointing to the Prosecutor's table. Proinov continued deftly, as Lashkov had done, to enumerate accusation after accusation that was based upon hearsay or that lacked documentation.

Looking up from the papers he had relentlessly studied throughout the trial, Gichev squirmed ever so slightly in his chair. For the first time I thought I saw some brief hint of emotion in Gichev's stoic features.

I found myself admiring Proinov's eloquence, wishing that he were a believer using his gifts for God's glory in the pulpit.

Gesturing again at our table, Proinov said, "Both of these men have proper documents proving that they are pastors. Christo and Dimitar Kulichev wanted only to protect the interests of their church. They courageously tried to protect the rights of the church members so that they would not be violated by Pavel Ivanov!"

Proinov's voice rose as he said, "The proper rights and interests of religious communities throughout our nation were attacked by Mr. Tzvetkov and Pavel Ivanov when they acted improperly and without authority. We're told that Mr. Ivanov brought twenty people into the church from outside to support him in his efforts to take over the pulpit. Yet with all of these efforts to disrupt the church and discredit these pastors, he still is not accepted by the congregation! Why then, I must ask you, are these two men even being brought to trial today? It's an injustice!

"Let me remind you, Comrades, that Dimitar Kulichev's responsibility has been to work with the finances of the church. Dimitar Kulichev has not mismanaged funds, nor has he been 'impersonating a minister.'"

Moving closer to Gichev's table, Proinov pointed to where Tzvetkov had once sat. He continued, "But look carefully, and you'll see a man, Mr. Tzvetkov, who has personal and political interests for promoting Pavel Ivanov. Look carefully, and you will see Pavel Ivanov pretending that he has been appointed by the Committee. Look carefully, and you will see that Mr. Tzvetkov was so intent upon his own personal agenda that he didn't have time to properly document his actions as a responsible public servant should. Look carefully at the law, and analyze it in light of all of the facts we have gathered and now lay before you. Look carefully, Comrades, and you will have no choice but to declare these defendants not guilty!"

For a moment it seemed that Proinov had finished, but then he continued to speak in a personal, almost an informal, tone. "Comrade

Judges, these men who sit before you are hardworking men. As you will recall, one witness testified that when Christo and Dimitar Kulichev worked as foremen on a construction project, they strove to do excellent work, the very best they could do. Such qualities are valued in our society. Dimitar Kulichev has three children, and yet he and his brother have been held in prison for three full months. Three months, when they've done no wrong! Let's not be quick to gloss over that important fact!"

Lowering his voice, Proinov concluded, "I can assure you that these men, Christo and Dimitar Kulichev, will not seek revenge for this injustice nor come seeking reparations. They are peace-loving men. All they want, and all that I am requesting of you now in the name of justice and the law, is that you declare them to be not guilty."

Our Chance to Testify

The closing moments of our trial were now upon us. Dimitar and I had prepared ourselves to use this opportunity to speak of our commitment to Christ and our rights to serve him as the church called us to do.

When asked if he would like to address the court, Dimitar stood and spoke.

"Let me say at the outset," my brother began, "that I'm grateful for the opportunity to speak on my own behalf." Dimitar thanked the judges for allowing our attorneys to speak freely in presenting our case.

"My only regret," Dimitar continued, "is that it was necessary to conduct this trial behind closed doors, thereby depriving so many concerned citizens of an opportunity to see justice in action."

At this point the chief judge interrupted, advising Dimitar that his right to speak was limited to defending his own conduct and that he was not to comment upon the conduct of others or on the trial itself. This had been our concern, that perhaps only legal concerns could be expressed, disallowing personal convictions regarding our faith or rights.

Dimitar adjusted quickly and continued, "Please allow me to testify today as one who is a witness for the gospel of Jesus Christ. I am a servant of Christ and have not intended to do anything that would harm the church I was called to serve—or anyone else, for that matter. To the contrary, I've always stated openly that my purpose in ministry is to strengthen our ties of fellowship and to serve others in Christ's name."

The judge held his gavel but did not use it to stop Dimitar from speaking of Christ. That was a good sign. "Equally important," my brother continued, "I've always taught that each Christian's responsibility is to be a good citizen and a productive member of society." Dimitar went on to stress that he emphasized moral behavior in his Bible classes. "Christians must always be on guard against the sins and temptations that come our way," he said, "so that we stand out among our neighbors as honest and upright citizens. It is our desire to improve the quality of life in our nation. I've always taught that there must be a consistent relationship between the things we believe and the lives we live."

Reaching his conclusion, Dimitar appealed, "In light of my motives and commitment to these ideals, I am standing before you to appeal that you render a decision of acquittal. That verdict will not only be consistent with the testimony given, but it will also honor this court and increase our people's trust in the judicial system of our nation."

When Dimitar was seated, the chief judge asked if I would like to speak as well. Moving from behind the defense table to the center of the courtroom, I began my closing statement.

"I'm standing before you with a clean conscience and full assurance that I have in no way violated the laws of our nation. My actions have been based entirely upon my Christian convictions. My responsibility as a pastor is to preach the gospel of Jesus Christ and to lead people in the Christian faith. That's what I have been doing—nothing more and nothing less."

This was a moment of high emotion. I offered a silent prayer for God's strength and wisdom as I began to speak publicly of my commitment to Christ before representatives of an atheistic government.

"My ministry and my preaching is to lay the gospel of salvation before all of mankind. As witnesses have told you, my life and preaching are committed to calling people to know God's righteousness, which will make this a better community, make people more honest, and help us relate to one another in peace. I find it strange that anyone would call this a crime against society!"

In rapid succession I refuted the charges against me: that I had turned the church against the Committee, that my registration to preach had been officially withdrawn, that I had obstructed justice, and that our church had foreign connections. Concerning the charge that I had violated public and personal interests, I emphasized, "There's no complaint from the church that I have imposed myself upon them. That is not the case with Pavel Ivanov, however. The church rejected his attempts to take over the pulpit. In light of that, who should be charged with violating the church interests?"

Watching to see if the head judge reached for his gavel, I said something I had long wanted to say: "And whose personal interests are harmed? Can any claim be made that Mr. Tzvetkov's personal interests are harmed when his plan to force Pavel Ivanov upon the church failed? Not at all. Mr. Tzvetkov has boasted that evangelical churches in Bulgaria will be totally done away with by the year 2000! This entire conflict resulted because of Mr. Tzvetkov's ambition to disrupt the church by his appointment of Pavel Ivanov as pastor. When his illegal efforts failed, he made accusations that I was violating public and private interests." At this point I inserted a line I had written in the cell two nights before, saying, "Personal interests? No, the issue at stake here is not one of personal interests but one of personal ambition."

Gichev, the Prosecutor, was sitting to my right. Out of the corner of my eye, I noticed he was nervously jotting notes. I continued without interruption, stressing the constitutional principle of the separation of church and state. "That principle makes it clear that evangelical Christians have the right to conduct their ministry under God's authority, to worship freely as the Spirit leads, and to call a minister as they feel led, without taking every detail to the Committee for approval."

To emphasize the point that my calling and installation to First Church was in accordance with the church's constitution, I couldn't resist adding, "Let me respectfully remind you that I've been preaching in evangelical churches for thirty years. I've been an ordained pastor for more than ten years. During all of that time it is noteworthy that I've never had conflict with the Committee on Internal Religious Affairs. To the contrary, it was Mr. Tzvetkov himself, together with pastors Assen Simeonov and Bozimir Kozuharov, who approved my serving as a delegate to the Church Alliance held in Skopje, Yugoslavia, in 1978. That was seven years ago, and now Mr. Tzvetkov has conveniently forgotten that fact in order to make his false claims more believable. Now he would have you believe that I am involved in 'illegal pastoral activities.'"

Having addressed Tzvetkov's complicity in all of this as much as I dared, I returned to my spiritual convictions. "Christ has called me to minister in his name, and I've always been sensitive to the wishes of God's people at First Church. The people of the church have encouraged me to preach the gospel of Christ and have received my preaching with respect. When Pavel Ivanov tried to impose himself upon the congregation, I offered to step aside if the people preferred someone else as their minister. I did not want to cause problems. The people of First Church made it clear to me—and to Pavel Ivanov—that they didn't want me to step aside.

"As you have heard, Comrades, there is no basis for the accusations made against me. If you convict me of something today, I hope you will convict me of doing my job as a Christian pastor and doing it well. Surely it is not a crime for a man to do his job well?"

I wanted my final words to be of Christ. "If I have seemed to be an obstacle, it's only because my first commitment is to Jesus Christ. Led by Christ's Spirit and instructed by God's Word, my deepest desire is to fulfill my duties as a Christian pastor. The Bible tells me to obey the laws of our nation as a respectful citizen—as long as they don't conflict with God's laws. And that is the reason I am asking you to declare me not guilty of these accusations. In doing so you will also confirm the promise made to all citizens that they have the freedom to worship according to their faith as promised in our Bulgarian constitution."

Silent Sentinels of Support

Within a few minutes of our closing statements, the head judge rapped the gavel sharply and announced that a verdict would be rendered the next day, and court was adjourned. The bailiffs came and put Dimitar and me in handcuffs to usher us back to the holding cell. The crowd of believers was still waiting faithfully outside of the courtroom, having remained there throughout the trial. As before, when the bailiff opened the door of the courtroom, the people stood silently and made room for us to pass through the packed corridor.

The crowds were as large now as they had been on the first day, and the gratitude that welled up in our hearts was just as great. The faith and commitment shining in the faces of those brothers and sisters in Christ made me realize that all we had gone through and were about to go through was well worth it. No earthly cost, in possessions or personal sacrifice, was too great to purchase our freedom to worship, serve Christ, and fellowship in his Spirit.

As we passed through the crowd that last day of the trial, one face in particular stood out. Sister Mihova, the daughter of a famous artist in our country, scurried along the perimeter of the crowd, trying to catch a glimpse of us as we passed. Recognizing her, I quietly spoke her name as we passed so that she would know her presence was appreciated. Her famous name made it especially risky for her to be seen among the crowd of believers. So many had taken risks and made sacrifices to stand with us as silent sentinels in support of the gospel.

CHAPTER NINE
A Proposal and Its Price

*Blessed are you when people insult you, persecute you and falsely say
all kinds of evil against you because of me. Rejoice and be glad,
because great is your reward in heaven, for in the same way they
persecuted the prophets who were before you.*

MATTHEW 5:11-12

*There is no remembrance more blessed, and nothing more blessed
to remember, than suffering overcome in solidarity with God;
this is the mystery of suffering.*

SOREN KIERKEGAARD

Throughout the trial we were given no hint by the judges as to what sentences might be handed down if we were convicted. As diligently as we had worked at presenting our defense, we were constantly aware that a conviction was almost a foregone conclusion. That was simply the way the judicial system worked under the totalitarian Bulgarian government. The courts were viewed as instruments to be used by those in power rather than as institutions to protect the rights of the people.

As much as I wanted to believe the prisoners at Kremikovtzi when they predicted acquittal, I knew how futile it was to hope for any such outcome. There was too much at stake for Tzvetkov and the Committee on Internal Religious Affairs. They would bend every ear and twist every arm necessary to secure our conviction.

Dimitar and I talked far into the night in the holding cell that had been our "home" during the trial. Dimitar's role was much less visible in all of this than mine, and I hoped that Tzvetkov would be satisfied with giving me a sentence and letting my brother go free.

Knowing how brutal and repressive the Communist regime had been with others, I felt fortunate that my life was being spared. Hundreds of people, some of them evangelical pastors, had just disappeared. How grateful I was to God for the thousands of letters received from abroad.[14] Had it not been for the international publicity my case

---

[14] Later we would learn that my name had been released by Amnesty International to the British Broadcasting Corporation and to Radio Free Europe, asking that letters be sent demanding my release. The BBC, we were told later, had filed a request to have a reporter present at my trial, only to be told that it was being conducted *in camera*, or in private chambers.

received, I might well have been among those who disappeared without explanation.

Don't Expect Anything Less

On the morning the verdict was to be announced, Dimitar and I had no sooner arisen and said our prayers than our attorneys, Lashkov and Proinov, appeared at the door of our cell.

Lashkov spoke first. "We thought we should meet in private before we go before the judges for the verdict," he said, watching our faces to gauge our response.

"The sentences in cases such as this are almost always six months and four months, respectively," Proinov said, nodding first to me and then to Dimitar. "There are always rumors swirling around trials such as this, and you should know what we're hearing."

After a few seconds of silence, he shrugged and said, "We did our best, and I'm sorry we can't promise you a better outcome."

Lashkov spoke again, "We just wanted you to know. Don't expect anything less." It was obvious that Lashkov and Proinov were preparing us for conviction.

"We're prepared spiritually and emotionally," I assured them. "God is with us, and we'll continue to serve him wherever he sends us—even if it's back to prison."

For the final time the bailiffs came to escort us through the crowd of faithful believers clustered in the corridor and into the courtroom.

The handcuffs were removed, and we had just been seated when the arrival of the judges was announced and we were on our feet again. The judges didn't look our way, which was a telling indication of the verdict to come.

The chief judge called the court to order, ordered us as the defendants to stand, and tersely announced, "In the case of the state versus Christo Kulichev and Dimitar Kulichev, the court's decision is in favor of the state. The defendants are found guilty as charged. Christo Kulichev is hereby sentenced to eight months in a medium-security prison. Dimitar Kulichev is sentenced to six months in a medium-security prison."

There was no discussion of the charges, no rationale given, just the verdict. With that blunt announcement, the gavel fell, and the trial was declared closed. It was as if Pontius Pilate had washed his hands and walked away.

We shook hands with Lashkov and Proinov, thanking them for

making a spirited defense of our case, and then turned to be handcuffed.

Additional bailiffs were present that day to escort us out of the courtroom. They obviously didn't know that, as evangelicals, we were pacifists.

When the doors swung open, our friends from the churches had already heard of the sentences. "God bless you, brothers!" someone shouted. "We're praying," said another. Tzvete, Stefan, Nebesna, and Toshko were all there with tears in their eyes, as were the members of Dimitar's family.

"Don't worry," I assured them quickly as I passed. "God will use this for his glory. That's all that matters." We walked down the corridor surrounded by a phalanx of bailiffs who took us back to our cell.

The Rule of the Ravens

"The judges didn't even explain why our sentences were more harsh than is the custom," said Dimitar when we are alone in the cell.

"This is how they build their reputation for being tough," I suggested.

While confident that the facts regarding both our personal conduct and the conduct of church business would exonerate us in a fair trial, both Dimitar and I had understood from the beginning that our chances of getting a fair trial were practically nonexistent. Too much effort had been invested by the state. Their aggressive actions in arresting us and forcibly entering the church building had put their integrity on the line. I had the feeling they would never have allowed our case to even come to trial if they hadn't already made sure the government officials, including the judges, understood this.

Most likely some kind of a deal had been made in advance to ensure our conviction. Tzvetkov had undoubtedly worked harder behind the scenes than he had on his court presentation to make sure that Pavel Ivanov's appointment would be endorsed.

We Bulgarians have a proverb that says, "The ravens never pluck the eyes out of their own young!" I believe there is a similar English proverb that says something like, "Birds of a feather flock together." The point is that the prosecutors, judges, and government officials were going to pull every string to make sure that their interests were served in this trial—with no regard for the interests of justice to us or to the people of the church.

I commented to Dimitar, "That's how they advance themselves in the system, by being tough and always approving whatever the government does, not by showing justice to a couple of evangelical pastors. But God will use us for his glory if only we will let him. Let's pray, brother, that God will use us even in prison to bring honor and glory to his name." And so we knelt and gave thanks to God for his promise never to leave us or forsake us.

We were left alone in the holding cell for several hours, doing our best to begin preparing ourselves for the experience ahead. The past months in prison had not been easy for us or our families. But spending time in even the worst of prisons would be better than renouncing our faith in Christ or cooperating with an atheistic government. Besides, there was always the hope that we might be placed in the same medium-security prison, which would make it easier to support one another.

As we were about to discover, that would not happen. However, something of a surprise was in store for us.

A Proposal

Another night passed in Central Prison. This was something of a surprise, since we had anticipated being shipped off to a medium-security prison soon after the sentencing.

Shortly after our prayers and the prison breakfast the following morning, a guard came and opened the door to our cell. "Follow me," he gruffly demanded. The guard led us through the steel door at the end of the cell block, around a corner, and into a small room containing only a table and four chairs. In one of the chairs, seated behind the table, was Vladimir Nikolov, an uncharacteristic smile on his face.

"Come in and be seated, Christo, Dimitar," Nikolov offered with all of the charm of which he was capable. I noticed he didn't bother to rise from his chair, however. "Well, your trial is over," he commented. State security agents had a way of stating the obvious. "I asked to be informed, since I've taken a special interest in your case."

Neither of us responded, waiting for Nikolov to get to the point. "The length of the sentences was something of a surprise," Nikolov continued, studying us carefully. "You've had almost twenty four hours to consider your sentence now. Perhaps you're a bit discouraged with such a long sentence, but I'm here to inform you there's still an option open to you."

Having anticipated that Nikolov was there to tell us of the details regarding our transfer, my first thought now was that he was toying with us. Again, neither of us responded.

"As you've pointed out," Nikolov nodded to me, "our prisons are crowded. The conditions are not pleasant, even in the medium-security prisons. Knowing this, I've discussed your case with the judges."

We were wondering where Nikolov was going.

"Fortunately for you, they've given me permission to make a proposal that could make a big difference to both of you." Nikolov was playing it for all it was worth, feeling important and in control. "If you wish to file an appeal, the judges have agreed to review it quickly. They would even be willing to allow you to return to your homes on bail while you make the appeals!"

I suspected that Nikolov was up to something. But what?

When neither of us responded, he continued, "That's why I'm able to offer you the possibility of going free this very day!" He paused dramatically, then said again, "This will be on bail of course, and only for a few days while you prepare your appeals."

Nikolov had finally gotten the bait out on the table. Now, I wondered, what price was he asking for the freedom he was offering?

"Are you interested?" Nikolov inquired, somewhat puzzled that neither of us expressed surprise or delight at his announcement.

"Of course we're interested," I replied. "But what conditions are required for our appeals to be accepted?"

"Let me first of all note that both of you have served time in prison for several months," Nikolov continued, not answering my question. "The time already served will certainly be taken into consideration. And I'm sure the judges would find in favor of an appeal, with only one condition."

I sensed what was coming. "And what is that?"

"Of course, when released you may do anything you wish with your families. You may travel for pleasure, you may move about the community." Nikolov was presenting his case as convincingly as he could. He paused and then continued, "But it wouldn't be allowed for you to go back to the church or to interfere with the appointment of Pavel Ivanov as the new minister." He shrugged. "That's a small concession when you consider the convenience of living at home with your families!"

My Call Is to Preach the Gospel

Dimitar and I looked at each other. I knew immediately what my response must be. My call to preach the gospel of Christ wasn't negotiable, and I could never promise the compliance Nikolov was asking for in my appeal. To accept freedom under these terms of surrender to

Ivanov and the Committee would destroy my integrity with the congregation and make the months I had already spent in prison meaningless.

My brother's case, however, was different. Dimitar was not directly involved in the preaching ministry of First Church, since he served as the financial officer for the Union of Evangelical Churches. I didn't want to speak until Dimitar and I had an opportunity to discuss the matter alone.

Looking back at Nikolov, I asked, "Would it be possible for my brother and me to have some time with our families to discuss these things?"

"Of course," Nikolov waved his consent, rising from the chair and moving toward the door. "As I said, it can be arranged for you to be at home while you prepare your appeals. There's the little matter of the bail while you're away from the prison, but get a taste of what freedom is like, and consider it carefully," Nikolov said agreeably. "And if you show respect for the Committee in your appeal, you may not even have to come back!" He was exuding confidence that we would accept his proposal. "I'll go call your families," Nikolov said. And with that he was out the door.

In a few minutes the guards came and summoned us to follow them to the induction area of the prison. With surprising speed our clothing was returned, and we were able to strip off the horrible prison garb we'd worn for months.

In another hour we were ushered to the door of the prison, where we found Tzvete and Stefan waiting to drive us home. A joyous reunion awaited us at our homes, which are situated adjacent to one another. Neither the thoughts of the appeal nor the conditions the judges were hoping to impose could diminish our gratitude for this respite from prison life.

The next days were a time of intense sharing with our families. I didn't even take time to attempt an inventory of all the things confiscated by the agents. It was far more important to spend time praying together and being a family again.

With government agents observing our every movement, this was not the time to attempt contact with church members or even those who had witnessed at our trial. And so we stayed at home, related the stories of prison, heard of the struggles our families had endured, and prepared for the decisions that lay ahead.

On the third day my brother and I met to consider the proposal the judges had made via Nikolov. "What do you think?" Dimitar inquired. "What chance do you think our appeal has of being accepted?"

"The pressure from abroad may be in our favor," I suggested, reminding my brother that Nikolov had been disconcerted by the letters demanding my release. "Now they'll report they've set us free—though it's not true freedom if we can't return to our ministry," I added.

"Do you think the judges might compromise?" Dimitar asked.

"On the length of the sentences, perhaps," I speculated. "But it's certain they won't compromise the Committee's authority. As it stands now, there's no way I can accept this proposal for myself. It's clear they're demanding total removal from the church, which is unacceptable for me. But your case is different."

"What do you mean?" Dimitar asked.

"My call is to preach the gospel of Christ. The church has called me to the pulpit, and that puts me into direct conflict with the Committee and Pavel Ivanov. Your work with the finances and visiting the believers isn't as visible. You went to prison because you supported me. They feared you might step into the pulpit in my absence, which you never planned to do anyway."

But What about You?

"What are you proposing?" Dimitar inquired.

"You could agree to their terms," I suggested. "Then, when their scrutiny drops off a little, you might begin meeting with believers in their homes to encourage them. Others can fill your position as the financial officer for the Union; in fact Tzvete says it's been filled already. As I said, it's not a highly visible position. It's the pulpit at First Church they're after. That's why you may go."

"But what about you? We're in this together," Dimitar said.

"Yes, I know, but even if you go back with me, we may not be together in prison. If you accept the conditions, you can help both our families. That's an important consideration, too. Pavel Ivanov's not after your position, though; he is challenging me for the pulpit of First Church."

Our discussion went on for an hour or so, weighing the pros and the cons. We recognized it was important for me to take a strong stand for the sake of the believers. To capitulate for the sake of my personal convenience would set a bad example for others at a time when few were willing to stand firm against the powers at work to destroy the church. A compromise for convenience would not only restrict my ministry but could also discredit me personally. It wasn't the same for Dimitar who was in a less visible role and had not been called to the controversial pulpit of First Church.

Think about Your Family, Man!

Our appeals were brief. Both of us maintained our complete innocence. The primary difference was that Dimitar said nothing in his appeal about returning to the church, while I asserted my rights as the minister who was properly called to lead the First Evangelical Church of Sofia.

Appeals in hand, we approached Nikolov's office and surrendered them. The clerk who accepted them asked us to wait, disappeared into Nikolov's office, and then reappeared a few minutes later. "It'll take a few days to consider your appeals," he informed us. "You may return home and wait for our call. It may take as much as a week," he suggested.

The days passed rapidly, although we were given two weeks at home rather than the one the clerk had predicted. I enjoyed the time with my family, spending precious hours reading Tzvete's Bible, which the agents had returned to her after threatening to confiscate it.

At the end of the second week, Nikolov's inevitable telephone call came. "You are hereby instructed to meet me at my office tomorrow at nine o'clock. A decision has been reached." The tone of his voice didn't sound promising.

When we arrived, Nikolov entered the room with our appeals in hand. "These appeals cannot be accepted as they are now worded," he began. "There must be an agreement to respect the Committee and to stay away from the church! I thought I'd made that clear to you!"

My many interrogations had taught me never to reply prematurely. Often the opening words of an agent were a ploy to intimidate me or to throw me off guard. Only time would tell which direction he might take. Would it be an extension of our bail with time to reconsider, or would it be prison? The wisest course was to wait and see what would be proposed.

"Still, we are prepared to give you one last chance," Nikolov said tentatively. Improbable as it seemed, the government seemed eager to compromise, or at least to negotiate! Was it because of pressure from the foreign letters we had heard about? Whatever it was, a window of hope was kept open by Nikolov's offer of "one last chance."

"Since your appeal wasn't properly worded," he continued while looking at me, "we've taken pains to put this petition together. It's really very simple. You give the Committee the freedom to operate the church as they see fit, and you'll have your freedom. The judges are confident that you'll see how reasonable this is. Are you ready to sign the petitions?" Nikolov asked, extending them toward us with pen in hand.

I looked at Dimitar, who glanced at me and then at Nikolov.

Dimitar spoke. "I have some questions," he said. "If I sign the petition, does that mean my family and I will have freedom to move about as before? For instance, can I visit in the homes of other believers?"

"As long as you're not plotting against Pavel Ivanov and the Committee," Nikolov summarized.

Dimitar spoke again, "I cannot support Pavel Ivanov, as you know. My brother will always have my full support. But I would like to be free to fellowship with the believers. I've made my stand in regard to Pavel Ivanov and the Committee, and I have nothing further to say. Under those conditions, I will sign."

"What about you?" Nikolov turned hopefully to me. He had not even acknowledged Dimitar's response, which spoke volumes. It was me, the pastor of the church, that he was after.

"You offered me this proposal months ago," I reminded Nikolov. "I couldn't accept it then, and I can't accept it now. The wording of my appeal is precisely where I stand. There's no freedom in walking the streets if my right to minister to the people of my church is taken away. God has called me to preach, and the church has appointed me to be their legal pastor. I'll not barter away my call to preach for a false freedom. I must obey God and not men," I said firmly.

Nikolov, clearly frustrated, raised his voice. "The court has already made the decision. Pavel Ivanov is the pastor, and that's final! Think about your family, man!"

"The Bible says," I replied calmly, 'Anyone who loves father or mother more than me is not worthy of me; anyone who loves his son or daughter more than me is not worthy of me; and anyone who does not take his cross and follow me is not worthy of me' (Matthew 10:37-38). My family and I will trust God to take care of us. My brother's circumstances are different, but I will not sign the petition."

The decision was made. Dimitar would be released. He would remain on bail for the duration of his sentence, but would be able to move freely among the believers' homes. We prayed together and said our farewells before his release that afternoon. He promised to take my greetings, as well as explanations for everything, to my family and to the believers.

Transfer to Plovdiv

The next day I was transferred by train to the prison at Plovdiv, Bulgaria's second-largest city after Sofia. Located southeast of Sofia in the south-central part of the country, Plovdiv was a three-and-a-half-hour drive away.

The trip was uneventful except that one of the prisoners shackled next to me told me he had heard my name in a radio broadcast.

The procedure in the receiving areas of the prisons was becoming familiar, although the people and their response to my story always differed. At Plovdiv, the young officer completing my admission form refused to accept "pastor" as a valid entry.

"'Pastor' is not an accepted occupation in Bulgaria," he insisted. "What education do you have? Perhaps that will tell us what you are trained to do."

I told him I was a graduate of the University of Sofia with a major in Slavic Philology.

"So you really don't have any theological education," he said scornfully. "We'll write down that you are a teacher."

Protesting, I tried to convince him I was not a teacher and told of being dismissed from my teaching post in Bansko some years ago. "They dismissed me for talking to students about my faith in Christ. That's when I became a pastor," I maintained. "That's what my whole life is committed to."

Nevertheless, the young man ignored my plea and wrote down whatever pleased him, which I suppose was "teacher."

Overcrowding at Plovdiv was horrible. While at Plovdiv I was assigned the number 7179. Since each prisoner was given an ascending number upon their admission, we could monitor the number of prisoners being admitted. Prisoners who had been there for some time calculated that four prisoners were admitted each day. Even allowing for the fact that some prisoners were transfers and others were habitual criminals circulating repeatedly through the system, they estimated that roughly one-half of the admissions were new to the prisons. Extrapolating those figures, prisoners calculated that if this kept up at the current rate, approximately one-half of the entire Bulgarian population would soon pass through a prison cell somewhere in the country.

My placement in Plovdiv was temporary, since the prison administration there had been given oversight for a number of labor camps scattered throughout central Bulgaria.

On my third day in Plovdiv, I found myself back in the administrative wing of the prison being processed out again. When I checked in, I had placed twenty-nine *leva* in the security envelope. Only five were missing, which was surprisingly generous of the thieves who worked in the administrative wing.

Handcuffed again, I was placed in a state automobile along with two others and began the trip northward. Our destination was a labor camp at a smaller town named Sopot, an hour north of Plovdiv.

Sopot is about two hours west of Sofia, somewhat closer than Plovdiv. My hope was that my family would be able to visit me as they had done at Kremikovtzi. I soon discovered that wouldn't be allowed. The order, of course, came from Vladimir Nikolov, who was apparently hoping that I might still reconsider. He wanted me to come begging and didn't understand that his little games wouldn't work with someone whose life was committed to Christ. I was reminded of the saying:

> Some will die in shackles,
>
> Some will die in flames,
>
> Some will die, inch by inch,
>
> Playing little games!

Can This Christ Change Lives?

It was at Sopot that I had my most interesting conversation with a warden. We had just been processed into the camp when one of the guards motioned me to follow him down a hallway. "The warden wants to speak with you," he indicated.

Inside the warden's nondescript office sat a large man; his graying hair contrasted with bushy black eyebrows. His associate, a slender man of medium build and several years younger than the warden, was seated to one side of the desk.

The warden's first question indicated he had read my file. "Your case is an unusual one," he began. "Can you explain to me what all of this means?"

I explained briefly my beliefs as a Christian pastor, emphasizing the evangelical tradition of each church choosing its own minister, and sketched out the events that had led to my arrest. When I mentioned that the Committee had forced Pavel Ivanov upon the church, several more questions followed.

It was clear from his questions that the warden at Sopot was confused as to why I was being held. More than that, both he and his assistant had spiritual questions.

The warden asked incredulously, "Do you actually believe there is a God?" I had only begun my answer when he pressed further, "How can it be? What made you come to believe this?"

What was amazing about the warden's questions was that he was asking them in front of a subordinate. In an atheistic socialist society, there was a long list of controversial topics one did not risk discussing openly for fear of reprisal. Religion was at the top of that list.

This situation was even more peculiar in that the warden's assistant participated in the questioning. It was as if he were an equal. Clearly these men had talked with one another about religious beliefs and felt comfortable discussing spiritual things with me in one another's presence.

"How can believing in someone who lived two thousand years ago make any difference in how we live today?" the warden asked curiously.

When I explained the Resurrection and that Christ is a living Savior, present with us in his Holy Spirit, more questions followed. "Can this Christ change lives? Have you seen lives actually changed by this Jesus you preach?" the warden asked.

As a partial answer to his question, I used a story that I've told often. It's the story of a Christian brother named Ivan Babulev. Ivan was not a believer when he was the commander of the police force in the city of Petrich, Bulgaria. His life was totally changed, however, when Christ spoke to him. He thought at first that he must be hallucinating, but Ivan actually experienced his own "Damascus Road" experience, similar to that of the apostle Paul!

I repeated the story as Ivan had told it to me: "Christ appeared to Ivan and said, 'Ivan, tell your superiors I'm alive. Tell them they're fighting against me but will not succeed. If they continue, they'll be punished for their sins! Tell them to put their faith in me!'"

Telling of the dramatic change in Ivan's language, behavior, and marriage, I concluded, "Ivan's new behavior gave evidence that his life was truly changed in a way that only God could change a person."

When I finished, the warden and his assistant were incredulous, as one might expect. The warden commented, "I'll believe God is real on the day when—let's say for example—I'm traveling in my car on the road to Sofia and suddenly crash into a steep canyon and yet emerge unharmed!"

Both men seemed eager to believe and yet, like the people of Jesus' day, they wanted a sign.

"Even if a miracle occurs," I pointed out, "it's doubtful you will become a believer if your heart isn't ready to make the commitment of faith. You probably would say to yourself, 'What a coincidence I wasn't hurt! I must be lucky!' God wants you to trust him by faith and live a life that honors him. He isn't interested in just having you believe in his existence; he wants a personal relationship with you!"

Our conversation went on for almost two hours. The men asked their personal questions as if I were the authority and they were under my control. Their spiritual hunger was so great that for a time we were no longer prisoner and wardens, just fellow human beings seeking to know the truth about God and his plan for our lives.

Thinking the men might make a commitment right there, I emphasized that they already had enough evidence to believe in God. "The Bible teaches us, 'What may be known about God is plain to them. . . . For since the creation of the world God's invisible qualities—his eternal power and divine nature—have been clearly seen, being understood from what has been made, so that men are without excuse' (Romans 1:19-20)."

To press my point home I suggested, "Can't you see that any person who looks out at the expanse of the universe and contemplates its precision has to conclude that there is something or someone behind it all? That someone is God. God has revealed himself in Creation and also in the Bible. But most important, he has revealed himself to us in his Son, Jesus Christ."

Nervous about the consequences, neither man made a commitment. As we concluded, the warden asked me not to talk about these beliefs among the prisoners.

Before I could reply, his associate interrupted and said perceptively, "We certainly can ask him not to talk about his beliefs, but it's clear to see that his principles are such that he's not going to tell a lie if a prisoner asks about religious beliefs."

The Prison Culture at Sopot

Since the labor camp at Sopot was a medium-security prison, conditions were more favorable than at Central Prison or Kremikovtzi. Sopot was presented as a model institution for visitors from outside of the country. Overcrowding was less of an issue—prisoners slept in single beds, not bunk beds, in the barracks. Food was more plentiful and of better quality. The prison uniforms were nicer than those I had seen before. Prisoners were allowed to develop relationships and even address one another as "Comrade," which contributed to a sense of civility and human worth.

Prison guards throughout the Bulgarian system, even at Sopot, were from the lowest level of society. Most were poorly educated and desperate for work. It released their frustration or gave them a sense of superiority to talk down to the prisoners. My two days at Plovdiv were especially abusive, with guards constantly shouting "pig" or "cow" at prisoners. There was little of this at Sopot, however, which provided a more relaxed atmosphere.

But even in Sopot there were irregularities and abuses under the surface that I found myself learning very quickly. As was common in many prisons, there was a strange system of hierarchy and barter at Sopot. The long-term prisoners at Sopot, for instance, had established a monopoly that allowed them to control the small cabinets in some of the cells. The cabinets were for storing uniforms and personal items.

There weren't enough cabinets to go around, and some were of better quality than others. In order to get a cabinet, a prisoner had to actually pay one of the prisoners who controlled the supply.

When I was admitted, I saw a cabinet near my bed and assumed it was for my use, storing my clothes and personal belongings in it. But when I returned to my bed from lunch the next day, I found my clothes and belongings lying on my bed. When I asked the guard responsible for our cell block what had happened to my cabinet, he informed me, "Oh, someone came and took it. He told me it was his."

As I soon discovered, the prison economy included more than just cabinets. Since I had no cabinet in which to store my clothes and other belongings, I had no choice but to leave them lying in plain view. It wasn't long before my working uniform disappeared.

There was a prisoner named Ljubo in the bed next to mine, a tall, thin man with a thatch of thick, black hair. When I mentioned to Ljubo that my work uniform was missing, his dark eyes flashed with sympathy. "I should've warned you," he said, clasping his forehead. "Those are popular with the thieves, and they take them from new inmates."

Adding insult to injury, it wasn't uncommon for a prisoner to approach the new inmate a day later and offer to sell him back the uniform just stolen from him! It was a humiliating way of letting new inmates know they were low on the prison pecking order. It also provided a few extra *leva* for the thieves as they continued to practice the tricks of their trade.

Because Sopot was considered a model prison, attempts were made to give structure to prison life under the pretense of having prisoners "govern" themselves. There was a president and a committee made up of prisoners who were supposed to enforce discipline. All sorts of illegal activities were carried on right in front of the president and committee members, however.

Gambling, though strictly forbidden, was widespread in the labor camp. It was tragic to watch the compulsive behavior of some prisoners, losing all of their meager funds in one night. The entire cell block knew they would hang around the canteen begging for the next several days. Not surprisingly, the prisoners' committee and president didn't bother to try to control the gambling at all. I watched one night as the president passed by a group of gambling prisoners, only to say, "Try to be a little less noticeable, please."

A few prisoners at Sopot had been able to save money to buy far more than they needed. When the canteen didn't open on Sundays and holidays, their extra supply of items came into view, and the prices went as high as they dared push them.

While Sopot offered greater freedom in most respects, it didn't allow smoking in the barracks. Most prisoners were addicted to smoking. At Kremikovtzi, the guards recognized how desperately prisoners needed to smoke and allowed them to go at night to the end of the room to smoke near the bucket—only to use the prisoner's addiction against him in order to control him at a later time. But at Sopot smoking in the barracks was not permitted, though some prisoners would get up in the night and try to sneak a cigarette in the toilet area or under their blankets. A fire would have been devastating, since all of the doors and windows were locked. The prisoners would have been trapped in a deadly inferno.

Sundays and Solitary

Sopot was a labor camp, which raised the issue of Sunday as a day of worship and rest. I viewed Sunday as the Sabbath and had vowed early in life to keep Sunday as the Lord's day. In a Communist culture, which puts great emphasis upon the merit of labor, I've always taken great care to set Sunday apart for worship and rest.

Complications arose quickly. Prior to my arrival there had been a loss of electrical power, and the factory where prisoners made furniture had been shut down. In an attempt to make up for lost production, the warden had informed prisoners that they must work on Sundays until production was back on schedule.

On my first Sunday at Sopot, when I respectfully refused to work because of my commitment to Christ, I was punished with three days in solitary confinement.

The cell where I was held in solitary was underground and without windows. The only available light was from a single bulb outside of the cell door. There was no furniture in the cell except for a thin mattress thrown on the damp floor, which provided a very uncomfortable place for sleeping. The hours dragged by, making it difficult to guess what time it was and, eventually, what day it was. I prayed and recited as much Scripture as I could, reverting to the disciplines that had kept my mind occupied while in Central Prison.

Witness under a Wagon

As difficult as solitary confinement was, I was grateful to serve that time as a means of witnessing to my Christian commitment. God blessed my time in solitary and my commitment to him in an unusual way.

Upon returning to the general population, I quickly realized that every prisoner working in the furniture factory now knew there was an evangelical pastor among them. They also understood that I was remaining faithful to the Lord's teachings even in the face of suffering.

When it became known that I had skills in the building trades, I was moved from the factory to a work detail building a storage shed. While pouring the foundation one afternoon, a sudden thunderstorm swept through the area, and work stopped because of the weather.

A group of us took shelter under a wagon, talking idly as we waited out the storm. Spontaneously one of the prisoners asked me a question about my belief in God. The most effective opportunities for witnessing often came like that—without warning and in rather strange settings.

While the opportunity to influence lives was great, because the conversation started so unexpectedly, I proceeded cautiously. One of the guards had also sought shelter under the wagon, and so I turned to him and asked, "Do you mind if I answer these questions?"

His reply was, "Yes, you may. Go ahead." But then he left the group, perhaps not wanting to bear responsibility if a superior learned we had been talking about religion.

When the guard had gone, all kinds of questions of a spiritual nature rained down upon me, almost as numerous as the raindrops falling around us. "What do you believe about Christ?" "What's it like to attend a church service?" "How is the service conducted?" "What is a sermon?" I had only begun responding to one question when another surfaced.

Breathing a prayer for God's wisdom, I explained that our sermons varied from Sunday to Sunday, stressing that I shared how the Bible speaks to the needs and problems we face in life. As the prisoners listened, I told them that the Gospels in our New Testament tell the story of Jesus Christ and his coming to earth to take away our sins so that we might have eternal life. When we believe on him, I stressed, God changes our hearts, making us new creatures. Growing bolder, I even told them that it was faith in Christ as Savior and Lord that united Christians in times when it was dangerous to be a Christian.

In prison or out, I've found the most effective way to witness is to simply tell the story of Jesus. Continuing to share under the wagon, I pointed out, "The Bible tells us that there is no one who has ever lived, except Jesus Christ, who can make the claim that he is without sin. Certainly none of us can. Because Christ was without sin he was able to offer himself as a sacrifice on the cross for our sins."

As the rain continued, I went on explaining basic Christian beliefs, telling them Christians aren't perfect, just forgiven. "We confess our sins and ask Christ to forgive us and become the Lord of our lives." Some had heard the phrase "being saved," and I explained that when a person received Christ's forgiveness and new life, that person was saved from sin.

The Line between Good and Evil Oscillates

If there was one thing that the prisoners seemed to understand, it was the struggle between good and evil. Famous Russian author and human-rights spokesman Aleksandr Solzhenitsyn is said to have written that the line between good and evil doesn't pass between nations, classes, or even individuals; instead, it oscillates within each human heart. My experience, in prison and out, has borne out the truth of that statement.

The struggle between good and evil was evident in the men's faces as I continued talking. I spoke of the story of Adam and Eve and how Satan deceived them into believing they could be like God. "Satan is a deceiver, and he convinced them they didn't have to obey God's commandments." Heads nodded as I pointed out, "Just as Adam and Eve fell into sin, so each of us has also fallen into sin."

As the rain came down steadily, I told the story of Satan's trying to deceive Jesus just as he had Adam and Eve. The story of Jesus out in the wilderness, hungry and tired, was a story with which the men around me empathized.

"He could've used his power to turn rocks into bread? And who would have known?" one man exclaimed.

"The point of the story," I stressed, "is that we are tempted to trust ourselves rather than God. When we selfishly ignore God's commands in an attempt to meet our own needs, we sin, and sin blinds us to the consequences of ignoring God's will."

The men listened in sober silence.

"Certainly we all have natural needs," I said. "But some of us are here in prison because we didn't believe God's law is for our own good. We didn't trust God to provide for our needs. We foolishly took matters into our own hands, thinking that if we could earn more money or steal or cheat or take advantage of women, somehow these things would make us happy. But these things are sin. God warns us not to do them because they not only hurt others and ourselves, they separate us from God!"

What the prisoners needed most was to hear that there was another way. "Jesus refused to be deceived by Satan," I said. "When he was tempted to meet his own needs, Jesus answered, 'Man does not live on bread alone, but on every word that comes from the mouth of God' (Matthew 4:4)."

At this point I stopped to ask, "Do you understand what Jesus was saying in those words?"

Perceptively, one of the men said, "Is it because our hunger for God is supposed to be greater than our hunger for bread?"

Smiling, I commended him, "That's a good way to look at it!"

When I had an opportunity to witness as I did under the wagon, I concluded with some great promise of Scripture. "Remember," I would say, "the Bible invites you to 'cast all your anxiety on him because he cares for you' (1 Peter 5:7)." Speaking to men who had committed rape, robberies, or worse, I knew that if anything could touch calloused hearts, it was the truth of Scripture. I often quoted passages such as Matthew 6:25, 33:

> Therefore I tell you, do not worry about your life, what you will eat or drink; or about your body, what you will wear. Is not life more important than food, and the body more important than clothes?
>
> But seek first his kingdom and his righteousness, and all these things will be given to you as well.

Life Is a Work of Art

The rain had washed the earth clean and stopped just as I finished talking under the wagon. Everyone had listened carefully. One man spoke up quietly and thoughtfully, "Pastor, you make it so practical."

After more thoughtful silence, another of the men suggested, "Pastor, I'd like to talk with you more, but I don't want to get you into trouble. Everyone may not be happy listening to our conversation and may fry you." The expression "fry" was prison jargon for "bringing the heat down" on someone, turning him in to the authorities.

And the men did come to talk! Every day after work, and on Saturdays after lunch when there was free time, or on Sundays, my time was filled with all kinds of conversations, talking to men individually and in groups. God had blessed my time in solitary confinement by giving me the opportunity to begin a counseling ministry in prison!

Sasho (not the same Sasho with whom I had briefly shared a cell in Central Prison) was just one example. Sasho was a tall, athletic young man with handsome, chiseled features. His wife was a beautiful woman known throughout Bulgaria as a famous sportswoman. Sasho, like many prisoners, was insecure and afraid his wife wouldn't wait for him.

When Sasho poured out his fears and suspicions to me, I tried to counsel him. "Sasho, you were on trial for taking money, and you told me you were taking it to help your family. You must confess everything to your wife. Tell her the whole truth and nothing but the truth! If your wife knows everything, she'll understand. Most women won't turn away if they know you love them and are trying to help—even if you've gone about helping the wrong way. When you marry someone, you must pray that God will make you one. That means you must share everything, even those things that are difficult."

"Ah, Christo!" Sasho retorted. "You know nothing about life."

"I know that life is like a work of art and that we can create whatever we desire out of it. The choice is ours. We can live honest lives that will help us trust one another, or we can cheat on one another. But when a man and a woman stand before God in a wedding ceremony, they promise to love and care for one another in sickness and in health, for richer or poorer, for better or for worse."

Continuing, I urged Sasho, "Confess your sins to God, then confess them to your wife and ask her forgiveness. Then ask her to pray with you that God will guide and bless your marriage. Do this, Sasho, and things will be different. I promise!"

It became something of a problem for me to keep in touch with everyone who wanted to meet with me, and before long I began to hear men saying, "Pastor, we were waiting for you to come and talk with us last night! Where were you?" or "Pastor, have you forgotten about us? When will you come back so we can talk some more?"

Spiritual Blindness and Spiritual Thirst

The food at Sopot was better than anything I'd eaten since my arrest. We were given tea for breakfast, and there was no limit to the bread we could eat. Prisoners were always asking for more food, and occasionally we would be given delicacies such as fruit preserves, cream yogurt, or chopped cucumber soup. Because we were working, however, prisoners still complained of hunger and constantly tried to get more food.

One evening as Ljubo and I were leaving the eating area, we asked a worker cleaning a nearby table if he could arrange to get us some preserves. To our delight he did, and we relished every bite, watching carefully to be sure we weren't observed by the guards. If the guards had spotted us, it might have gotten both us and the worker into trouble. Other prisoners watched us as we ate this treat, but they didn't say anything since they knew how scarce these delicacies were.

With more comfortable living conditions, less crowding, and better food, the months passed quickly at Sopot. I looked forward to my release on September 8. Counting the time I had spent in prison prior to the trial, that date would mark one day short of eight months of imprisonment.

As the summer months passed, it became evident that Vladimir Nikolov was not allowing my family to visit. This was just another of his attempts to pressure me into reconsidering his proposal. With the condition that I must accept Pavel Ivanov's right to occupy the pulpit of First Church, even talking to Nikolov wasn't a consideration.

As the word spread that an evangelical pastor was concerned about prisoners, men became more bold in seeking spiritual help. I prayed God would give me the strength and wisdom to not only endure the prison experience myself but also to reach out and help those who would say, "Pastor, can I have just a minute?"

As these conversations continued, I was grateful for the evangelism and counseling ministry God was allowing me to carry on. Ljubo, the dark-haired man whose bed was next to mine, had been a driving instructor. He had been discovered accepting bribes to give a driving permit to someone who otherwise might not have passed the exam.

Ljubo's spiritual blindness was typical of most prisoners. Ljubo was caught in a cycle of denial and self-justification: "Pastor, I just wanted to help the people! I was giving them a driver's license so they would be able to drive. They have put me into prison just for trying to help people." This spiritual blindness existed side by side with spiritual thirst. With Ljubo and others, I often quoted 1 John 1:9-10: "If we confess our sins, he is faithful and just and will forgive us our sins and purify us from all unrighteousness. If we claim we have not sinned, we make him out to be a liar and his word has no place in our lives."

Ljubo and I talked earnestly and at length about the fact that his "helping" people involved accepting illegal money in return, and that some of the people to whom he had given driver's licenses probably posed a threat on the highways. "Ljubo," I said, "you must recognize that those people could cause accidents and even the deaths of innocent people. You must confess you were doing something wrong, just to meet your own desire for more money."

He responded, "Pastor, now you're talking just like my interrogator!"

Not all responded positively, but I was still thankful to be able to do the work God called me to do by pastoring those men in the prison. When I lay down at night, I reflected on God's mysterious ways—making me as useful to God's kingdom among those needy men as I would have been in the pulpit of First Church.

Some of the men with whom I spoke, particularly the younger ones, had hearts that were open to the gospel. I'll never forget them. To this day, I continue to pray that God will use my witness in prison to bear eternal fruit in their lives.

Young Christo

One young man placed in the barracks with me for a time was also named Christo. I used to call him "my namesake." His bed was two spaces away, and each evening he came to the medicine cabinet close to my bed to take his medication.

"Young Christo," as the prisoners called him, worried about what was going to happen to the rest of his life as a result of his conviction and imprisonment. He would say, "I don't know what to do! In six months I'll be released, but how will I make a living? My nerves have been completely shattered by this experience. I can't sleep or concentrate anymore."

One evening I responded, "My dear namesake, you're speaking to a man who believes in God. Whenever I have problems or needs I take them to my heavenly Father in prayer and ask his help."

"I believe in God, too, Christo," the young man replied. "But what should I do?"

Knowing he had observed me when I knelt in prayer each morning and evening, I said, "You've seen me pray. But it's not necessary for you to pray on your knees like me. The important thing is simply to open your heart and talk honestly with God. Tell him what you're feeling, share your needs with him, ask him to protect your life and health, and then ask for his peace to come into your heart. I'll pray for you, too, but it's most important for you to pray and believe God will help you."

Young Christo seemed genuinely interested and asked innocently, "Pastor, would you write out a prayer for me to pray?" I explained that my church didn't use written prayers in a prayer book. I emphasized that all he needed to do was to share his own thoughts and feelings with God.

Later I did write a short prayer for Young Christo, as I had done on occasion for other prisoners. In a few days my young namesake approached with a broad smile and announced, "Pastor, I don't know how to thank you! I'm well now. My nerves are much calmer since I began praying, and I'm sleeping like a baby!"

I reminded Young Christo, "Please remember what you've learned from this experience. Our God is a living God who cares for us. Now you must thank him for answering your prayers and try to live a life pleasing to him."

Heartbreaking Stories

Almost every man I spoke with in prison had family problems. Some told tragic, heartbreaking stories like the man I will call Charlie.

Charlie was approximately forty years of age, of medium build, and balding. He was supposed to be released from prison in a few months, after serving a sentence of four and one-half years.

Charlie had a quiet, brooding presence about him that made me uneasy. When I spoke with Charlie, I found he was disturbed and angry because his eighteen-year-old daughter had died of an illness while he was in prison. Disappointed that his wife hadn't done something to prevent this tragedy, Charlie was refusing to see his wife.

One day Charlie told me he had decided to look for an apartment for himself and his teenage son when he was released. "I'll take my son with me, but I plan to divorce my wife," Charlie insisted. "She neglected her duties to our family, and that's why my daughter died! My son has also lost a year in school because she's caring only for her own needs!"

One constant of prison life was the stress and worry inmates had about their marriages and families. In many cases arrest and imprisonment put additional strain upon already troubled relationships. Difficult problems left unresolved were nearly impossible to address with the physical and emotional distance prison created.

The frustration of prison almost always grew into a gnawing suspicion that the prisoner was being abandoned. That suspicion, in turn, usually ended in accusations of unfaithfulness—sometimes imagined, other times well-founded.

Young prisoners were especially prone to believe their wives wouldn't wait for them. Often this suspicion would become an obsession, until their criticism drove their wives away.

They're Serving the Sentence Right Alongside Us

Charlie was facing the same problem as Sasho but was more depressed and was determined not to see his wife again. I prayed as to exactly how I should approach him.

Finally, one day when we were alone, I ventured to speak. "Charlie, you've been in prison much longer than me, and I don't know if you'll agree, but I've observed that those of us who are locked up can fall into the trap of thinking only of ourselves." I remained silent to see how Charlie responded.

"What do you mean, Christo?" he inquired.

The door was open. "We need compassion from our families so badly, and we want their help to such an extent, that we forget to look at the situation from their perspective."

Charlie didn't speak, but he didn't seem to be defensive either.

"Few of us stop to ask ourselves the question, 'What's life like for my family, for my wife, struggling to keep the family together?' It must be hard for them to make both ends meet without a husband to provide. Sometimes I think our families have more hardships than we do."

After a few seconds of silence, Charlie spoke. "Prison destroys most marriages," he began. "In one sense it's destroyed mine, I think." Tears welled up in Charlie's eyes. Then he got to the heart of what he was feeling. "I feel so guilty! If only I'd been there, my daughter wouldn't have died! Now I feel like a man without a family. Sometimes I feel that I'm not even a man!"

"That's a natural response, Charlie," I sympathized, "but you can't blame yourself—or your wife. Your wife is probably blaming herself, and maybe your son feels guilty as well. We're human—all of us. Most tragedies are beyond our control even if we *are* present."

"I suppose you're right," Charlie said softly.

"Families need each other at a time of loss and grief," I insisted. "It's so much harder to be alone. If you leave your wife, it'll only cause another great loss, and everyone will be more lonely."

Charlie had lapsed into a thoughtful silence. But he was letting me speak, and he seemed to be interested in what I was saying.

"We need to remember our families. In a way, they're serving the sentence right alongside us!" I had said more than I intended and dared not say more. I would wait prayerfully to see if Charlie's attitude changed.

She Lost Her Husband and the Love of Her Parents

One day a young man in our barracks named Vanjo received a letter from home. Vanjo brought it to me and asked if I would discuss it with him. The letter was from his wife, who was six months pregnant; she had written to share the problems she faced.

Vanjo was in prison for stealing an electric motor worth only ninety *leva*. While he was in prison, his wife's parents had turned against him, criticizing their daughter for marrying someone so worthless. This hurt both Vanjo and his wife deeply.

Because Vanjo was in prison, his in-laws tried to run his wife's life for her. When she resisted, they shamed her by telling her she shouldn't have chosen such a worthless husband. Vanjo's wife was feeling hurt and alone, having lost her husband and the love of her parents as well.

Vanjo's wife wrote, "I know it isn't easy for you in prison, but please don't think that it's easy for me either!"

A few days later, without identifying the family, I shared that story with Charlie and said, "That young man felt sorry for himself in prison, but he soon came to see that his wife had it just as hard."

Charlie responded, "I've been considering what you said the other day about thinking only of myself. But I think my situation may be different."

"Charlie," I ventured, "I know you're upset because of your daughter's death. But don't accuse your wife when you don't really know all the circumstances. I hope you'll try to work things out with her."

Charlie looked thoughtful but said only, "It may be too late."

Allowing some silence to pass, I continued softly, "Charlie, you and I both know your daughter's death had to be hard for your wife to bear. She's lost a daughter also! Don't start assuming she's done something wrong and threaten her with divorce on top of this great loss."

"My biggest concern is for my son now. I would like for him to come live with me, but I don't think it'll work with my wife," he said, shaking his head.

"You want your son to come live with you? Do you think that will work?" I asked. "He's spent his entire life at his mother's side. He loves her and is accustomed to her ways. He'll rejoice when you're released from prison, but don't drown his joy in the sorrow of forcing him to choose between his mother and father. Think about the future. Will you always live alone, or is there a possibility you may find another woman? If so, she'll never be your son's mother. If you try to force the relationship, you'll lose him. He may not want to come spend time with you. What you're thinking of doing would hurt your wife, your son, and even yourself!"

While Charlie didn't argue, he continued to refuse to see his wife. I was worried, but I had said all that I could say. All that was left for me to do was pray.

Impressionable Young Hearts

Medium-security prisons were meant for young, first-time offenders, and many of the prisoners at both Sopot and Kremikovtzi fell into that category. As I had seen before, social aspirations drove many of these young men to the petty crimes that landed them in prison. When I asked how they ended up in prison, the typical reply was: "My girlfriend and I wanted to enjoy life. There were so many fun things to do—if only they weren't so expensive. I tried to save money to take her to a disco, but an evening like that cost fifty *leva,* and my salary was too low."

There were many opportunities to talk with such prisoners about their lives and what hopes and dreams they had. The harsh prison experience sometimes softened young hearts and made them receptive to counsel. Again I shared passages of Scripture, pointing out how easy it was to get priorities in life confused, trying to meet one's own needs rather than depending upon God.

"The world deceives us," I would say, "but Jesus tells us that God will never deceive us." I often quoted Matthew 7:9-11: "Which of you, if his son asks for bread, will give him a stone? Or if he asks for a fish, will give him a snake? If you, then, though you are evil, know how to give good gifts to your children, how much more will your Father in heaven give good gifts to those who ask him!"

"God gives us what we need," I would explain, "not what the world tells us we should want. It may seem painful at the time—just as a wise father's discipline is not easy—but in his love God meets our deepest inner needs. All we need to do is ask God to forgive our sins and come into our lives."

Again and again I invited the men to trust God for their needs: "Ask and it will be given to you; seek and you will find; knock and the door will be opened to you. For everyone who asks receives; he who seeks finds; and to him who knocks, the door will be opened" (Luke 11:9-10).

Old Man Christo, Let's Talk

While the hearts of many prisoners were soft and impressionable, other prisoners were hardened criminals. Some of the scams the con men tried were laughable, but they managed to take advantage of enough prisoners to keep them trying. On one occasion a prisoner I didn't know approached and called me by name. "Old Man Christo, let's talk." His easy familiarity put me on guard.

Sitting down next to me, my new "friend" showed me a wristwatch. "Christo, I know you're an honest man. You're a pastor, and I can trust you."

My suspicions mounted as I noted that this fellow knew my name. He'd done his research!

"Please take this watch," the smooth talker continued. "Give me twenty *leva* for it, just as a pledge that it'll still be here when I come back on Wednesday. When you return it on Wednesday, I'll then give you twenty-five *leva*, which will give you a nice little profit! You can't lose!"

I asked the obvious question. "Why are all of these transactions necessary?"

Chuckling as though my question were elementary, I noted that he nimbly glossed over the heart of my question to say, "Well—just because I'm asking a favor of you, I'm willing to show you my appreciation by helping you make five *leva* of profit."

Aha, I thought to myself, *the age old appeal to greed.*

"But I see no good reason for making such a complicated deal as this," I told him.

"Look," he whispered, making it seem that I was getting privileged information. "I found this nice watch worth at least fifty *leva*!

Now I only have thirty *leva* myself, and I don't want to let it get away. That's why I need the extra twenty *leva* from you. I promise to pay you back on Wednesday."

There were still essential details missing. I continued to question.

"How are you going to find an additional twenty-five *leva* so you can pay me back as you promised?"

The inevitable answer of the con game surfaced: "Don't worry, I'll find it. And I promise you'll get five *leva* for no work at all. Think of it! Besides, if I don't return, you still have the watch."

I explained the obvious, that I already had a watch and didn't need two. Then I noticed something of interest—this man who was so desperate to buy watches already had one on his wrist! Pointing this out, I suggested, "Since both of us have watches that are working, this deal doesn't seem to be necessary!"

Seeing his plan wasn't going to work, the con man turned on me. "Oh, you're the one who's supposed to be such a good man, are you? And you aren't even willing to do me a small favor!"

Taming the "Dog"

Valeri was the name of a young man only one year older than my son Stefan. Valeri was known as a troublemaker, harrassing everyone with whom he came into contact. Other prisoners didn't give him the dignity of using his name; they simply called him "Dog."

We were returning from a work project on a bus one day when Valeri began smoking. When some of the prisoners objected, Valeri became irate and threatened those who were shouting at him.

Underneath the crude exterior, I sensed Valeri was a fragile young man. I waited for an opportunity to be alone with him. Finally, two days after the bus incident, when we were alone for just a few moments, I said, "Valeri, the other prisoners may call you 'Dog,' but you're a human being just like me. You were created by God, and God loves you. You know that I was among the prisoners who objected to your smoking on the bus, but I don't want anything to stand between us."

Valeri looked at me with a mixture of surprise and fear, waiting for some time before answering, "We'll talk about this some other time. I'm too busy now."

We never did talk about the incident on the bus, but from that brief conversation our relationship changed, and Valeri's behavior began to change as well. I became Valeri's confidant. He often came and talked to me about what he was thinking or things he wanted or wished he could do.

As our relationship developed, Valeri regularly began to bring me his money, asking me to keep it with mine so that he wouldn't spend it all. It was a gigantic step of trust for one as rejected and isolated as he.

Valeri, "the Dog," much as Gosho the Red had done, gradually opened up. His trust allowed me to talk about spiritual things with him and encourage him to trust Christ as Savior and Lord. He always listened quietly, and I still pray that the Holy Spirit will continue to use what I shared to touch Valeri's life. To my knowledge, I was the only friend he had in prison.

A Gracious Answer to Prayer

When we offer a word of witness or counsel, and a seed is planted, we may never know if it grows or bears fruit. I thought that perhaps my talks with men like Valeri, Gosho the Red, Sasho, and Charlie might fall into that category. But by the grace of God, such was not the case with Charlie.

At the end of August, when I was about to be released from prison, Charlie came to see me one evening. It was obvious that Charlie wanted to say something. *Perhaps he is trying to say farewell,* I thought.

After a short silence, Charlie stuttered and mumbled before finally saying, "Pastor, when you're out of prison would you call my wife for me? Please tell her I would like for her to come and see me."

Joy swept over me. It had been difficult to speak candidly to Charlie, but I had felt God leading me to intervene and ask Charlie to consider things that weren't easy. "Of course I will, Charlie. You're doing the right thing! Give me your wife's telephone number, and I will call her."

There obviously had been a change in Charlie, and I breathed a prayer of thanksgiving. The Holy Spirit was working in Charlie's life. The very idea that he wanted to meet with his wife brought me happiness.

As Charlie handed me his wife's name, address, and telephone number scribbled on a scrap of paper, I promised, "I'll be praying for both you and your wife!"

There were tears in his eyes as he turned to go.

Few of the prisoners responded as openly to my witness as Charlie did. Prison conditioned people to suppress feelings, concealing them from others. Emotional openness in prison led to vulnerability, which could lead to danger. Because of that it was difficult to assess how many lives were touched and changed by the witness I shared. But that was not important, since it was the work of the Holy Spirit and something for which I cannot take credit. What was important was that the seed was planted. I left it up to God to water and bring the harvest.

I rejoiced in the cases where arrest and imprisonment opened hearts and minds to the gospel in special ways. Because their human ingenuity had finally failed, some prisoners were ready to turn to God for guidance and healing. All I could do was to be as faithful as possible in sharing my witness, leaving the results with God. As the Bible teaches in Matthew 13, some seed falls upon rocky soil, some among thorns, and some is snatched away by the evil one; but some falls upon good soil, takes root, and bears fruit.

Preparing for Release

Finally, notice was given confirming that on September 8 I was to go home to be with my family. It was an exciting prospect after the ordeals of prison life. The prisoners were always aware of release dates, and several were counting the days with me.

As the date of my release approached, I became more introspective, reviewing the things God had taught me in prison. First and foremost, I had learned that I was never beyond God's love. As bleak and dismal a place as prison was, it was still a venue where God's care and help could be known by those who sought his strength in their lives.

Secondly, I learned that God's strength and wisdom make it possible to be a witness for Christ in prison and that witnessing and service are at the heart of true Christian experience. Christianity isn't just a set of beliefs but a way of life. God's grace isn't just something intended for us to receive; it's given so that we might share it with others.

Another spiritual reward was seeing God touch and change lives. We should never presume that even our smallest, seemingly most insignificant word of witness won't be used by God to touch lives. Unlikely lives such as Valeri's, Charlie's, and Assen's can be impacted by what we say and do. The important thing is to remember that the work is done by God working through us; it's not something we can take credit for.

As I looked forward to my release, I vowed not to forget those still in prison. I didn't want to be like Pharaoh's cupbearer, who was imprisoned with Joseph. When they were captives together, the cupbearer vowed that, when he was released, he would remember Joseph.

Yet when he left prison, he relished the good life restored to him and forgot his promise to Joseph (Genesis 40).

When the suffering and discomfort of prison were behind me, I knew it would be easy to forget those who had shared the experience with me. It was vital that I continue praying for, writing to, and visiting the men I had come to know in prison.

Much of the seed I have sown in prison has yet to bear fruit. My prayer is that God will protect that seed. It is not seed that is intended to bring me honor, for I am only a lowly servant of my Lord. What was sown was sown by his grace, and it can be preserved by his grace so that it might bear fruit to God's glory in God's own time.

Pastor, Would You Pray for Us?

My commitment upon release was not just to maintain contact with those I had developed relationships with in prison but to reach out to other prisoners as well. Jesus calls us to visit those who are in prison (Matthew 25:36-40). Having experienced the debilitating effect of prison life firsthand and knowing the confusion and distress that occupies the lives of prisoners, I realized that I was in a unique position to minister where I had not been able to before.

The joy of being released was clouded somewhat by the uncertainty of returning to First Church in Sofia. I was very much aware of the ongoing conflict between the church and Pavel Ivanov. My resolve to stand beside the church could very well lead to further charges from the Committee on Internal Religious Affairs. There was, I knew, the real threat of another imprisonment.

During the last few days before September 8, one prisoner after another came to talk. Some asked if I would return to visit, which I hoped to do but wasn't certain would be allowed. Other prisoners, like Charlie, asked me to contact loved ones or gave me messages to convey. Some, like Assen, asked if they could contact me when released. Many just said, "Pastor, would you pray for us?"

My own prayer to the Lord as September 8 approached was, "Lord, bless my witness to these men. Water the seed that has been planted here by your grace. You're the Lord of the harvest. May glory be brought to your name as lives are changed by the power and presence of Christ in the hearts of those open to your love."

Looking to my own uncertain future, I prayed, "May I be faithful to these men I'm leaving behind: faithful to pray, faithful to write and visit as I am able, and faithful to minister to others in prison. Most of all, Lord, may I always be faithful to you. Help me to be strong and faithful as I go back to the church and the problems to be faced there. Even if I must return to prison, Lord, may you always find me faithful!"

CHAPTER TEN

Release!

I eagerly expect and hope that I will in no way be ashamed,
but will have sufficient courage so that now as always Christ will
be exalted in my body, whether by life or by death.
PHILIPPIANS 1:20

When sufferings come upon us, we must utter thanks to God,
for suffering draws us nearer the Holy One.
RABBI ELEAZAR BEN JACOB

On September 7, I was transferred from the work camp at Sopot back to the prison at Plovdiv. I spent my last night in prison in a reflective mood.

Knowing I was about to leave, the prisoners back at Sopot had asked, "How does it feel to know you will be free again?"

Not all prisoners are excited at the prospect of freedom. Those who've spent much of their lives in prison are institutionalized and feel anxious. One older man at Sopot died of a heart attack the night before his release. Those who feel abandoned by their families, or whose wives or sweethearts have left them, usually feel depressed by the idea of returning home.

My feelings were a mixture of joy and gratitude. My heart was rejoicing at the thought of being with my wife and family. My heart was hungry and thirsty to have fellowship with them and other Christian brothers and sisters. At the same time, I was grateful for my prison experience.

It's Better to Die Right Than Live Wrong

Having chosen to serve my time rather than compromise my principles, I felt gratified that I had remained faithful in the face of the Committee's pressure. It was also gratifying to know that God had used my witness in prison. Strangely enough, even without a Bible or Christian fellowship, I felt my faith had grown in many respects.

More than anything, prison had given me a new perspective on life and faith. God had shown me through my arrest, trial, and imprisonment that my calling was to advance his honor and glory even if it meant suffering and loss. Suffering and loss are only temporary, but God's glory is eternal—and someday we'll live in the light of that glory! The words of 2 Corinthians 5:4 came to mind: "These tents we now live in are like a heavy burden, and we groan. But we don't do this just because we want to leave these bodies that will die. It is because we want to change them for bodies that will never die" (CEV).

This new perspective God gave me through my prison experience made me want to be holy rather than happy. It made me want to see things, as much as humanly possible, as God saw them—even if it humbled me. My constant prayer in prison had become that God would help me make *eternity* judgments rather than *time* judgments, to live outside of the pull of this world while making decisions based upon the values of the world hereafter. Paradoxically, as I left prison, I found myself cherishing life to a greater degree than before, and yet I was eager to offer it up to God. More than ever I was determined to maintain a faithful witness for Christ, risking death rather than living selfishly. Things that are right and true resonate in the soul when we live in harmony with them, and I knew I could never barter truth away for an extra few days in this world.

The Sweetest Family Reunion

The process of release at Plovdiv was short and simple. The officials allowed me to call my family to come pick me up, and I was delighted to hear Tzvete's voice over the telephone. We hadn't spoken in all the months I had been at Plovdiv and Sopot.

"It's good to hear your voice," Tzvete said through her tears after I told her the good news that I was free to go. "Praise the Lord! It's as if a load has been taken from my shoulders. Stefan will get a car, and we'll come as soon as we can!"

The wait at the prison entrance seemed interminable, but a few hours later Tzvete, Nebesna, and Toshko, along with our granddaughter Mimmi, came bounding out of the auto driven by Stefan. We embraced with tears, squeezed into the car, and offered a prayer of thanksgiving to God for bringing our family together again. It was the sweetest family reunion we'd ever known.

To my surprise Stefan didn't turn toward the highway leading back to Sofia and home but toward the center of the city of Plovdiv.

"There's a youth meeting in Assenovgrad," Tzvete informed me. "We knew they'd want to hear you talk about your prison experience, so we'll be staying in Plovdiv overnight."

All kinds of news, not all of it good, came tumbling out as we drove toward the city's center. "We aren't welcome at the Plovdiv church right now," Stefan said over his shoulder as he drove. "Pastors Marin Marinov and Nikola Raichev took a strong stand against Pavel Ivanov. They've been replaced by puppets!" Stefan spoke with derision in his voice.

My gaze swung immediately to Tzvete. Marin was her older brother, and I knew she must be deeply concerned. "Where are they now?" I asked.

"They're traveling constantly, visiting in the homes of believers and challenging them to remain faithful," Tzvete informed me. It was just like Marin to stand firmly. As a young man, because of his outspoken witness, he had been ousted from medical school just prior to getting his degree. At one time he had even been held in prison because of his strong witness for Christ. He was a dear brother in Christ and not just my brother by marriage.

But God Meant It for Good

Word of my release spread quickly, and that night a group of believers from the Plovdiv church gathered in the home of a Christian couple to pray and to share. After thanking God for the bond of Christ's love that held us together in good times and in testing we began to share. There were scores of questions about my prison experience, and the brothers and sisters were eager to tell me what had happened in their church and others in the Union of Evangelical Churches.

Some of the pastors had buckled under the pressure applied by Pavel Ivanov. His threat to have the Committee remove them from their pulpit, as they had done to me, made some fearful. Others, like Marin and Nikola, had remained firm. Many had paid the price for maintaining their convictions. "There are some in each church who have remained true to Christ and not given away their freedom to the Committee," one brother assured me.

It was hard to hear news of brothers and sisters becoming fearful and giving in. Ivanov and the infamous Tzvetkov were working hard to bring conflict wherever they could. Pentecostal pastors were forced upon non-Pentecostal congregations and vice versa. Baptist churches were forced to receive pastors who used other modes of baptism and vice versa. The resulting confusion made it easier for Tzvetkov and the Committee to assert their agenda.

But there was good news as well. Tzvete told of reports in Sofia that the BBC in England and also Radio Free Europe had mentioned my name and the date of my trial. As the news spread, thousands of letters poured in from abroad demanding my release. Although listening to foreign radio stations was forbidden, several of the believers in the group told of hearing my name mentioned in broadcasts that they had heard from overseas.

"Our closing thought," I suggested, after a long and emotional meeting, "must be that it is Christ's church. It's not our responsibility to protect the church. Christ will protect his church. He calls us to be faithful. Christ is our Redeemer, and he's able to redeem the most difficult situation. Who knows? Perhaps someday, we'll look back and see that God has brought blessings out of the confusion we're seeing. We shall smile and say, 'Pavel Ivanov meant it for evil, but God meant it for good.'"

What Are You Going to Do Now?
The next day we drove to Assenovgrad, a few miles to the south, to meet with the youth gathered there. As much as I wanted to return home after the months away, my place was with these young ones. Some of these brothers and sisters had attended youth camps in the mountains, and many had prayed faithfully for me while I was in prison. Several had traveled to Sofia to stand vigil outside of the District Court at the trial, and I wanted to express my gratitude.

The story in the Assenovgrad church was just as I had been told. A pastor forced upon the congregation by Tzvetkov was hindering the church. Surprisingly, however, I found the people's spirits high. Twenty-five young people from half a dozen churches in the area had gathered in Assenovgrad. One Christian family owned one of the larger homes in the area, and we met in their living room. Most of the youth sat on the floor, while parents and others stood at the perimeter and in the doorway. Over forty were present in all.

As I began telling the story of my imprisonment, I realized how impossible it would be to give all the details. All I could do was tell a story or two to represent something of what my experience was like. The young people laughed when I told them that some prisoners, almost as young as they were, called me "Old Man Christo." Some wiped away tears as I told of being held in solitary for not working on Sundays. Most of all I emphasized that our purpose as Christians was to glorify God, not to live for our own convenience. I ended by quoting the song that says, "The prison becomes a palace when I'm there with Christ."

The questions went on for over an hour. A nervous silence settled over the room when one young woman asked, "What are you going to do now?" Everyone present was aware that the conflict with the Committee and Pavel Ivanov was not over.

I glanced at my wife. Since we hadn't had an opportunity to discuss the matter, I answered slowly and thoughtfully. "As Christians we can't resort to violence," I began. "We don't fight against flesh and blood, but against principalities and powers. While I haven't had time to make specific plans, I'm sure the Lord will open doors for me to minister. I'll go where the Lord leads. I don't fear Pavel Ivanov and the Committee, and I will return to my church in Sofia. But I will not attack them. When I go to the church, I'll sit in silence and pray; that will be my protest. Our weapons must be spiritual weapons, for we can be confident that God will deal with our enemies in due time."

Home Again

When we returned home the following day, Dimitar and I were joyfully reunited. We would spend many hours during the next few days sharing our experiences and enjoying fellowship again.

In the house, I quickly took inventory. As my family had reported, all of the Christian literature and books were gone, as were my personal files. Even my Bible had been confiscated, never to be returned. Nevertheless, it was refreshment for my soul to pick up a Bible and begin reading and studying again.

There was much work to be done. I had longed for months to be able to write down my thoughts about prison and the lessons God had taught me. There were letters to send to friends far and near, and there were the contacts with Charlie's wife and the families of other prisoners I had promised to make.

Many members of our Christian family came to visit—including Jordan Milanov and Vasil Kozuharov, allowing me to thank them for offering testimony at the trial. We went to see others such as Bozhimir Kozuharov and Reverend Assen Simeonov; I thanked the latter for the Communion service on Easter Sunday.

When I thanked Reverend Simeonov for his thoughtfulness, I mentioned also what an encouragement his prayers and support of my family had been. Gracious as usual in his response, Pastor Simeonov shared something I hadn't known.

"The name of Penkov was known to every Protestant minister in 1949," he said. "Chavdar Penkov's father was the judge who sentenced the ministers to death! He was known for being harsh, and later he committed suicide. You were dealing with some tough people!"

Protesting Pavel Ivanov

Difficult as it was, I knew I must attend First Church. Pavel Ivanov was still there, and secret agents from the Committee also attended the services to observe and speak favorably of Ivanov.

The great majority of people were loyal, however, and resented Pavel Ivanov's intrusion. He had forced himself into the pulpit but not into the hearts of the people of God. The true church was the people, filled with God's Spirit, and it was for their sake that I returned.

Ascending the steps of the church for worship that first Sunday, I wondered how things would go. Pavel Ivanov had to be aware of my presence, and I was sure that he was far more nervous than I.

We entered as the people were singing, and tears began coursing down my cheeks. To finally be able to sing of God's faithfulness with brothers and sisters in Christ who had proven faithful—to sing of our oneness in Christ—was a joy. The hymn they were singing was one I had sung alone in prison. Then, my memory had recalled voices in the congregation. Now that I was in the congregation, the hymns reminded me of God's faithfulness in bringing me out of the barren prison cell.

When we finished the hymn, I started to sit in the pew, only to notice the entire congregation was still standing. As I rose again, applause began spontaneously. As friends turned to smile, I realized the people were praising the Lord for my safe return. Pavel Ivanov blanched and busied himself with notes on the pulpit. Rather than diminishing, the applause rose to an ever-greater crescendo as Vasil Kozuharov appeared with a bouquet of flowers, motioning for Tzvete and me to step into the aisle.

As we stepped into the aisle, I couldn't help but notice Pavel Ivanov's white knuckles gripping the pulpit, no doubt fearing that the congregation might try to take the pulpit by force as he had done. We had resolved, however, to leave Pavel Ivanov and his conduct with the Lord and to carry on the ministries as God led. Holding the lovely bouquet, we bowed before our Christian family, and I spoke briefly to give God the glory for bringing us safely together again.

During that first service and each service I attended over the next months, I bowed in prayer during Pavel Ivanov's address. Bozhimir Kozhouharov attended worship weekly but routinely walked out of the service when Ivanov stood to speak. A young man named Mircho had recently begun to walk out also. At the conclusion of each service, I sat with head bowed when Pavel Ivanov gave the traditional blessing. When friends asked why, I replied, "The hand that betrays Christ's church cannot bless Christ's church." Soon others began to join me in this silent protest.

Preaching Again

The most refreshing aspect of my return home was to pick up a Bible and read it slowly and deliberately, meditating upon its truths in light of the new perspective God had given me in prison. My family had managed to find a new Bible, which was not easy in Communist Bulgaria. I found myself not only reading it each morning, as had been my custom, but also returning to it for hours each evening.

I quickly resumed contact with churches that were part of the Evangelical Union. If the church had been taken over by a state-appointed pastor, the contact was made with loyal lay leaders. Traveling to places such as Krichim, Popovitza, Bansko, and Merichleri, I attempted to encourage the believers. It was so good to be preaching again, even though I knew the government agents followed me everywhere I went. We met in church buildings when possible or in the homes of believers if the Committee had taken control of the building.

My message was usually the same, that we must remain faithful to what God has taught us in the Word: "Then I will answer the one who taunts me, for I trust in your word" (Psalm 119:42). I urged the believers not to doubt in the darkness what God had taught us in the light. "Let him who walks in the dark . . . trust in the name of the Lord and rely on his God" (Isaiah 50:10). The message of endurance was central, for "to him who overcomes and does my will to the end, I will give authority over the nations" (Revelation 2:26).

Letters were sent to churches I couldn't visit, thanking them for their prayers and for the greetings they had sent after my release. As I wrote my letters, I knew agents would scrutinize every memorandum leaving my hand, with copies eventually finding their way into the hands of the Committee. I was resolved to continue my ministry, however. It meant nothing to be out of prison if I couldn't be free of the Committee's intimidation.

Word of my release had circulated through the Christian community in Bulgaria, and I was pleased when the pastor of the Baptist church in Sofia came to visit. Assuring me of their prayers, he observed, "Your arrest and trial, with the agents entering the church by force, has put the Committee in a delicate position. They can't afford to create another scene like that until those memories fade!"

When I encouraged him to ask his people to stand firm, he replied candidly, "Some of us are taking a strong stand, but there are always those who are afraid. Please pray for us. As I look back I think we could have done more to help you, my brother. It's so easy to surrender without a fight."

Surprise Visitors

A couple of months after my arrival at home, Tzvete knocked gently on the door of the room where I was studying. "There's a call for you. It's from a man named Assen."

As I walked to the telephone, my mind raced. *Could it be Assen? My closest friend at Kremikovtzi, who by God's providence had come from Dimitar's cell to spend time with me? Could it be?*

"Pastor," he said. I could tell from his resonant voice that it was Assen. "I hope you don't mind my calling you?"

"Not at all, my friend," I exclaimed.

We talked of our experiences after we had been separated, the dates of our releases, and how good it felt to be out of prison. Recalling how Assen had worried over his wife and how exalted he had been when her letter arrived, I asked Assen about her.

"We're together," he assured me. "That's why I called, to thank you for your prayers. I don't think we could've made it without your prayers."

Assen came to meet me at my home, and we enjoyed a wonderful time of fellowship. "My wife tells me, 'Christo had such a positive influence on you, Assen,'" he said with a smile. "She reminds me, 'When he was encouraging you, you wrote often. After he left prison, your letters became less frequent, and I could tell you were more discouraged.'"

At our first meeting I gave Assen a New Testament, which he promised to read. We met again two or three times after that, and I felt it was clear that God was working in Assen's life. When we met, I told Assen I had prayed for him often, asking that somehow God's Spirit would open his heart and life to Christ. He was pleased.

Before we parted at our final meeting, I asked Assen, "Would you like to pray for Christ to be a part of your life as you go?"

Assen nodded, and we bowed together as I prayed for his new faith in Christ and for his marriage.

Assen and his wife had been so traumatized by his imprisonment that they were fearful of attending a public worship service. Attending First Church as my guest wasn't an option. Ivanov's "sermons" would only confuse them, and they would live in fear of the government agents who were watching me closely. All I could do was try to stay in contact with them by phone and letter and pray for them.

I had prayed faithfully for the men I was with in prison, and Assen's call and visits encouraged me to begin writing regularly to some of them. Letters went out to Young Christo, my namesake, who had asked me to write a prayer for him, and to Ljubo, the driving instructor whose bed had been next to mine. The letters weren't long, and any religious content would most likely be caught and rejected by censors. More than anything else I tried to let them know they weren't forgotten and that God loved them.

Writing to Metodi, the man who had once worked for the foreign ministry, I assured him that I continued to pray that he would be reunited with his family. Young, dark-eyed Tzeko, who treated me kindly when I needed clothes, received a letter telling how much I appreciated him.

The letters to Mitko, who had literally climbed the walls of Central Prison trading for cigarettes, and Raijko, who had gotten us the job as "sweepers," were both returned. Perhaps censors rejected the letters, or Mitko and Raijko were not able to be located. With each letter I lifted a prayer that the seed I had planted would grow and someday bear fruit.

A few weeks after Assen had called our home, another call came from Charlie, the man who had asked me to call his wife. I was delighted to learn that Charlie had been released and was living with his family. We invited them to our home as we had invited Assen.

Charlie arrived with his lovely wife, and we sat around our table having a cup of tea. Charlie was a worrier, and I could see he was as serious as always, but they were together!

"Seeing you together is an answer to prayer," I reminded Charlie.

They told us of the tragic death of their daughter and how troubling it had been to both of them. "When a tragedy such as that makes you feel helpless, it's easy to blame one another," his wife observed. "I felt like blaming Charlie for not being there, for being in prison."

Charlie looked at me sheepishly and admitted, "You were right, Pastor, when you told me she must be struggling. I confessed to her that I was wrong not to see her."

What joy it was to hear them share out of the depths of their hearts. "Remember," I said, "it's by God's grace that broken relationships are healed."

Tzvete and I spoke to them of eternity and of the hope Christ gives of seeing our loved ones in heaven. Before they left we prayed for continued healing in their marriage and for Christ's presence in all our lives.

Our meetings with Assen and Charlie and his wife were affirming. Seeing changes in their lives was confirmation that my witness in prison had touched hearts. More than ever I was convinced that if my proclamation of the gospel was accompanied with *praxis*, living out my faith, God would bless my witness and change lives. But my meetings with friends such as Assen and Charlie wouldn't continue for long. Storm clouds were gathering.

Another Round of Interrogations

As I had surmised, it was only a matter of weeks before the telephone rang. "Vladimir Mladenov here," the unfamiliar voice informed me. "I'm the assistant to Mr. Tzvetkov at the Committee on Internal Religious Affairs. We would like to arrange a meeting with you at once. Please plan to be at my office tomorrow morning at nine o'clock. I believe you know our location?"

"Yes, I know it," I responded, my heart lurching with the thought of starting interrogations again. The party loyalists in these government bureaucracies loved to play mind games, and it was such a waste of time to answer their questions hour after hour.

The appointment with Mladenov went about as I expected. He tersely informed me that the Committee frowned upon my memorandums to the churches. "Our friends in the churches, and we have many of them, are reporting that your writings are stirring up trouble."

"My letters go only to those believers who contact me and ask for my assistance," I pointed out. "The reports coming to me are that the believers are offended by what the Committee is doing to deprive them of their right to choose their own pastor."

"It's not your place to advise the churches," Mladenov argued. "Pavel Ivanov has been lawfully elected by the Committee to carry out that responsibility. Tell your friends, these 'believers' as you call them, to send their inquiries to Ivanov. Do you hear?"

Objecting to Mladenov's assertion that Pavel Ivanov was lawfully elected by the churches, I repeated the same points I had made over and over again with Chavdar Penkov, Vladimir Nikolov, and at the trial.

When I questioned Ivanov's election, Mladenov challenged me, "Prove it."

Mladenov didn't have the polish of Tzvetkov, Penkov, or Nikolov. Sensing an opportunity, I took his challenge literally and decided to test him by attempting to leave. I stood and reached for my jacket. At worst, he would stop me.

"That can be done," I said, moving toward the door. "It's not my personal rights that I am seeking. I'm asking for the triumph of justice for the Christian churches in Bulgaria, a country that promises freedom of religion."

Mladenov was irate at this point. "Prove it or it may cost you. It may cost you your life!"

"I'll gladly stake my life on it for the sake of Christ's gospel. In fact, I'll stake my honor as a minister of the gospel. My calling is more dear to me than my life!"

Mladenov, in his frustration, was shouting obscenities by this time. I continued to move toward the door, even though he hadn't dismissed me. With the door of his office open I turned and quoted a famous line from Botev, one of Bulgaria's national heroes, "'Lies and slavery reign over this wasteland!'"[15]

A look of irony passed over Mladenov's features. "Botev said that!" he responded, as if I were quizzing him for a history exam.

"That's good!" I exclaimed. "Since you know Botev said it, maybe you'll think twice before charging me with insulting the government."

Continuing the conversation was futile, so I closed the door and walked away, conscious that Mladenov could have me summoned back in a moment. He made no attempt, and I continued to walk away.

The Declaration

Mladenov's challenge to "prove it" was all I needed. The Committee wasn't happy that I was traveling and preaching at the churches again. What I was considering would risk irritating them more.

When I reached home I immediately contacted Vasil Kozuharov, asking him what the leaders at First Church would think about sending a letter to all the churches asking for documentation of the fact that no election putting Ivanov into office had ever been held.

When Vasil told me he thought they would agree to the idea, I began working on the letter. Vasil and the other leaders would gladly have signed the letter, but knowing the Committee would hold me responsible, I put my signature at the bottom.

What I was considering, if the response to my letter was what I hoped, was composing a declaration. It would state that Christ was the

---

[15] Christo Botev was a poet and national revolutionary who lived from 1849 to 1876.

head of the church and that the conduct of the Committee and Pavel Ivanov was improper.

In two weeks the responses started to come in from the churches.

"The annual elections were not held as scheduled."

"Our church knew of no elections."

"We haven't participated in any elections having to do with Pavel Ivanov."

The response was the same in church after church. Only a handful of churches—those cooperating with Ivanov—failed to respond.

Immediately we began working on the declaration. As agreed, Vasil and Jordan asked the board members of First Church to read and sign the declaration. The word began to go out, notifying believers throughout the country that assistance would be needed to circulate a declaration.

The declaration began by stating that Christ was the only true head of the church and that God's Word declared that all things be done decently and in order. It went on to point out that the board members signing the declaration were the last to be duly elected at a regularly scheduled annual meeting of First Church. Five points followed:

1. That the church had not held an annual meeting that year and that this was a violation of the constitution.
2. That since no election had been allowed as required by the constitution, those appointed as board members by Pavel Ivanov were self-proclaimed and not elected in the proper congregational manner.
3. That Pavel Ivanov, without being elected pastor, had taken the position by force; therefore, those claiming he had been "lawfully elected" were, in fact, acting illegally.
4. That no budget for the church had been approved as is required annually, making the current expenditures directed by Ivanov and the Committee improper.
5. That the member churches of the Evangelical Union had not been allowed to conduct elections, making the claim of Pavel Ivanov to be the head of the Union false.

The declaration closed with these words: "We declare that those responsible for these unauthorized actions, by putting private interests before the interests of God's kingdom, are violating the clearly stated principles of God's Word, the historic practices of Christ's church, and statutes of the Evangelical Churches of Bulgaria."

The declaration went out immediately with a request that it be posted in or near each church. We were taking a risk in sending it, but our spiritual principles left us no choice.

The declaration was posted by the loyal members in plain view at the entrance of First Church early Sunday morning. Amazingly, it remained there throughout the service until Pavel Ivanov's wife saw it afterwards and tore it down.

Early Monday morning the call came from the Ministry of the Interior, summoning me to report at nine o'clock the next day. Stefan, Nebesna, Toshko, and Mimmi gathered with Tzvete and me early in the morning to pray for God's protection as I went. The prospects of returning to prison were very real. Stefan warned me, "If I were you, I would wear warm, comfortable clothes in case they take you away."

Failing to heed Stefan's advice, I wore my Sunday best, determined not to be in old clothes while surrounded by agents in nice suits. We knelt to pray, embraced, and said our farewells.

"God is with me," I said, offering a smile as I departed. "Please don't worry. God will be with you as well. We must be faithful."

Another Encounter with Nikolov

When I reached the offices of the Ministry of the Interior, Vladimir Mladenov brusquely informed me that I was to wait in the corridor. "We'll call for you when we are ready," he said.

Such treatment was typical of government agents; they used tactics such as this to establish an adversarial relationship. They hoped that by making me stand in the corridor I would feel at their mercy. I smiled to myself, remembering 1 John 4:4, "You, dear children, are from God and have overcome them, because the one who is in you is greater than the one who is in the world."

After fifteen minutes of being rooted in one spot, I heard the sound of plodding footsteps on the stairs. It was Vladimir Nikolov, the agent who had teamed with Chavdar Penkov to work me over on so many occasions. Penkov had dropped out of sight, and Nikolov had handled all of the interrogations immediately prior to the trial by himself. Nikolov had always been surly and impatient, and this day was no exception; he walked by without a word or a glance.

Another fifteen minutes passed before the door to the office opened and a young clerk asked, "What's your home telephone number? Are any members of your family there now?"

Giving the number, I informed her my wife was working. The door closed. Now my curiosity was piqued. If they thought Tzvete could be brought into the interrogations to apply pressure on me to stop my ministry, they were wrong.

Nikolov walked out of the office, down the stairs, and back again. Still he did not acknowledge my presence. An hour dragged by, then another fifteen minutes. Finally the door to the office opened and Nikolov stepped out, looking directly at me. "Follow me," he announced.

I descended the stairs behind Nikolov, then followed him down a long, dark corridor until he turned sharply, opened a door, and motioned for me to enter. I found myself in a standard, dusty, institutional office typical of government agents. Seated behind the metal desk was a man I had never met. He was dressed in a gray suit, not as distinguished as the suits most agents wore. A police officer was standing behind him, and the thought occurred to me that this did not bode well.

There was an icy silence in the small room. "Good morning," I offered, looking at the man seated behind the desk. His nod in response was barely perceptible. Nikolov ordered me to be seated. The only seat was on a very low sofa, situated in front of the desk. Because the sofa was so low, I was forced to look up at the man behind the desk. Standing, Nikolov and the police officer towered even higher.

The man in the gray suit began abruptly, "How long are we going to have to deal with this case of yours, Kulichev?" There was a look of contempt on the man's face even though I had never met him before. The outcome of our meeting was obviously prejudiced from the start.

As calmly as I could, I answered, "I'm only a humble pastor called to preach the gospel of Jesus Christ. I don't know why you spend your time dealing with me."

Looking at Nikolov and then at me, the man in the gray suit announced in an authoritative tone, "Perhaps you'll understand when you've spent some time at Nozharevo!" Looking at the file to make sure of my name, he pronounced, "Christo Kulichev, I hereby sentence you to three years' exile in the camp at Nozharevo! Notice of your deportation must be on this desk within three days." He slapped his palm upon the desk.

Nikolov looked at him with astonishment and leapt into action, "No! He's to go immediately! He's not to be given time to do anything but must be taken directly to Nozharevo." It was obvious that

Nikolov was in charge here. This compliant official had been given his lines to speak and still hadn't gotten them straight. He hardly knew my name, and knew less of my case.

Turning to Nikolov, I asked, "How can you do this without formal charges being filed? This is no trial! When will I be given a chance for appeal? Even a person sentenced to death is given the right of an appeal!"

"The order for you to be interned at Nozharevo has been signed personally by Stoyanov, the Minister of the Interior. You may file an appeal when you reach Nozharevo," Nikolov said adamantly. With that, Nikolov opened a file and extended a pen. "Here, you may see the signature! You're required to sign just below it, acknowledging that we've informed you as to where you will be going."

With Nikolov hovering over me, his hand firmly holding one side of the document, I signed before asking, "Where's my copy of the document?"

"Don't worry," Nikolov sneered. "We'll send it to you at Nozharevo."

Only What God Allows, Nothing More

Things began happening quickly. Nikolov informed me that my wife was waiting in the lobby downstairs with my clothes and that I would be sent immediately into exile. Tzvete and I were given no time to say farewell. She pressed the small suitcase she had hastily packed into my hand. Assuring her of my love, I reminded her, "Don't forget what I said this morning!" I was hustled out the door and into a police car.

Once the car had begun to move, Nikolov snatched the suitcase off my lap. "This will have to be searched," he said. "It will be returned when you arrive at Nozharevo."

I couldn't resist saying, "You treat me like I'm a common criminal, but you're the ones acting unlawfully."

Nikolov shot back, "Everything *is* lawful! You've been told not to preach, but you continue to do so!"

"And why has no one been able to show me the written order documenting that I've been forbidden to preach? I've been asking to see it for over a year, and I asked to see it at my trial. There is no such order!"

"I'm sure Tzvetkov has a copy of it," Nikolov insisted.

Nikolov couldn't walk away as the police car sped through the streets of Sofia, so I persisted. "One of our Bulgarian historians wrote about this dangerous precedent in describing our revolution. He wrote, 'Dishonest men avoid issuing written papers, so that it's easy to say later, "I didn't say that!"'"

Nikolov shrugged and turned away to peer out the window.

"You know that you carry on these practices all the time, making your plans secretly, in darkness, always fearful that the light of justice will expose you. The Bible tells us that Jesus said, 'I am the light of the world. Whoever follows me will never walk in darkness, but will have the light of life' (John 8:12)."

Still looking out the window, Nikolov repeated, "We do everything according to the laws."

"Then why have you taken my Bible and notebooks, refusing to return them even after I've served my sentence?"

"Because you would continue to disseminate those foolish ideas of yours that the church is free from government control," Nikolov argued. He was clearly losing patience, looking over the driver's shoulder in hopes we were getting close to the Central Prison of Sofia.

"Nikolov," I said earnestly. "You have me under your control, just as you want. It appears that you're trying to destroy my family and me. But I'm not afraid, because I know there is a far higher power than yours. It is God's power. My life and yours are in God's hands, and whatever you do to my family and me, it will be only what God allows and no more. Even if you take my life, God will use it for his glory. We must all answer to God someday, and you cannot change that. Knowing you will someday answer to God allows me to release my anger and forgive you for everything."

Sneering, Nikolov responded, "According to your gospel, right?"

"Yes, that's right. With God's help I live according to the gospel."

The Trip to Nozharevo

We arrived at Central Prison of Sofia, and I found myself packed into a large cell with over two dozen other inmates. My suit made me look more like one of the government agents than a prisoner. Familiar with the crowded cells of Central Prison, I moved to the corner and found a space to sit down.

Soon after I arrived, four more young men were pushed into the cell. They had been arrested, as many young people were, for being in Sofia without a residence permit. We squeezed together like sardines to accommodate them, only to have other prisoners join us periodically. Soon over forty men were pressed into the cell which was about two meters wide and three-and-a-half meters long.

Struggling to make our time in such confined quarters tolerable, prisoners began to share experiences. Most were being detained, as I was, for deportation to other prisons. Others were being shipped to their home districts after abortive efforts to find work and places to live in Sofia.

Difficult as it was, I knelt in the corner and prayed for God's protection in the trying times ahead. Rising, I introduced myself to another prisoner, mentioning that I was an evangelical pastor.

Another man three or four people away overheard the conversation and spoke up. "Kulichev? The evangelical pastor? I was listening to a radio broadcast and heard a foreign correspondent tell about your case!"

We were given bread to eat, and I stuffed some into the breast pocket of my suit in case I became hungry later.

The next morning, six of us were handcuffed together and taken in a police van to the train station. After a night slumped against other prisoners and hardly any sleep, we were a disheveled bunch. Predictably, our motley crew drew stares as we were escorted to a train bound for the northern reaches of Bulgaria and placed in a compartment with two guards posted outside. My good suit looked horrible, and I recalled Stefan's advice that I wear different clothes.

The prisoner handcuffed to me on my left was a Muslim doctor sentenced to eighteen years of imprisonment for refusing to drop his Turkish name for a Bulgarian name. Another prisoner had run away from Nozharevo, but he was more interested in sleep than in answering my questions about the camp. A third prisoner was a young fortune seeker who had come to Sofia without a permit. He was being returned to his Muslim village in the north. The remaining two men smelled strongly of alcohol and slumped lethargically in their seats. I suspected they were being sent away for detoxification, a practice common in Bulgaria.

Stopping and starting, the train proceeded to the station at Gorna Oryahovitza, then on to the city of Varna. It was impossible to find a comfortable position while handcuffed to four other men.

Taken from the train in the late afternoon, our guards turned us over to the local police, who marched us to a nearby prison. Finally the cuffs were taken off, allowing us to soothe our chafed wrists. As usual, pockets were emptied, and belts and shoelaces were taken before all six of us were pushed into one small cell. We looked at one another in astonishment, seeing only one small cot in the corner with no mattress. When we commented on this to a passing guard, he returned with five blankets, stuffing them through the bars.

We were given water to drink, but the prison kitchen had

apparently closed for the day. The bread I had stuffed into my pocket was so moist and crumpled as to be barely edible.

Only the Muslim doctor seemed interested in any kind of conversation. He too spoke of hearing my name on the radio and expressed an interest in studying various religions.

When he asked questions about clairvoyance and the occult, I told him of a man in one of our churches who had been involved in the occult. "When he read our Bible," I witnessed to my new acquaintance, "he discovered that there are pure and impure spirits. The impure spirits lead us into sin, but Jesus Christ came to purify us from our sins."

The Muslim's dark eyes danced with interest.

"When evil men crucified Christ, who is God's son, God raised him from the dead to defeat sin and evil. If we trust him, Christ frees us from the power of the evil spirits, and we need never fear them."

The Muslim and the others watched with clinical interest as I knelt to pray.

We spread three of the blankets on the floor to serve as the thinnest mattress I've ever slept upon. Pulling the other two blankets over us as best we could, we huddled on the floor for warmth. Somehow we made it through the night.

Back on the train, with new guards escorting us, we continued our journey. Stopping overnight in the city of Rouse, we again went through the familiar routine of being taken to the local prison, searched, our belts and shoelaces confiscated for the night, and put into a cell.

The cell in Rouse was excruciatingly small, only about four feet wide and ten feet long, and already had two occupants. There were eight of us now, and the cell had very poor ventilation. Again, no provisions had been made for food. The crumpled bread I'd eaten the night before now seemed enticing. This would be my third night sleeping, or attempting to sleep, in my good suit, which would never be the same.

I managed to kneel briefly for prayer in the crush of the small cell, and then we somehow managed to settle ourselves. The cell was so narrow that we had to place our feet up on the wall to stretch our legs. It was either that or curl into a fetal position, which meant my knees were poking another prisoner in the back.

The Back Roads of Bulgaria

Arising at seven the next morning, we were given tea and bread to assuage our hunger. Equally as pleasing was the fact that we would no longer be handcuffed. Loaded onto a bus without the cuffs, we could finally sit separately. Another runaway being returned to Nozharevo joined us.

The bus didn't take us to the train station but departed Rouse on a route east of the city. The Danube River, which serves as a border with Romania, was just a few miles north.

Every hour or so the bus would stop, usually to meet the local police and dispatch one of our prisoners to his home district or another detention camp. Eventually five of us remained, including the returnees, myself, and the two men who had smelled of alcohol.

The villages were now all Turkish. Arriving in the village of Toutrakan, we were joined by a sad-looking girl whose dark eyes betrayed Turkish descent. She had been sent to the wrong village in the belief that her husband was held under house arrest there. Upon arrival, she found the camp for exiles closed and was now making her way to Nozharevo with us.

Bouncing over the back roads of Bulgaria, I was interested to see what my new home would be like. This northern part of Bulgaria had a long history of conflict and ethnic cleansing. At various times it had been occupied by the Greeks, Slavs, Turks, Romanians, and Bulgarians. In 1940 the Treaty of Kraiova had ceded the region back to Bulgaria. When the Communists took over the government on September 9, 1944, Stalin had funded the building of several prisons and concentration camps in this region.

The bus jostled over the last rise in the road, and a sign announced we were approaching Nozharevo. It was now the fourth day since Nikolov had arrested me. It was good to finally be off of the bus, but the dilapidated buildings and broken tile roofs told me life was not easy for anyone in these parts.

Finally reunited with our baggage, which had been kept secure in a rear compartment of the bus, the five of us and the girl with the sad eyes stood outside of what appeared to be the municipal building of Nozharevo. A small crowd slowly gathered to stare, some in the crowd evidently exiles living here under house arrest, others obviously residents of Turkish descent.

A Human Garbage Dump

A tall, slender man with blue eyes approached. Dressed better than most, which required little effort in Nozharevo, he introduced himself.

"My name is Karov," he announced. "As steward of this detention camp, you will report to me every morning and every night.

Otherwise you're free to move about the village. In an hour I'll take you to your rooms in the hostel. Until then, your baggage will be guarded in my office inside the administration building. For the next hour you're free to walk in the village."

It wasn't the most hospitable of welcomes, but it was better than Central Prison, Kremikovtzi, and Sopot. Some of the exiles offered to give us a tour. Most of them were unwashed and unshaven. Some smelled of alcohol. Places such as Nozharevo were the government's answer to chemical dependency and the homeless. People who were drunk and disorderly or who failed to pay child support ended up here.

Our guides showed us where we were to sign in each morning and evening, just inside the administration building into which Karov had disappeared. They walked us to the small post office, the dilapidated cinema, and then to a general store where the exiles could buy food and a few other basic necessities. The police station was unimposing, and it was clear these exiles weren't detained by force, only by threat of capture with an additional sentence. Several exiles, I quickly learned, had spent time in various prisons and considered Nozharevo to be quite comfortable in comparison.

The exiles pointed out the home of the mayor of Nozharevo, prominent among the cluster of residences in the village. He and his wife were the only permanent Bulgarian residents in a village that was entirely Turkish.

When I asked about telephones, one of the guides pointed to the small post office. "It's a direct connection to Sofia, and they'll let you use it if you don't abuse the privilege," I was informed.

The guides had also pointed out the hostel on the edge of the village. When at the end of an hour Karov led us to our rooms, even the cracked and broken steps of the hostel, covered with refuse, couldn't prepare me for the disheveled state of my room on the second floor.

The small room was in terrible shape. The door to the room hung precariously on a single hinge. The single bulb dangling from the ceiling revealed that someone had begun to sweep the floor, only to leave a pile of dirt and refuse and the broken broom in one corner. Empty beer and vodka bottles were under the bed. A three-legged chair, padding protruding from its seat, balanced precariously in a corner.

The previous residents had obviously been heavy smokers. A thick film covered everything and clouded the single window, which could hardly be called transparent. One broken pane allowed both light and air to enter. The small sink smelled of urine; no doubt it had been used as a toilet by someone who didn't want to walk to the bathroom at the end of the hall.

Without a word Karov handed me a single towel and a blanket, motioning casually toward my room. The small bed had a thin mattress but no sheets or pillow. With my small suitcase in one hand and the towel and blanket in the other, I stood, rumpled suit and all, to contemplate my new home.

It was as if I'd been thrown into a human garbage dump—which was undoubtedly the way Vladimir Nikolov wanted me to feel. What Nikolov didn't understand was that I was the child of a King, clothed with the armor of God and the breastplate of righteousness. Under the sovereign rule of God, who would never leave me or forsake me, this prison could be turned into a palace also. The bed squeaked a strange welcome as I knelt to pray.

Calling Home

The next morning, as early as I dared, I made my way to the post office and asked permission to call home. Nebesna answered and immediately called Tzvete to the phone.

"Do you mean you've been traveling all these days?" Tzvete asked with astonishment. "How will we ever be able to visit you?" Assuring her our route had been slow and circuitous, I estimated that she could make the trip in a full day by taking the express train and a bus.

"What shall we bring?" Tzvete offered, always concerned for me. "Are you in a cell? What's it like?"

I dared not tell Tzvete of the filthy room, but I assured her I wasn't wallowing in a cell like the ones in Central Prison.

"Each one has a room to himself," I explained. I refused to call it a hostel as the other exiles did. "I'll call again next week when I'm settled to suggest an item or two you might bring."

Returning to my room, I began by fixing the broken door. There was no lock on the door, but a solid door firmly closed would at least give the impression that visitors should ask permission to enter. When the bottles were removed and the floor was swept and mopped, I began washing the unbroken panes of glass in the window.

That evening when I signed in, I asked Karov for materials to fix the window and patch a hole in the wall—the latter apparently caused by someone throwing a bottle.

"I'll have to inspect it, before I can give permission," Karov said rather officiously.

I smiled at the irony of Karov's "inspections" of our quarters, but when he came the next day, he took some interest in the fact that I was cleaning my room.

"Certainly we can give you a pane of glass and some putty to fix the window. The plaster to patch the wall will take a day." His eyes swept to the corner where my few clothes were neatly arranged. "If you keep this room clean so we can bring the boss to see it when he visits, I might even give you a strip of new carpet for the floor."

Obviously I was pleased with any help Karov might give, but it was clear that he was thinking of himself. The typical Communist method, whether in a commune or a detention camp, was to provide a well-maintained model for visitors to see. This was especially important when government inspectors arrived, but even they knew the models displayed an ideal while disguising a multitude of actual defects.

A Hostile, Religious Fanatic

On my first Saturday in Nozharevo, a few days after my arrival, Karov summoned all of the exiles to a general meeting in the cinema. Several government officials and their assistants were present, strutting on the platform as if this were a meeting of the parliament. When the disheveled crowd had gathered, the drunks slouching in their seats, a representative of the Ministry of the Interior and a prosecutor, both from Toutrakan, addressed us.

"You will present your passports to be stamped with your new residence," they informed us. "If anyone attempts to hide his passport or claims to have lost it, he will be punished."

I had heard of this practice at Kremikovtzi from some prisoners who had been sent there after being caught fleeing a detention camp. If a prisoner could avoid getting his passport stamped, it would be more difficult to prove that he had run away from his place of exile.

The man from the Ministry of the Interior concluded the speech, saying, "You're all here to be reformed! Remember that, and conduct yourselves accordingly. There's to be no drinking, no black marketing, and—oh yes—it's forbidden to preach any religion in Bulgarian prisons or detention camps."

The last comment, I was confident, had been added for my benefit.

After the meeting a Lieutenant colonel named Kostadinov, an important official with the Ministry of the Interior, stamped my passport. Examining it closely, he commented, "This entry says you worked for a church?"

"Yes," I answered. "The First Evangelical Church of Sofia."

"They're all the same," he said impudently. "How long are you here?"

When I told him I'd been sent here for three years, he replied, "Watch it, we'll meet again. Remember, there's to be no preaching! Good behavior may allow you to return home early, but it depends upon you."

"By the way," I hastened to interject, "the agent in Sofia promised to give me a copy of the written order for my detainment. I haven't received it yet. Do you have a copy?"

Rustling through the files on his desk, Kostadinov opened a file with my name upon it. Turning a page, he held out a copy and inquired, "This is your signature, isn't it?"

It was my signature. Nodding my assent, I noticed the order wasn't just one page as I had thought. Asking to see it, I examined it and quickly realized how deceptive Nikolov had been. The page I had signed was nothing more than an acknowledgment I had been informed I was to be detained at the village of Nozharevo. Nikolov, hovering over me, had been holding the paper as I signed it, and now I could see that he had concealed another page that was full of print!

Reading the page concealed from me, I saw my name, address, and passport number. Following those lines was written, ". . . a hostile, religious fanatic, a self-proclaimed pastor from the First Evangelical Church in Sofia, who, in spite of his conviction for performing illegal activities, continues to perform such and to level aspersions and libel at the Committee of Internal Religious Affairs."

Reading on, I saw, ". . . a person of antisocial acts . . . against the social order . . . and a threat to the security of the country."

Even though Nikolov had told me I could file an appeal when I got to Nozharevo, there before me were the words, ". . . subject to immediate execution and shall not be subject to appeal." Nikolov had concealed this information and boldly lied to me!

Where Was God in All of This?

Never, never would I have knowingly signed such a document! I had been naive not to look more closely before signing. The lack of my signature, however, would undoubtedly not have changed my exile.

"I was never allowed to see the second page of this document," I informed Kostadinov. "Can you arrange for me to have a copy of the full document?"

Although a copy of the written order was eventually given to me, there was no hope of justice in pursuing the matter. The document was worthless except as evidence of Vladimir Nikolov's treachery!

It would have been easy at such a low point to become obsessed with revenge. I could seek to expose and embarrass Vladimir Nikolov and get even with him, or I could trust God to use my situation for his glory. To focus my thoughts and energies in such a negative way, I had learned, would be counterproductive. As Romans 12:19-21 teaches, "Do not take revenge, my friends, but leave room for God's wrath, for it is written: 'It is mine to avenge; I will repay,' says the Lord. On the contrary: 'If your enemy is hungry, feed him; if he is thirsty, give him something to drink. In doing this, you will heap burning coals on his head.' Do not be overcome by evil, but overcome evil with good."

Convinced that God had a reason for my being at Nozharevo and that he would use my time there for some good purpose, I waited and watched. Where was God in all of this? Would God use me in some special way at Nozharevo? What purpose could this strange, unclean place play in God's plan for my life? Why was I here? Faith told me the questions would all be answered . . . eventually. But initially I had to wait. And trust.

CHAPTER ELEVEN
Nozharevo

There was given me a thorn in my flesh, a messenger of Satan,
to torment me. Three times I pleaded with the Lord to take it away
from me. But he said to me, "My grace is sufficient for you,
for my power is made perfect in weakness."
2 CORINTHIANS 12:7-9

Suffering out of the love of God is better than working miracles.
ST. JOHN OF THE CROSS

The days passed slowly. We signed in at Karov's office every morning and evening, but the hours in between provided few options for doing anything productive.

Karov had brought the strip of carpet he'd promised. Placing it alongside of the bed, I could at least put my bare feet on something clean when I rolled out of bed each morning.

When my room was as clean as I could make it, I called Tzvete to suggest a few things she could bring when she came. A Bible and food were highest on my list of priorities. The exiles at Nozharevo were responsible for their own food, and most of them bought it at the general store with money their families sent. Tzvete promised to try to come the following week.

Having made the call, I began walking through the village. Although the government had made it illegal to speak Turkish, wear the loose Turkish trousers, or have a Turkish name, evidence of Turkish culture was everywhere. The women wore dark head scarves unique to their culture, and the Turkish accent was undeniable.

When I walked into the general store to buy yogurt, I overheard a heated discussion in forbidden Turkish coming from the back of the store. A person could be fined for speaking the language, and seeing me, a young man stocking the shelves began scolding the men for speaking Turkish.

My purpose in walking the streets of Nozharevo was to see if I could find work. Exiles were allowed to work and keep the wages they earned, but Nozharevo was an impoverished village and offered no employment whatsoever.

"Not much here in the way of work," Karov informed me when I asked. "If you find something, they'll only give you a shot of vodka for half a day's work!" He advised me that there was a bus that went to the town of Silistra, 120 kilometers away, and that some exiles had found work there.

In my mind I was already resolving myself to the fact that I had no choice but to go to Silistra and try to find a job there when Karov spoke up.

"Do you have any skills?" he asked.

"I'm good at carpentry," I responded. "I was trained by my father and have worked at it most of my life."

Karov's face lit up. "You're just the man I'm looking for!" he exulted. "I've needed someone with skills such as yours, but most of the people sent here are drunks. Your carpentry skills can be used right here. There's no need for you to go to Silistra!"

Arising early the next morning, I made my way toward Karov's office to see what type of carpentry he wanted me to do. As I passed the bus stop, I saw half a dozen men waiting to go to Silistra.

"What kind of work do you do there?" I asked one of them.

"It's dirty and doesn't pay well," the man said. "The locals get the best jobs, leaving us to sweep the streets and collect garbage."

As I began repairing the broken furniture Karov asked me to attend to, I felt fortunate to have something more dignified and closer to my room.

Georgi and His Winter Coat

After a few days I observed that none of the exiles worked regularly. The pattern, I discerned, was to work a day or two, then buy some vodka or cheap wine and spend the next days in a drunken stupor. Drunks could been seen everywhere. Some slept it off in the hostel; others collapsed along the road outside of the village and could be seen wallowing in the grass.

The locals in Nozharevo exacerbated the problem. As Karov explained, they used the enticement of a drink to get several hours of work out of the exiles. Some of the locals drank with the exiles, keeping a keen eye out for an exile who might have recently received a package from home. Exiles addicted to alcohol would receive a package containing clothing or food and immediately barter it away for a fraction of its worth. Sitting outside of the general store, the drunks pawned whatever they had. All they wanted was enough for a good stiff drink that night. The locals loved it, since every deal was a good one from their perspective.

Georgi was one of the exiles I'd gotten to know my first day in camp. Georgi was from the Samakov region of Bulgaria and had been sentenced to a year in exile for his alcoholism.

Having not seen Georgi waiting at the bus stop for a few days, I knew he must have saved enough money to buy some vodka and stopped going to Silistra. Leaving Karov's office one evening, I saw Georgi walking toward the general store with a nice winter coat in hand.

"Where're you going, Georgi?" I inquired.

Georgi silently held out the winter coat and pointed to the general store where most of the bartering took place.

"You're going to sell your winter coat?" I asked incredulously. "You'll get hardly anything for it there, Georgi!"

"You wanna buy it?" Georgi held it out to me. He had a desperate look in his eye.

"It's a nice coat, Georgi," I commented. "But I would be taking advantage of you. Besides, I know you'll take whatever you get for the coat and use it to buy vodka. It wouldn't be right."

Turning, Georgi walked resolutely toward the crowd outside the general store. He was determined to go through with it.

"Stop, Georgi! Think about what you're doing," I said, trying to persuade him. "You worked hard to earn enough to buy that coat. Don't do something you'll regret later!"

The young men sitting outside of the general store were watching Georgi and me. Georgi answered me, waving at the sky, "The weather's warm now. I don't need a heavy coat like this!"

The young men laughed and knew they had their victim. One of them stood up and announced, "Let's see that coat. I may be interested!"

When I protested, asking the young men not to take advantage of Georgi, the group laughed again. "Look! Are we forcing him to sell his coat?" one of them insisted. "He brought it here of his own free will!"

The exchange was made in a minute, with Georgi accepting the first offer made. It gave him enough *leva* to buy a few drinks, and that was all that mattered.

Tzvete's Visit

As promised, Tzvete came to visit me at Nozharevo the week after I called home. Our son-in-law, Toshko, graciously arranged to get a car and drive Tzvete to the camp. It was a long, hard drive, and they drove up to the hostel late in the evening.

Having stopped in the village center to ask directions, they had already seen the filth and the drunken exiles. There were tears in Tzvete's eyes, as there had been when she first visited me at Kremikovtzi.

"What are they doing to you?" she exclaimed. "How can they send you to a depraved place such as this?"

"I'm counting the days," I told Tzvete and Toshko. "I must spend 1,095 days in this place, but I know God will be here with me each and every day."

The gifts Tzvete and Toshko brought were a blessing and made my little room more like a home. They brought an electric heater to take the chill away at night, a hot plate and a pot to cook with, but most precious of all their gifts was a Bible to read. Tzvete surprised me by bringing a Tzarigrad edition of the Bible, prized for being a more exact Bulgarian translation and having excellent study notes.

Introducing my wife and son-in-law to Karov, I asked if he knew of a place where they could stay overnight. The hostel with its carousing drunks, especially on weekends, would make sleep impossible even if we put a pallet on the floor. To my amazement Karov agreed to place two beds in his office and allow Tzvete and me to sleep there. Toshko agreed to sleep in the hostel to guard my things.

"Besides, it'll give me an idea of what exile is like in case I get arrested again," he said, smiling.

Unlike most days at Nozharevo, the two my wife spent with me passed in a flash. We walked through the village, and I introduced Tzvete and Toshko to the mayor and his wife, whom I had gotten to know. The mayor was probably one of the most educated men in the village and seemed to enjoy conversing with me. He and his wife spoke at length to Tzvete about the long journey from Sofia and wished them well on the return trip.

I also went out of my way to introduce my family to some of the other locals. Few wives visited their husbands at Nozharevo. The few women the locals saw visiting exiles were usually prostitutes, and fights were common as the men clamored for their attention.

I was eager for the people of Nozharevo to see that my family and I were different. My hope was to be able to witness to these people as I had done in other prisons. There was also the possibility that I could get more work in Nozharevo when I finished the jobs Karov had given me.

On Sunday morning, Tzvete, Toshko, and I had our own little worship service in my room at the hostel. We prayed, read Scripture, and sang a favorite hymn or two even though our singing raised howls of protest from drunk exiles trying to sleep off their hangovers.

As we shared our prayer concerns and items of praise, I told Tzvete and Toshko how deeply grateful I was for a godly family to support me. "God has given me a faithful and loving wife," I said with tears in my eyes, "who doesn't wait to be encouraged but encourages others. What a source of strength you are!

"And God has blessed us with obedient children, Nebesna and Stefan, who've committed their lives to Christ." Turning to Toshko, I said, "God has blessed us in leading you into Nebesna's life. You're a man who understands what it means to live for Christ in a world that is hostile to God. My prayer for Stefan is that he'll find a Christian wife and that they'll be as committed as you and Nebesna."[16]

Standing beside the car as Tzvete and Toshko prepared to return to Sofia, we embraced and prayed again. Tzvete had tears in her eyes again as she lamented, "It's so hard to go away and leave you in a place like this."

"Surely God has a reason for my being here," I assured her. "I'm not sure why God has placed me here, but it will become apparent as time passes. The rulers of this world have no power greater than God's power. Even though they throw me into the fiery furnace, the lion's den, or 'the valley of the shadow of death, I will fear no evil, for you are with me' (Psalm 23:4). Don't worry about me. Our God is faithful, and he will be here with me."

A New Beginning in Nozharevo

It was difficult to watch them drive away. My spirits dropped further when I returned to my room to discover I had been robbed of all of the food that Tzvete had brought. Someone had been watching and had taken advantage of my being distracted while saying farewell to Tzvete and Toshko.

The Bible had been untouched, for which I was grateful. Better to have spiritual food in these circumstances. Food for the body was more easily replaced than a Bible would have been in these Muslim villages.

The morning after Tzvete's departure, I awoke, said my prayers, and resolved to make a new beginning. Karov had me remodeling a building that he wanted to use as a kitchen, but that job would be finished in a few weeks.

---

[16] My prayers for Stefan were answered four years later when he married our wonderful daughter-in-law, Danielle, establishing a home that is centered upon Christ.

When Karov's work was completed, the winter had passed. As springtime approached I resolved to get better acquainted with the people of Nozharevo and to build a reputation among the locals as a hard worker. There was surely plenty I could do around the village that would provide income while also giving me opportunities for witnessing. Still, several hours each day were reserved for Bible study and prayer.

Striking out with new resolve, I began looking at Nozharevo from a new perspective. Rather than looking with disgust at the dilapidated buildings and shattered lives, I asked God to help me see the possibilities for witness and service. There were needs everywhere; surely I could do something to help, even if the residents had no money to pay me.

Going first to the home of the mayor, I noted that what had once been a garden was now overgrown with weeds. I knocked at the door. When the mayor answered, I presented my plan to him.

"You and your wife were so kind to befriend my family while they were visiting, and I would like to repay you in some small way."

The mayor eyed me suspiciously.

"If you would allow me to use your garden tools," I said, "I would be happy to pull the weeds and turn the soil in your garden. Do you have a hoe I could use?"

"Well . . . uh . . . yes, I suppose you could use our hoe," the mayor responded cautiously. He seemed to be thinking there had to be a catch, wondering what I might demand in return.

"Don't worry," I assured him. "I enjoy doing this kind of work, and there'll be no charge. It's just a small way of showing my appreciation."

As I began working the garden, I occasionally saw the curtains in the mayor's kitchen window move ever so slightly, making me aware that I was being watched. The exiles in Nozharevo weren't known to offer free labor.

When the weeds were removed, the soil cultivated, and the seed beds prepared, I put the hoe back on the mayor's back porch and walked toward the center of the village. With the money Tzvete had brought, I went to the general store and bought some seeds. Early the next morning I was back in the garden, planting beans, cucumbers, onions, tomatoes, and eggplant. I was finished before the heat of the day.

When the rows were clearly labeled, I returned to the mayor's back door and asked his wife for a bucket of water to water the seed beds. Thanking her, I promised, "I'll be back from time to time to tend the garden. You should have some produce in just a few weeks."

The garden quickly became a project the Lord and I worked on together. I planted and weeded the garden, and God watered it and miraculously gave the increase. While the plants were growing, I found other projects around the village: fixing a broken door, repairing shutters, and painting a faded and peeling fence. The whole village could have used at least a coat of paint, so there was always something that needed to be done. I asked for no compensation, and word of my skills soon spread throughout the village.

Content Whatever the Circumstance

As I had hoped, villagers began asking if I would make a repair or help with some improvement to their properties. When asked what I charged, my response was always the same, "Please pay what you feel my work is worth." Some paid with money, others with food from their cupboards, and others said, "Come and take whatever you would like from our garden. Help yourself as often as you'd like."

Karov approached one day and asked, "Would you be interested in making some repairs to the municipal building? We have materials, but good labor is hard to get in these parts. You've made such a good name for yourself, and I've been so pleased with the construction work you did for me previously, that I would even be glad to pay you for it." Before I could accept, he hastened to sweeten his offer: "If the pay isn't enough, there are other ways I can make your life easier. There's an abandoned storage shed behind the municipal building you can use as an apartment if you want to fix it up and live there."

It was an offer I couldn't resist. The hostel was an impossible place to live, with exiles stealing from one another and the drunks disrupting life. It wasn't uncommon to awaken in the middle of the night to the sounds of fighting and cursing. On more than one occasion my door had burst open, interrupting my sleep, as an inebriated figure stumbled into my room, thinking it was his. If I could arrange to make the storage shed my own little apartment and secure a lock, it would be a great improvement.

A few days later, I began working on the municipal building as Karov had requested. It felt good to be productive. The lime needed for making cement was stored some 200 meters from the construction sight and had to be brought in by wheelbarrow. It was heavy, and the sweat trickled down my back as I moved wheelbarrow after wheelbarrow to the cement mixer. The locals in front of the general store watched.

On one trip, as I paused halfway to rest, one of the local men spoke up. "You're not like the other exiles," he observed. "You accomplish more in an hour than most do in a day. You don't smoke or get drunk. What's a man like you doing here?"

It was the opportunity I'd been waiting for, an opportunity to share my faith and tell the story of being arrested for preaching the gospel of Jesus Christ. The Turks of Nozharevo weren't receptive to Christianity, but they fully understood religious persecution. My story of persecution, combined with my hard work and honesty, gave me credibility and many subsequent opportunities to speak of my faith in Christ.

The conversation finished, I trudged on, pushing the wheelbarrow filled with lime, thinking, *Thank you for sending me here, Vladimir Nikolov, to share my faith in Christ with this man.* Smiling to myself, I mused, *You sent me here to make me miserable, Nikolov, but what you meant for evil, God intended for good. I'm learning to "be content whatever the circumstance. . . . whether well fed or hungry, whether living in plenty or want. I can do everything through him who gives me strength" (Philippians 4:11-13). My calling is to share the gospel of Christ, and I can do that wherever I go, not just from a pulpit in Sofia!*

A Wholesome Rhythm

As promised, Karov allowed me to clean out the abandoned storage shed and convert it into a private room. Its thick masonry walls were covered with wood siding inside, providing excellent insulation for the winter months. The one-room shed was wired for electricity, with utility costs paid by the municipal budget. A grove of mulberry trees surrounded my new quarters, providing fruit for my cereal each morning that autumn, and the lilac bushes outside my door wafted a wonderful fragrance over my new home. The latter was a blessed antidote to the smell of a nearby pig farm that pervaded the area.

Life was attaining a rhythm I found both wholesome and pleasing. Mornings were spent in prayer and extended Bible study. I could accomplish more work in a single afternoon than other exiles could in an entire day, and so after an early lunch I went to work, doing several hours of manual labor.

The work kept me physically fit, and I slept well in my new room. The mayor shared produce with me from his garden, as did other locals in payment for my work, and I was eating as well as if I were at home in Sofia. I remembered the words from Deuteronomy 6:11, where God promised the people of Israel that they would eat, drink, and be satisfied from vineyards they had not planted and wells they had not dug.

Free to sing familiar hymns and Christian songs in my little apartment without disturbing anyone, I found myself humming and singing more and more throughout the day. One song that particularly expressed my feelings was:

> Every day and every hour,
>
> God on us his help will shower,
>
> There is joy, joy, joy within my heart.

As weeks and months passed, I began to realize why God had allowed me to come to Nozharevo. For years I had been traveling, working to support my family, leading the ministry at First Church, as well as leading the Evangelical Union. The clandestine nature of the ministry had taken its toll. The emotional pressure of the trial and eight months of imprisonment had also been difficult. The physical and spiritual renewal I was finding at Nozharevo was making up for it all.

It was a practical discovery that led me to understand that God was giving me this time of exile to rest and be restored spiritually. The realization came not like some brilliant revelation or vision but as I began to feel a return of the emotional resilience and spiritual strength I had expended in the previous year.

Only as I recovered my spiritual bearings did I realize how perilous my condition had been. It would have been dangerous to have thrown myself back into ministry after my time in prison without this time of refreshment and renewal. God, who often works in mysterious ways, was meeting my need through the exile—improbable as that may have seemed.

That, I realized, was how God worked in my life most often. There had been times when I dreamed dreams and even felt that I had been given a vision. My theology, however, required that everything be validated by the teaching of God's Word before I went racing out to proclaim, "God has spoken to me!" It was my conviction that if God did speak to someone in a dream or vision, the message was intended for that person alone and was not to be given as some grand pronouncement to others.

I have seen churches divided by opinions about dreams and private revelations, and I'm convinced that Satan sometimes uses them to confuse God's people. One of the truths reaffirmed during my study and prayer in exile was that everything we preach and teach, always, must be based upon the Word of God. It's the only true and trustworthy guide for our faith and life. As Paul warned, even if an angel descends from the sky and preaches something, if it's different from the gospel proclaimed by Christ and the apostles, we must not listen to it (Galatians 1:8-9).

The "Revival Process"

Tzvete returned to visit every two or three months. Whenever possible, she saved her days off at the clinic to be able to spend several days at a time with me. On one occasion I met her bus in Silistra, where we went directly to the bank to withdraw funds she had transferred there. It wasn't safe for her to be carrying money while traveling such a long distance alone.

Upon leaving the bank, we returned to the bus station for the trip to Nozharevo. While waiting for the bus there, I met a young man whose face was familiar. Recalling that I had taught him how to make shutters for a home that we had built several years before in the Sofia area, I approached and reintroduced myself. "Your name is Ahmed, isn't it?" I asked.

"It *was* Ahmed," he replied with a pained look on his face. "Because of laws against Turkish names, I now give my name as Anton."

This attempt at changing Turkish names and customs to a Bulgarian equivalent was called the "Revival Process" in government propaganda.

In theory the Revival Process was a program that was supposed to unify our country. In practice it was a dismal failure, arousing deep resentment among minority ethnic groups whose languages and cultures were being blatantly assaulted. Ironically, it tapped a vein of anger among the Turks and produced an even deeper national consciousness among the Turkish population.

My parents had experienced the same kind of prejudice at the hands of the Greeks many years ago. When the Greeks tried to forcibly "Macedonianize" the Bulgarians living in the area around Gorno Brodi, many of them, including my parents, had simply left. These human programs designed to bring social change can't change people's minds or touch their hearts. Only God can transform lives and make us love our neighbors as ourselves.

Tzvete brought news of the family, including pictures of little Mimmi, our granddaughter, and news from the churches as well. The people at First Church continued to maintain Bible studies and to fellowship in their homes even though they were forbidden by law.

The youth ministry, Tzvete reported, was continuing under the leadership of young people such as Nick Athanasov and Emanuel Tinev, with guidance and counsel from my brother Dimitar. Tzvete's brother, Marin, was preaching in various churches that refused to be controlled by Pavel Ivanov. The Lord had timed it so he could pick up where I had left off.

The only time Pavel Ivanov was seen was on Sunday mornings. With his usual wit, Vasil Kozuharov had said, "He's invisible six days of the week and incomprehensible on the seventh!" Some protested his presence by bowing in silent prayer as he preached, others made their exit after the reading of the Scripture. Even though Ivanov's presence in the pulpit was resented, the people realized Sunday worship was vital and provided a valuable point of contact with other Christians.

During Tzvete's stay, we enjoyed the fruit and vegetables given to us by the locals. She also brought a lock to provide security for my room and a Bible that had been requested by one of the other exiles. We had everything in abundance: watermelon, muskmelon, stewed tomatoes, and delicious sweet corn. Tzvete helped me can beans and tomatoes for the winter.

Tzvete also had the opportunity to attend one of the periodic lectures conducted in the cinema by the Ministry of the Interior. The lectures against drinking alcohol were so futile that the words passed right by the drunken exiles slouched in their seats. Once again we saw the futility of human efforts to change the outer person without touching the heart.

My heart went out to the exiles who were addicted to alcohol. Like the possessed man from Gadara (Matthew 8:28), they were groveling under the power of the evil one. The lectures were only a pretense at educating alcoholics about the physical and emotional damage that addiction caused. No educational or social program could free a person from such an evil influence. Our sinful human nature is like a cracked bell. No cosmetic covering will restore the beautiful sound the bell was designed to produce. It's restored only when it is cast anew. Hearts can be made new—indeed we can be made new creatures—but only through Jesus Christ, our Lord and Savior (2 Corinthians 5:17).

Dealing with Complications

The wonderful days with Tzvete were over all too soon. She packed for her return to Sofia, our church, and her work at the clinic. I was able to send with her a large sack containing melons and vegetables given to us from the gardens in Nozharevo. Carrying her luggage and the sack of vegetables, I walked Tzvete to the bus and with a heavy heart kissed her good-bye.

As Tzvete boarded the bus for Toutrakan, Rouse, and Sofia, my final words were, "Take my love and best wishes to Nebesna, Toshko, Mimmi, and Stefan. Give my greetings in the Lord to the brothers and sisters at the church. Tell them I'm discovering that God has a plan for my life, even in the desolation of Nozharevo. Tell them I'm praying they will be faithful. I love you!"

It had been wonderful to have Tzvete pray with me and join me in my Bible studies. When she was gone, I returned to my routine of solitude and study each morning and physical exercise and labor each afternoon.

Life at Nozharevo was not without its complications, however. When the national elections approached in the fall, it was announced that all exiles were required to vote. Of course, only the names of candidates with the Communist party were allowed on the ballot, which made the whole thing a sham. My father had taught our family that Christians shouldn't vote in such elections. In refusing to vote, we saw an opportunity to tell others that our allegiance was to God's kingdom, not to an atheistic human government.

After Karov had made the announcement about the elections, I approached him and asked if we could talk. I told Karov I objected to voting for leaders who were utterly opposed to all that I stood for. "I prefer not to elect my executioners," I protested. Karov made no objection when I asked, "Could you please ask the mayor to leave my name off the voting list?

When the voting list was posted outside of Karov's office a few days later, my name wasn't on it.

During the winter months, Karov asked me to help him and his son-in-law Marin clean the supply room next to Karov's office. We were talking as we worked when Marin turned to Karov and asked, "Did you tell Old Man Christo what the mayor is requesting?"

Karov nervously busied himself with a stack of blankets he was moving but didn't reply. "What is the mayor asking?" I asked.

It was obvious Karov was nervous. "He asked me to offer you a job this spring. He wants you to erase the Turkish names from the tombstones in the cemetery." Erasing the Turkish names from tombstones was a part of the infamous Communist Revival Process.

"He should know better," I responded. "Everyone here knows I will not promote the prejudices of the government. Anyone with common sense knows this changing of names doesn't make a bit of difference in how people feel. I'll never consent to do it!"

Karov made no protest. "That's what I keep telling him," he shrugged. "But he doesn't seem to understand."

Review for Parole

As the months passed, and warm weather came, I resumed my work as a handyman. Tzvete came to visit from time to time, familiar with the bus routes by now and accustomed to the long journey to Nozharevo. When she couldn't come, the telephone at the post office made it possible to keep in regular contact with my family.

As another autumn approached, I was nearing the halfway point in my three-year sentence. When I went to sign in one evening, a cluster of exiles was looking at a notice on the board outside Karov's office. It stated that Lieutenant Colonel Kostadinov was scheduled to make a follow-up visit, and my name was posted as one of the exiles asked to meet with him to review my record.

Exiles were always excited when asked to meet with the officials, hopeful that they might be sent home. Rumors were flying that with good behavior, exiles were sent home after a year. I had been there for a year and a half. When the other exiles saw my name listed, one named Petko exclaimed, "If they don't release *you* for good behavior, then who?"

I, however, wasn't optimistic.

When the date came, I sat down across the desk from Kostadinov. Shuffling through my file, he finally looked up and spoke. "You've made quite a name for yourself here in Nozharevo," he began. "I've learned this not only from your file but also from talking with Karov and some of the other exiles. Unlike some others, the report in your file is proving to be true, not just words to fill in the required space."

Kostadinov's words were affirming. Difficult as it was to give witness in a remote Muslim village, God had helped me live an exemplary life. My guide was Philippians 2:14-16, which says, "Do everything without complaining or arguing, so that you may become blameless and pure, children of God without fault in a crooked and depraved generation, in which you shine like stars in the universe as you hold out the word of life." It was good to know that it was being noticed.

"However," Kostadinov said reticently, his gaze returning to my file, "these decisions about parole are made in Sofia. Unfortunately, those people aren't here to talk with the villagers as I've done. I'll send them my report, but all we can do is wait for their decision." As his words sunk in, Kostadinov watched me to gauge my response.

I thanked Kostadinov for his kind words about my conduct, something extremely unusual for a government agent, and our brief meeting concluded. Thinking that perhaps some word of my release might come in response to Kostadinov's report, I waited hopefully. Going about my daily routine, days and then weeks passed, but still there was no word. Hope dwindled, and I found myself thinking about the possibility of release less and less. Then something happened that raised a far greater concern.

The Black Shade Descends

The cold weather was upon us. Having agreed to help a widow in the village, I was chopping firewood one day, stacking it near the back door of the house. I paused to rest when suddenly and without notice there was a pain in my right eye. With the pain came a sudden darkness. It was as if someone had pulled a window blind down in front of the eye. The black shade descended, receded, and then descended again.

Taking out my handkerchief, I wiped my eye, thinking perhaps something had gotten into it. I was hoping the darkness would go away, but it did not. The pain was not excruciating, but obviously something was not right. As I rubbed the eye, it was as if the blackness began to crystallize. A little light filtered through the blackness, giving the effect of a net being thrown over the eye. This was no improvement, since I still couldn't see out of the eye. Evidently the condition wasn't going to pass.

Going directly to Karov's office, I described what had happened and asked for medical attention. "I'll make a few calls in the morning to see if we can get someone in Toutrakan to take a look," he answered nonchalantly.

After a restless night of wondering what was happening to my precious eyesight, I loitered outside of Karov's office while he made the calls as promised. Emerging with an address and telephone number on a piece of paper, he informed me I should go to the emergency entrance of the hospital in Toutrakan.

It was a two-hour bus ride to Toutrakan, where I asked a taxi driver to take me to the hospital. After an extended wait, a nurse called me to follow her to an examination room where I waited again.

Finally, in the middle of the afternoon, an older physician came into the room, heard the account of what had happened, and proceeded to examine my eyes. While the physician seemed interested in my case and spent several minutes questioning me, in the end he concluded, "Strange things happen to our eyes as we get older. This darkening of the eye is nothing more than a natural result of aging. Be thankful you still have the sight in your left eye. Don't worry, you'll get used to it in a week or so."

The physician's explanation didn't seem plausible, but I had no choice but to return to Nozharevo. Arriving after dark, I reported to Karov's office, signed in, and returned to my apartment. The uncertainty about my parole was dwarfed now by my concern for my eyesight. As I knelt for prayer that night, I struggled to remain open to the possibility that God could use even this grave health concern in his plans for my life and ministry.

Surprising Reprieve

When I arose the next morning, I headed straight for Karov's office. Explaining the unsatisfactory examination in Toutrakan, I asked Karov to call the authorities in Sofia. "Surely there's some possibility for an emergency medical leave," I pleaded.

Karov's response was surprisingly low-key. "Why should I have to contact Sofia?" he asked. His tone of voice was smug, as if he were taking minor offense at my assumption that he didn't have the authority to deal with such a matter himself. "It's within my jurisdiction to release exiles for up to ten days for health or family concerns. Of course, this depends upon their good behavior, but why wouldn't you qualify?"

"Is that possible?" I asked incredulously. "Could I return to Sofia to receive medical treatment there?"

"Of course," Karov replied. He seemed pleased to see my gratitude for this surprising reprieve.

"When may I leave?" I questioned Karov further, hardly able to believe his words were true.

"As soon as the next bus departs," he smiled, waving toward the bus stop down the street from the general store. I had underestimated Karov's authority! Resisting the temptation to ask why he hadn't told me of this option yesterday, I thanked Karov profusely, returned to my apartment, and began packing for the trip.

My heart leapt with joy as I packed my clothing for the trip. Taking my belongings to Karov's office, I asked, "Would you keep these in the storage area until I return?"

As Karov took my things into the storage room, where I hoped they would be secure, I continued, "There's some food in my apartment you may have if you like. The door's unlocked. I left it on the table for you. Thanks, again."

On the way to the bus stop, I passed the mayor's home. "Are you leaving Nozharevo?" he asked when he saw my luggage.

"Just a ten-day medical leave," I responded. I didn't have time to go into all the details. "I'm on my way to the post office to use the telephone to call my family."

Tzvete was ecstatic to learn I was coming home.

"It's only for ten days," I cautioned. "It's a medical leave."

There was a tone of concern in her voice as she began asking questions I didn't have time to answer.

"It's a problem I'm having with one of my eyes," I offered, trying to sound as casual as possible. "Don't worry. We'll talk about it when I get in late tonight."

The arduous trip to Sofia required bus connections in Glavinitza, Toutrakan, and Rouse. Finally, I boarded a train in Rouse that took me to Sofia. The journey gave me a renewed appreciation for Tzvete and her trips to visit me. It was eleven o'clock that night when I arrived at the bus terminal in Sofia and hurried to call for Stefan to pick me up.

Nabesna, Toshko, and Mimmi were waiting with Tzvete when we arrived home. The embraces and kisses were joyful, but I could sense the subdued concern for my health. We prayed, thanking God for the safe journey and the joy of being together again, and then I tried to answer their many questions.

"I've put you on the schedule to see one of the physicians at the clinic," Tzvete informed me.

The Medical Academy

We arose early the next morning, and I went with Tzvete to her clinic to keep the appointment. The news wasn't good. After a brief examination the physician calmly suggested my case was something that should be handled by the Medical Academy at the University. "We're a regional clinic," he explained. "They handle more difficult cases there. I can assure you, however, that this is not something that's a part of the normal aging process!"

Going directly to the Medical Academy, I was fortunate to see one of the eye specialists who had already been contacted by the regional clinic. After the customary wait, the ophthalmologist, Dr.

Tannev, looked into my right eye for only a few seconds before stepping back and asking, "How long have you had this condition?"

I told him the black shade had descended five days ago.

Dr. Tannev became flushed and asked, "Why didn't you come to us sooner?"

I told him I was being held in exile for my religious beliefs, and he explained that my right eye had apparently experienced hemorrhaging. "This is a very serious condition. Even with the new laser treatments, it's unlikely we can do anything to improve your sight in the damaged eye. The greatest concern now is that when one eye is effected, there's the probability the other eye may experience a similar episode. We need to observe you for several days and begin preventive treatment for your left eye immediately."

When I told Dr. Tannev that I had been given only ten days' leave, his impatient tone returned. He was the chief of the department and not accustomed to having orders questioned. "This will take at least a month of observation. I'll give you a letter. It will explain how serious this condition is and excuse your absence. Plan to check into the hospital tomorrow."

During the next two days in the hospital, I was given thorough exams. All my life God had blessed me with good health. I'd seldom taken medications, and my eyes had been unusually good. Many people my age had worn glasses for years, at least for reading, but I'd never needed them.

The tests concluded, Dr. Tannev told me that an artery in my right eye's retina had hemorrhaged. "We're not sure what caused the hemorrhaging," he said, turning a page in the medical chart. "Your blood pressure and other vital signs seem to be normal. We can't promise to improve your sight, but we would like to try using a new laser treatment. We'll need you to stay for two or three days for the treatment and then return once a week for observation." He handed me the letter excusing me from returning to Nozharevo and a written order scheduling my return for treatment.

Contending with Nikolov Again

Vladimir Nikolov wasn't pleased with my presence in Sofia. Within hours of taking the physician's letter to the Ministry of the Interior, the telephone at our home rang. It was Nikolov. "On what grounds are you remaining in Sofia rather than returning to Nozharevo?" he demanded.

"It's spelled out in the letter written by the physician at the Medical Academy," I explained calmly. "I took the letter to the Ministry of the Interior this morning."

"Be at my office at the Ministry of the Interior tomorrow at 9 A.M.," Nikolov demanded. "I'll be looking into this."

The meeting that ensued was the most contentious one I'd ever had with Vladimir Nikolov. Stomping to remove the snow from my shoes, I climbed the steps to his second-floor office.

No sooner had I entered than Nikolov assaulted me verbally. "What makes you think that you have the right to be living in your home here in Sofia? You're supposed to be in Nazharevo as ordered!"

These interrogations were always unpleasant and usually left me feeling upset and disgusted with the way the agents spoke and acted. By God's grace I found that God gave me an unusual sense of peace and strength. Convinced that whatever they did to me, God would use it for his glory, I had slept well the night before. That morning I had prayed that this would be an opportunity to show Nikolov what a difference faith in Christ made in my life. I calmly answered, "You may read Dr. Tannev's letter for yourself. I delivered it to the offices of the Ministry of the Interior, just as I'm required to do."

"Who is this Dr. Tannev?" Nikolov demanded. "We'll see what he has to say after I've talked with him! I can see nothing wrong with your eyes. Besides, you could've gone to the clinic at Varna, which is much closer to Nozharevo!"

Remaining composed, I countered, "The agent at Nozharevo contacted the police there, and they approved a ten-day leave to come to Sofia. Dr. Tannev has scheduled me for treatments that will take at least a month. You'll find out when you speak to him."

"This is ridiculous," Nikolov interrupted me. "I know your type. You've deceived and manipulated these people to get their approval. You're back here to interfere in the church again!"

Nikolov's attack upon my integrity, after dealing dishonestly with me the last time, made it impossible to resist countering, "You've no right to talk about dishonesty and manipulation after using your back-handed methods to get me to sign those slanderous accusations against me! I've always spoken and acted truthfully, and you know it. You also know that I'm rightfully appointed as pastor of First Church and yet you wrote that I am 'self-proclaimed' and 'a troublemaker.' Then you deliberately hid the whole page of accusations from me when I signed what I thought was an order transferring me to Nozharevo. Don't speak to me of deceit and manipulation!"

"The Chief of the Ministry of the Interior signed that document, validating that it's true!" Nikolov shouted.

"That's even worse," I insisted. "Now you've implicated your superiors in your dishonesty! Neither you nor anyone else can document that I've 'interfered in the life of the church.'"

"We know you've spoken against the Committee on Internal Religious Affairs from the pulpit!" Nikolov insisted, his face red with anger.

"That's a foolish charge, and I have witnesses to prove it!" I rejoined. "I preach the gospel of Jesus Christ. The people are hungry to hear God's Word preached. That's why they have supported me and resent the political influence of Pavel Ivanov! The church members will tell you it's Ivanov and the Committee who are interfering!"

Truth Is Truth

Nikolov sneered at my mention of the gospel of Christ and freedom of worship. "It's that kind of talk that sent you to prison!"

Regaining my composure, I answered, "You'll recall that the reason I didn't accept your offer of freedom was because you insisted I could no longer preach or witness to my faith in Christ. It is a privilege to suffer for Christ and his kingdom. I'll continue to share my faith in Jesus Christ—in prison or out!"

"You're trying to make yourself a martyr!" Nikolov scoffed.

I laughed. "You're making me look like a martyr! I'm just an ordinary minister, preaching the gospel of Christ, and you've made me known to people in other countries. If you insist on putting a halo upon my head, I'll try to wear it with dignity!"

"Don't tell me," Nikolov stammered, "that you and your so-called 'believer' friends haven't been campaigning to win sympathy in foreign circles! It's not easy to get your name on a station like the BBC. That's no ordinary station—"

"You obviously don't understand the power of a free press. Not just the BBC but others have come asking why Christians in Bulgaria aren't free to preach Christ without government interference. Don't give our little churches more credit than they deserve. If you hadn't sent me to prison, neither the BBC nor anyone else would be interested in me. Thank you for making me a celebrity!" I smiled as I said it.

Nikolov was astounded. As I countered him point by point, I was amazed at the freedom with which I spoke. Usually I thought carefully before speaking, trying to calculate how my words might be interpreted. I took care not to implicate others, and I was careful to maintain control. On this occasion, however, I threw caution to the wind and spoke directly from the heart. Truth is truth, and I was more determined than ever to speak it no matter what the consequences.

Writing down the name of my physician, Nikolov dismissed me, warning, "You'll be hearing from me; you can be sure of that."

We Have Only Done Our Duty

My return to Sofia had come just prior to Christmas. The next few days passed quickly as we celebrated the coming of Christ into our world. To my surprise, however, days and then weeks passed without any word from Nikolov.

The freedom I had felt in speaking with Nikolov translated to the rest of my life as well. Avenues of ministry opened up to me in surprising ways.

The impending return to the hospital for treatment didn't allow me to travel. In the next few days, however, evangelical pastors from across the country called or came to pray.

I quickly noticed that the tentativeness the pastors had once felt was gone now. Mikhail Gorbachev's book *Perestroika* had just been published, outlining many policies of reform and raising everyone's hopes. The pastors wanted to discuss how they could support the cause that First Church and I had come to represent. I sensed a new boldness and a depth of commitment that had been absent for decades.

There were also literally hundreds of letters to answer. They came from Christians all over the world, saying such things as "Don't lose courage!" and "You are not alone!" Believers in Bulgaria wrote to say "We're with you!" and "Keep heart, we are praying for you!" Christians from abroad, much to my amazement, had even heard of my medical problem and wrote to encourage us, promising to pray. Several offered, "Please tell us what kind of medicines you need, and we'll send them."

It was humbling to know how many people were praying for me. There was strength in knowing that we were part of God's worldwide family and an inner satisfaction in knowing that we had been faithful.

It had never been my goal to become anyone's focus of attention. All I had ever aspired to was faithfulness in my commitment to Christ and the gospel. My aspiration was not to gain fame and fortune but to live a consistently holy life in the Lord's service. When friends and acquaintances spoke well of me, I reminded them that Satan would tempt us to feel pride and superiority. There could be none of that in Christ's church, for it is by his strength and for his glory that we serve. As Christ himself taught in Luke 17:10, "So you also, when you have done everything you were told to do, should say, 'We are unworthy servants; we have only done our duty.'"

Among my visitors those next few days was Ingulf Diesen, a Christian leader with the Evangelical Covenant Church in Norway, who had written letters and called my family while I was in prison. Shortly after my return from Nozharevo, Mr. Diesen called to say that Christians in Norway had been praying for my release and were celebrating the answer to their prayers.

Ingulf Diesen had applied to the Bulgarian embassy for permission to see me while in Sofia on business and visited our home a few days after my heated discussion with Nikolov. It was a delight to finally have contact with a Christian from the free world after all of the years of enforced isolation. Our spirits were invigorated as my family and I listened to Ingulf's account of the ministries of the Evangelical Free and Covenant churches in Scandinavia.

Lessons Learned in Exile

As we savored every minute of fellowship with Ingulf, I realized that just as I had been in exile from my family and friends, so our evangelical churches had been in exile, isolated from the global body of Christ. Like Israel in the time of Jeremiah and Daniel, our exile purified our faith. While Christians in Bulgaria were fewer in number after the horrible Pastors' Trial of 1949 and the subsequent years of persecution, I knew those who held true were more bold in their witness. As I look back upon our experience as Christians under Communist rule, my memories are not so much of the suffering, but of God's faithfulness to us and of our striving to remain faithful to him.

As we conversed, Ingulf asked, "What lessons did God teach you during your time in prison?"

I responded, "There are many lessons we may learn from suffering. Perhaps first among them is that the things hardest learned are longest remembered. God can only teach so much through fellowship and instruction. The most significant lessons must be learned through actual experience, from falling down and getting up again, from the challenges in life."

As we shared, I realized how much God had been working in my life during my years in prison. It was one thing to say "I believe," but it was something far different to test those beliefs in the crucible of life-and-death circumstances. I opened my Bible and showed Ingulf and my family where I had underlined passages such as David's song of praise in 2 Samuel 22:2:

> The Lord is my rock, my fortress and my deliverer; my
> God is my rock, in whom I take my refuge, my shield
> and the horn of my salvation. He is my stronghold, my
> refuge and my savior—from violent men you save me.

Having committed those words to heart, I recited them again and
again when preparing for the grueling interrogations.

What had begun as an evening of conversation and Christian fellowship ended in reverent gratitude and worship of our redeeming
God. Ingulf Diesen prayed with us before departing. We thanked God
for our fellowship and thanked God for all he was teaching us, even in
difficult circumstances. I recall Ingulf's prayer, as he asked that God
break down the barriers separating Christians behind the Iron Curtain
from brothers and sisters in Christ abroad. Little did we know how
soon those barriers would begin to fall.

CHAPTER TWELVE

The Greatest Reversal of All!

For just as the sufferings of Christ flow over into our lives, so also
through Christ our comfort overflows. . . . We have conducted
ourselves . . . in the holiness and sincerity that are from God. . . .
not according to worldly wisdom but according to God's grace.
2 CORINTHIANS 1:5, 12

O Christ, convince us by your Spirit, thrill us with your
invading love, lay on us the burden of the world's suffering,
drive us forth with the apostolic fervor of the early church.
JOHN WILHELM ROWNTREE

When I returned to the hospital to begin laser treatments, Dr. Tannev entered the room and began explaining the procedure.

When I had opportunity, I commented, "You may receive a call soon from an agent who works with the Ministry of the Interior. He's questioning my need to come to this hospital for these treatments."

Dr. Tannev's eyes never left the medical charts in which he was making notes. "He's already called," he responded. "But don't worry about it. To hear him tell it, you're a low-life criminal living in the city dump, but he isn't going to influence me." Looking up, Dr. Tannev continued, "I told him, 'Listen, if you think Kulichev's a criminal, prove it. As for me, Christo Kulichev is in need of medical attention, and I'm treating him.'" He didn't smile, but there was a lilt in Dr. Tannev's voice that told me he was confident Nikolov wouldn't be interfering in my treatments.

When I returned home from the hospital, there was no change in my eyesight. It was becoming apparent that I would go through life with sight in only one eye. The troublesome "net" that seemed to be draped over my right eye admitted some light, but it was impossible for me to focus on anything; I was unable to read or even identify someone standing in front of me. By God's grace, my left eye quickly began to compensate for the loss of vision in the right eye. To this day, I still don't need glasses and can read as rapidly as before.

The Reforms of Gorbachev
On January 8, 1988, Mikhail Gorbachev, General Secretary of the

Communist party and president of the USSR, held a press conference. For a Communist leader, a meeting with the press was unusual in and of itself. What the personable and photogenic Gorbachev had to say was even more astounding, sending repercussions throughout the Soviet bloc and the world.

Gorbachev used his meeting with the press to call for *glasnost,* or a new openness in economic and political decisions. To our amazement and delight, he was advocating the free flow of information within all government agencies. This, Gorbachev pointed out, would allow for an open and more democratic discussion of what was truly in the best interests of the people.

We could hardly believe our ears! The proposals by the General Secretary of the Communist party quickly reverberated throughout the Communist world. Would Gorbachev's proposal lead to positive changes? We would watch and wait —and pray!

Gorbachev's earlier speeches and writings on *perestroika,* or restructuring, had called for reforms. He had even gone so far as to issue a decree calling for freedom of conscience and religious faith! Years later, in his memoirs, he candidly addressed the problems of ethnic prejudice and religious persecution, writing, "Both my grandmothers, Vasilisa and Stepanida, were religious. Grandfather Andrei was also a believer, and Grandfather Pantelei, a Communist, considered it a personal obligation to respect believers. On the other hand, we 'party cadres' followed the instructions of the party Central Committee and carried on high-pressure anti-religious propaganda, more often than not in violation of the constitutional guarantee of freedom of conscience . . . thereby causing unnecessary dissatisfaction among ordinary people."[17]

Gorbachev's sincere desire to have true freedom of worship without persecution had raised hopes, but Communist history had taught us to embrace hope cautiously. This same term, *perestroika,* had once been used by Stalin decades ago, only to lead to repression and further loss of freedom. Millions had lost their lives in that "restructuring."

This proposed *glasnost,* however, was calling for the exact opposite of what Stalin had imposed. To hear the prime minister and party Secretary talk of openness and free access to information was an evidence of reform we could not deny. Could this be an answer to our prayers? Was it possible that freedom of religion and the end of our persecution was at hand? Like the exiles in Babylon who dreamt and

[17] Mikhail Gorbachev, *Memoirs,* (New York: Doubleday, 1995).

wept and hoped and prayed for return to Jerusalem (Psalm 137:1-6), we waited to see.

My Ticket Out of Nozharevo

Each time I kept an appointment with Dr. Tannev, he examined me, asked a few questions, and then concluded, "We'll see if there's any change when you return next month." I always asked him to write out his recommendation in case I was arrested again. Those monthly appointments were my ticket out of Nozharevo!

Dr. Tannev's orders to return month after month extended my time with family and friends in Sofia and kept me away from the rigors of Nozharevo. The respite had come just in time to allow me to celebrate Christmas with my family. Over the following weeks, we enjoyed fellowship with Christian brothers and sisters. We also continued to attend worship at First Church, where the symbolic protests against Pavel Ivanov continued.

With Dr. Tannev's permission I began to travel, preaching and teaching in churches and the homes of believers within easy driving distance of Sofia. On some occasions my brother Dimitar and I traveled together as we had as young men. It was exciting to encourage the believers again, work with young people, and keep the churches in fellowship with one another. Stefan accompanied us much of the time, driving us if a church couldn't dispatch one of their men to pick us up.

Everywhere we went there was a scarcity of men in the congregation. Christian men, especially those who were active in a church, had been targeted for discrimination. Many had lost jobs or had been demoted to the most menial of positions. Those who remained faithful were a great inspiration to everyone.

Youth groups were small but made up in quality what they lacked in quantity. Teenagers met for prayer and Bible study each night, encouraging one another to remain faithful. The witness of teens was, proportionally, far more effective than the adults', as they shared their beliefs with inquisitive friends. Some of our young adults, such as Nick Athanasov, had become believers when Christian friends had had the courage to give them a Bible.

In most congregations, the few young women of marriageable age remained single rather than marry unbelievers in accordance with the teaching of 2 Corinthians 6:14. In the congregation at Assenovgrad, a young single woman named Mimi had adopted a little girl so that she could still experience the joys of being a Christian mother.

The churches had problems, and we spent much time praying and seeking the counsel of God's Word. There were spiritual victories also, and we celebrated God's grace in those early days of *glasnost*. What a joy it was to be moving about in ministry again!

Faithfulness Is Not Calculated by Percentages

Vladimir Nikolov didn't call again until late in the winter of 1988. When I answered, his voice had an officious tone, but there was no hint of the antagonism of our earlier meeting when he had threatened, "You'll be hearing from me!" It had been almost three months since he had taken the name of Dr. Tannev with the intent of sending me back to Nozharevo.

As he began to speak, Nikolov's manner changed drastically. "We've decided that it would be better for you to spend the winter in Sofia rather than back in Nozharevo," he intoned, using a bland bureaucratic style.

I smiled and resisted pointing out that winter would be over in another week or so. Experience told me to wait and see where Nikolov was heading.

"There's even the possibility," Nikolov emphasized the words deliberately, as if to entice me, "that you could be dismissed before your sentence is completed."

Nikolov paused, waiting for me to respond. I enjoyed waiting silently, knowing that Nikolov was laying the groundwork for something and was looking for an early indication as to whether his offer was appealing.

"All that we ask in return," Nikolov continued with his script, "is that you sign an agreement not to cause conflicts in the church or take leadership positions offered to you."

Nikolov's manner may have changed, but his objective hadn't. Just like Penkov, Tzvetkov, and the Committee, Nikolov wanted to control me, to entice me to swap my calling to serve Christ for earthly freedom.

When I remained silent, he added, "Agree to these simple requests, and we can stop these unpleasant calls and long meetings!"

That was tactic number two. If enticement didn't work, use fear. Nikolov was implying that the horrible interrogations would resume if I didn't agree. His tactics were typical of Communist agents.

When Nikolov had laid out everything, I responded calmly, but with firmness.

"No, I won't sign your agreement," I began. "First, let me remind you that I'm a man of spiritual principles. I would rather return to Nozharevo than agree to stop preaching and teaching the gospel. Second, let me remind you that I signed your paper saying I had been given notice of being sent to Nozharevo, only to find you were using deceit to slander me. I would be foolish to enter into any agreement with a man who has proven to be untrustworthy."

Nikolov was not pleased with my response and ended the conversation abruptly.

When word of my conversation with Nikolov got out and people learned that I had turned down yet another offer to commute my sentence in exchange for compliance, some of our Christian friends came to see me.

"You've made your point," one of them said. "Don't bring more suffering upon yourself than is necessary."

Another man asked me to reconsider as well. "We can't remove Pavel Ivanov," he commented, "but it would be better for us to have you here than in Nozharevo. We need you to advise and guide us quietly behind the scenes."

Still another sympathized, "You've got to consider your health!"

While I appreciated the good intentions of my friends, conscience would not allow me to back down from the stand I had taken. I had found no exception in my reading of Scripture that would allow me to minimize my commitment to Christ out of concern for my health. Neither could I exempt myself from present tests of devotion by claiming credit for past faithfulness. Faithfulness isn't calculated by percentages. We're either faithful or we're not. We're not called to be true to the Lord 80 or 90 percent of the time. God's Word says, "He who stands firm to the end will be saved" (Matthew 24:13), and "Be faithful, even to the point of death, and I will give you the crown of life" (Revelation 2:10).

To the Faithful You Show Yourself Faithful

The weeks and months passed quickly without a call from Nikolov or the Ministry of the Interior. Could it be that by God's grace the *glasnost* was having an impact upon the Committee on Internal Religious Affairs? Christians everywhere were praying but hardly dared talk about their hopes.

Believers from various churches in different localities were asking eagerly for Dimitar and me to tell of our prison experiences. Routinely I began by cautioning that there was danger in making early pronouncements about lessons learned in such turbulent times. "One thing is abundantly clear in every age," I would say, "and that's the fact that God continues to work in our world through his people as they are open to being used by the Holy Spirit. We do not witness by our wisdom or serve in our own strength, but the Spirit works in and through us as we faithfully follow in obedience to God's Word."

Psalm 18 had meant much to me as I meditated upon its familiar phrases in prison. When I had opportunity I preached upon its phrases. "The Lord is my rock, my fortress and my deliverer. . . . The cords of the grave coiled around me; the snares of death entangled me; the torrents of destruction overwhelmed me. . . . In my distress I called to the Lord; I cried to my God for help. . . . He reached down from on high and took hold of me; he drew me out of deep waters. He rescued me from my powerful enemy, from my foes who were too strong for me. . . . To the faithful, you show yourself faithful . . . with my God I can scale a wall."

Visits to churches outside of Sofia were not made in secret. Each time travel took me away from home overnight, I called the Ministry of the Interior and reported where I was going. I didn't want Nikolov accusing me of subversive activities. While I knew the Committee didn't approve of this itinerant ministry, there was never any attempt to prevent me from traveling and speaking at the various churches. God's protective hand was upon me just as it had been in another wilderness when he promised, "See, I am sending an angel ahead of you to guard you along the way and to bring you to the place I have prepared" (Exodus 23:20).

Pavel Ivanov's influence at First Church continued to be nominal. None of the leaders of the church would speak with him, and Bozhimir Kozhouharov continued to lead a small contingent in walking out as Ivanov stood to speak each Sunday. Others bowed in a silent prayer of protest as Pavel Ivanov spoke. It was clearly just a matter of time before Pavel Ivanov would be forced to leave. If it wasn't by his choice, it would be dictated by circumstances.

There was increasing talk of *perestroika* and *glasnost*. It still wasn't clear where all of this was leading, but more people were listening to foreign radio broadcasts in hope that true reforms were imminent. The fearful silence that had once permeated Bulgarian society was giving way to a cautious, quiet discussion of the possibilities. Several friends told us they had heard my name on foreign broadcasts. Bozhimir Kozhouharov reported hearing that the United Nations had asked the

Bulgarian government to give an account as to why Christo Kulichev had been held in exile. All of this was surely leading to something.

An Abrupt Turn

It was July 19 when Nikolov called again. It was a strange conversation that began with a threatening tone. "I understand you've been traveling outside of Sofia without permission," he began.

Grateful that I had called before each trip, I assured him, "Each time I've traveled, I've called the Ministry office and reported where I was going. The record of times and dates I've called is available if you would like to compare notes."

Nikolov didn't seem interested. Staying with his sweeping generalizations, he continued, "Don't think we don't know about these meetings you're holding in various locations. We're watching you closely."

Nikolov flitted from subject to subject, pursuing nothing in depth. At one point he told me that he had checked with the Medical Academy in Sofia. "They don't even have a file verifying that you're being treated there," he lied. When I told him that Dr. Tannev had told me of their conversation, the subject was quickly dropped.

The wrangling continued as Nikolov brought up the subject of Ingulf Diesen's visit. "What was the Diesen fellow from Norway up to? Why did he visit you?" he demanded.

"He's a Christian and came to encourage us," I assured him. "He also visited First Church on Sunday and spoke with Pavel Ivanov. Why don't you ask Ivanov since you believe everything he says?"

"We know that Diesen came to make you a member of his religious organization," Nikolov asserted. "But the Committee will never allow such a thing, and you know it!"

We had been sparring for some time in this manner when suddenly Nikolov made an abrupt turn. "We've been expecting you to submit an application requesting that the remainder of your sentence be dismissed for health reasons," he said in a civil tone. "Why haven't you?"

"If you're suggesting that I make some concessions in exchange for dropping the remainder of my sentence, don't hold your breath," I responded. "I would never file an application under those terms."

To my astonishment, Nikolov didn't drop the subject. "We know how stubborn you are!" he continued. "But think about it seriously. Put something into writing and bring it to my office on July 25. At least it'll give us something to discuss, and you never know where it might lead." He spoke as though this were a tempting offer that I would not possibly be able to refuse.

When I hung up the receiver after our disjointed conversation, I felt there were signs of a change. First, there had been the long silence, and now this. For whatever reason, Nikolov was serious about the possibility of reducing my sentence. Whether it was the pressure from foreign contacts, the talk of *glasnost,* or sheer frustration in dealing with me, something was pressuring Nikolov to bring closure to my case.

But How Should I Respond?

That evening I met with members of my family to discuss the call I had received from Nikolov. We agreed that the request to apply for dismissal was irregular, and that the political climate did appear to be changing. Just one month before, in June of 1988, the Nineteenth Party Conference had convened with *glasnost* as the key theme. Resolutions had passed approving Gorbachev's proposed reforms, including mention of freedom of conscience and religion.

"Maybe they want to close your case because of *glasnost,*" Stefan suggested.

"But how should I respond to Nikolov's call to bring in an appeal on July 25?" I asked.

Tzvete was cautious. "Be careful that you don't give them an opportunity to boast that they're showing you mercy," she advised. Then she pointed out, "Nikolov didn't say what you should write in the application. You can ask that the sentence be dismissed because the charges are false!"

We all agreed that my reply had to be carefully balanced—neither a manifesto of pride or stubbornness nor an opportunity for Nikolov to claim that I had compromised.

After further prayer and consideration, I began drafting a document. It was more of a statement than an appeal. It wouldn't contain the concessions Nikolov was hoping for, but there was good reason to be prepared to discuss matters. As he had said, "You never know where it might lead."

After discussing the draft with Tzvete, my children, and Dimitar and his family, the final wording was put into place. It acknowledged Nikolov's invitation to prepare a request for dismissing my sentence, and expressed gratitude for the opportunity. This provided a reasonable approach, not proud or confrontational, yet it clearly pointed out that Nikolov had taken the initiative in this and not me. The heart of the statement stood firmly in defense of my rights: ". . . because I have been imprisoned on the grounds of false accusations made against me, I am hereby requesting that all charges be dropped."

Caught in His Own Trap

The following Monday, July 25, I kept my appointment with Nikolov at his office. Nikolov's office was located on September 6th Street, which commemorated the date of Bulgaria's unification in 1885. Nikolov was waiting.

"So, Old Man Christo," he began, "where've you gone lately without notifying our office?" It was not an auspicious beginning, but I restrained myself to answer calmly.

"If I haven't given you notice, you can be sure I've been only in Sofia. I'm a man of my word."

"What do you have for me?" Nikolov asked, eyeing the statement in my hand. I handed it to him as he moved toward his desk. Before he had even sat down, he protested, "You're talking about 'false accusations' without any proof!" Like Penkov, he was assuming I had to prove my innocence. After all, the way of the Communist party was to force the accused to prove their innocence.

"The point is," I responded, "the law states I am innocent until proven guilty. There's no document showing that my right to preach the gospel was ever revoked. Our constitution promises freedom of religion, but I've been denied that right! I'm not asking for an apology, but I should be released to show that the government respects the constitution."

Nikolov laid my statement on the corner of his desk as if it were contagious. I had underlined the fact that it was in his interests to commute my sentence, yet he was silent. It was clear that Nikolov wanted to close the case but was frustrated that he couldn't get my signature on some document that could be construed as a victory for the Committee.

Rising from the chair, I moved toward the door. Nikolov didn't try to stop me. Surely he could see how counterproductive his efforts had been! He was now caught in his own trap. To emphasize the point, I smiled graciously and said, "Comrade, I'm grateful for all that you've done for me."

Nikolov looked up in bewilderment and said, "What?"

"I'm grateful for what you've done!"

"What do you mean?" he asked.

"By arresting me you've strengthened my faith and the faith of many believers in the churches! As for the broadcasts from the BBC and other stations, I'm as surprised as you are. It amazes me they've taken the name of a common pastor known to so few and made it known in other countries. Thank you. You tried to discourage us, but God is using it to bring glory to his name."

Nikolov's gaze dropped to the desk. As I opened the door and stepped out of his office I looked over my shoulder to see that he was sitting motionless.

I'm a Pastor, Not a Prostitute!

The next day Nikolov called again. "We will meet again," he informed me. "Tomorrow. The same time, the same place." He spoke matter-of-factly, giving no hint as to what he was planning. When I told Tzvete of the brief phone conversation, we looked at one another in bewilderment.

Nikolov began the meeting by saying, "We're going to lay this aside." He picked up my statement of the day before and then put it back on his desk. "There's no need to make this complicated," he said, reaching into a drawer and bringing out a fresh sheet of paper and a pencil. Laying them in front of me, he continued, "This can all be finished if you'll only make a brief statement that you're willing to obey the law of our country. That's a reasonable compromise, I'm sure you will agree."

Surely something was astir behind the scenes. Nikolov was hardly concealing his desire to commute my sentence. Perhaps he had been given orders from above to bring this embarrassing case dealing with religious freedom to a quiet close.

Nikolov's offer was tempting. As Dimitar had warned, however, it was the type of thing the Committee and Nikolov could possibly use to claim they were showing mercy.

"What's the logic of your request?" I responded. "Stop and think about it. There's no legal precedent for asking any citizen to declare in writing that they will obey the law. It's every citizen's duty!"

"Surely you're willing to sign that you will obey the law?" Nikolov was almost pleading now.

"Why?" I insisted. "You wouldn't think of asking a streetwalker to sign such a document. I'm a pastor, not a prostitute!"

The more I thought of it, the more opposed I was to the idea. "Give me a document that removes the false accusations, and I'll sign it. But not this. If I signed that I would obey the law, you would claim it implied that I've violated the law. But I didn't violate the law. It was Tzvetkov who slandered my brother and me by calling us thieves, and

Mladenov tried to label me a criminal. Ask them to sign your document promising to obey the law!"

"In that case you'll be returning to Nozharevo," Nikolov threatened. But his heart wasn't in the threat, and I doubted he wanted to complicate matters further.

"It's against your interests to send me back to Nozharevo, not mine," I pointed out. "My only concern is to be faithful in serving my Lord and Savior, Jesus Christ. I'll do that wherever you send me! Oh yes, it would be an inconvenience to go back, but I would rather do that than lose God's blessing by betraying his call to preach."

"Then you're refusing to make any appeal for your release?" Nikolov asked incredulously. "Why not make an appeal for health reasons?"

"I am saying," I articulated my words clearly, "that my life is in God's hands. If God wants me in Nozharevo, I'll gladly go. As you've seen, he will bless my going. If God wants my sentence commuted, he's able to do it without an appeal!"

Where Two or Three Come Together

Tzvete and Dimitar had spoken to the church leaders, asking them to pray for my return visit to Nikolov's office. That evening Vasil Kozuharov and Jordan Milanov came to our home, separately and after dark so as to not attract attention. When tea had been poured, Vasil said, "So, tell us what happened."

Reviewing Nikolov's request that I sign a promise to obey the law, I told them of my response. "It's in God's hands," I concluded. "Nikolov could have me shipped back to Nozharevo or he could call me back tomorrow with another proposal to sign."

The police didn't come, and Nikolov didn't call for the next few days. Our lives and ministry continued as before. If anything, Pavel Ivanov's tenuous grip on the pulpit of First Church was slipping. More people were joining the protests, and members were speaking more courageously to one another about petitioning the Committee again to remove him. The people planted in the congregation by the Committee to support Pavel Ivanov were drifting away one by one.

At this critical juncture it was important for me to be occupied elsewhere so that the Committee would recognize I was not stirring up the protests and discontent. As much as possible I traveled and spoke in churches within short driving distance of Sofia.

One of the churches I visited often was a small church in the village of Banja, two and a half hours south of Sofia. It was good to see that the little church was doing well. I could remember the days when it had almost passed out of existence.

Several years before I had gone into prison, the church in Banja had dwindled down to one older man who, all alone, had remained faithful. The old man had attended the church, as he said, "long before the Communists came." He wasn't about to give up. When he wrote for help in building the church up again, I felt God's leading to accept the challenge.

The first two Sundays I preached to the old man alone. No one else came. The third Sunday a couple joined us, and we had a congregation of three in addition to myself. Slowly the small church began to come back to life.

It was gratifying to see the Lord work in Banja. As I had seen before, when the situation seemed impossible, God did marvelous things when his people simply trusted him. Each Sunday I met with the small group of four or five people, I reminded them of the words of Jesus: "For where two or three come together in my name, there am I with them" (Matthew 18:20).

Returning to Banja after my prison experience, I was delighted to find that the church had not only survived but had actually grown to include thirty courageous souls who attended for worship. Most encouraging was that some were young people who came in spite of their parents' warnings that they might be arrested. What a thrill it was to see how God had blessed the seed we had planted!

A Surprising Return to Nozharevo

As it turned out, Nikolov did not call me, but I found myself calling him. An envelope in the mailbox one day informed me that a check had been drawn in my name to pay an allotment that was due me for sick leave. It was to be issued at Nozharevo. The check alone was hardly worth the long journey to Nozharevo, but I had left personal items with Karov that I hoped to bring home.

It was October 17 when I called Vladimir Nikolov, telling him of my purpose in traveling to Nozharevo and the dates I would be gone.

His reply was brusque and perfunctory. "Okay, Old Man Christo," he said. "Straight there and back. Nothing more." I thought it curious that Nikolov said nothing about meeting again.

It was late on October 24 when I arrived in Nozharevo again. I noted that nothing had changed as I made my way from the bus stop to Karov's home. My knock at the door of Karov's house prompted the scraping of a chair on the wooden floor and approaching footsteps. It was Karov himself who answered the door. "Old Man Christo," he exclaimed. "What are you doing here? You're a free man now!"

I could hardly believe my ears! Thinking that perhaps Karov was misinformed, I asked, "Are you talking about my medical leave? I came to pick up the check for my sick leave."

"No," Karov insisted. "You're free! The order came from Sofia!"

"An order dismissing the remainder of my sentence? Are you sure it wasn't a transfer back to Sofia?"

Karov laughed. "I recognize an order of discharge when I see one, Kulichev."

I was still numb with disbelief. "When did it come?" I asked.

"Over a week, ten days ago," Karov assured me. "Just a moment," he said, turning to pull a jacket out of a closet. "Come to my office, and I'll show you."

Sure enough, Karov produced a letter from the Ministry of the Interior announcing that my order of discharge had been issued on September 30! A surge of relief and gratitude to God swept over me. I could hardly wait to find a telephone to call my family.

Nikolov Knew!

I looked again at the date on the order of discharge: September 30, 1988. It had reached Nozharevo on October 14. I glanced at the bottom of the letter; sure enough, a copy had been sent to V. Nikolov! Nikolov had known about my discharge when I called him on October 17!

Vladimir Nikolov was too proud to tell me of my release. He had wanted me to come begging for it, trying to get some last minute compromise for it. I had told him that if God wanted me to be released that it would happen without an appeal, and it had! Nikolov surely knew that he and the Committee, along with Pavel Ivanov, had been defeated!

Typical of his deceitful ways, Nikolov had said nothing about my discharge before I left. Typical of the inhumane Communist mentality, he wanted me and my family to live under the threat of interrogation or possible arrest and exile for those few extra days. It was a relief to know that I wouldn't be dealing with the likes of Nikolov and Penkov again!

Turning again to Karov, I asked, "Do you have a copy of this for me?"

"I didn't contact you because I thought they would tell you in

Sofia. Kostadinov will give you the formal order with his seal upon it at his office in Toutrakan. If you're going back tomorrow, you can stop and get it."

Even though it was late, I ran to the post office and grabbed the telephone. "Tzvete," I was almost shouting, when my wife answered the telephone. "Good news! I've been discharged. Yes—I'm free. I just found out the order was given on September 30. Nikolov was withholding the good news from us. Call the children and Dimitar and tell them immediately. I'll be home tomorrow."

Through It All, I Learned to Trust in Jesus

My last night in Nozharevo was spent back in the storage shed I had converted into an apartment. As I knelt to pray, tears of joy came to my eyes as I thanked God not just for my release but for his presence with me through it all. God had sustained me through the suspense of the early interrogations. His Holy Spirit had strengthened me through the rigors of Central Prison. I thanked God for his presence with me at Kremikovtzi, where even the other prisoners had seen prayers answered and miracles performed. The solitary confinement at Sopot had been used by God in an extraordinary way to open doors for ministry. And Nozharevo, my place of exile, had become a place of spiritual renewal. My heart poured out praise and gratitude that God's presence had been so near and real through all of those trials.

As I rose from my knees that night, reflecting upon the times of testing my family and I had been through, a familiar Scripture passage kept going through my mind. It was Romans 8:37: "In all these things we are more than conquerors through him who loved us."

Someone had taken the heater, and that night was the coldest I'd known since the night of torture in Central Prison when the guard forced us to keep the window open. Cold as it was, it was a night of joy and thanksgiving, knowing that my life was in God's hands. I had trusted him, and he had taught me so much. Through it all, I had learned to trust in Jesus. The Lord had taught me that in every circumstance, no matter how painful, there are blessings to be discovered. Searching hearts will not find the deepest joy in a place of comfort but in the person of Christ, who is "God with us."

Meditating upon all that God had taught me, I recalled the words of someone, perhaps one of the martyrs, who had said something about looking not at the writhing flames about us but at the wreaths of victory that are before us when we are faithful to Christ. The idea surely expressed something of the thrust of James 1:12: "Blessed is the man who perseveres under trial, because when he has stood the test, he will receive the crown of life that God has promised to those who love him."

The Certificate of Discharge

Up early the next morning, I prayed again, paused to survey my humble apartment one last time, and made my way to Karov's house. Collecting the things I had left with Karov, I bundled the clothes and kitchen utensils into three collapsible nylon bags I had brought with me. The sun was just rising as I boarded the bus for Toutrakan.

Juggling the nylon bags in Toutrakan, I inquired about directions to the Municipal Building and walked the eight blocks. Kostadinov's office was on the second floor.

A young lieutenant was working behind the desk in the outer office.

"I've come from Nozharevo to get the certificate of discharge from Lieutenant Colonel Kostadinov," I informed him.

Looking at me somewhat uncertainly, he responded, "Stay here. I'll be back." He disappeared through the door behind his desk.

In a few moments the young lieutenant returned, spent a minute or so riffling through first one file drawer and then another, and pulled out a file that I hoped was mine. "Come with me," he said.

Bundling up the three nylon bags, I made my way around the counter, through a swinging door, and into Kostadinov's office. Kostadinov remained seated as the young lieutenant placed the file on the desk before him. As I awkwardly placed my baggage just inside the door, Kostadinov greeted me. "Kulichev, I didn't expect to see you again."

"I've come to get the certificate of discharge," I explained. "Karov told me that you have a copy for me."

"No one ever comes to get a copy of the discharge papers," Kostadinov said with a quizzical tone to his voice. "Did you think there had been some mistake?"

"Karov showed me the letter that had been sent to him and suggested I could stop in and pick up my own copy of the certificate. I'm returning to Sofia, and it's along the way. Besides, I'm curious as to the wording in the document, and the reason cited, if any, for my release. Nikolov has been pressuring me to sign an agreement to limit my freedom. I just want to make sure my release is unconditional."

Kostadinov was good-natured in his reply. "Of course, I can give you a signed copy," he said, placing his signature at the bottom of the document and then turning it for me to read. "Don't worry, I'm not going to hide it from you as Nikolov did!"

I was pleased that Kostadinov remembered the incident. He even sounded perhaps a bit sympathetic. "Don't blame you a bit under the circumstances. Here, take it. It's yours to keep."

My eyes scanned the certificate, picking up the relevant phrases. Under the seal of the Ministry of the Interior, it read, ". . . hereby certifies the cancellation of the order of detention . . . for reasons of health and for good behavior . . . it has been noted that the subject has been conscientious, disciplined, and an active worker." It concluded, "This writ is hereby authorized by . . ." and it had been signed by the Minister of the Interior and by Kostadinov as the Chief of the District Department in Toutrakan.

The document did not exonerate me of the false charges or give a reason for my detainment. On the other hand, there were no conditions placed upon my release, which Nikolov had been working toward.

He Saw Him Who Is Invisible

That night the certificate of discharge lay upon our dining table as my family and I joined together with Dimitar and his family to celebrate God's goodness in the midst of our trials. "We can never see very far ahead or know where God is leading us," I shared with my family. "But we may be certain that God will go with us, even if we 'walk through the valley of the shadow of death' (Psalm 23:4)."

Another passage I shared was one of the many I had meditated upon at Nozharevo, found in Hebrews 11:27. It tells of Moses, who pressed forward in faith and "persevered because he saw him who is invisible."

Later I would preach on that same verse, saying, "Moses didn't know the sea would part until he stretched out his hand. He didn't know the cloud and pillar of fire would lead them until he followed. He didn't know that manna would fall from the sky until he saw it. Moses persevered, trusting in an invisible God. So we must persevere also in times of testing, knowing that God is with us."

New Depths of Faith and New Heights of Service

My prison experience had taught me that proclamation cannot and must not be separated from the *praxis* of the gospel. Witnessing for Christ must include far more than speaking from the pulpit to hundreds of believers. True witness is given, I am convinced, only when we have loved our neighbors and given of ourselves to others when we are tempted to look after our own needs first. In short, we are to live for God's glory and not for our own convenience.

Prison taught me the truth of what we preach when we say, "We are never beyond God's love." Just as Isaiah wrote to God's people when they were surrounded by a pagan enemy, so we may know:

> Fear not, for I have redeemed you; I have summoned
> you by name; you are mine. When you pass through the
> waters, I will be with you; and when you pass through
> the rivers, they will not sweep over you. When you
> walk through the fire, you will not be burned; the
> flames will not set you ablaze. For I am the Lord,
> your God, the Holy One of Israel, your Savior.
> (Isaiah 43:1-3)

Then there are the lessons to be learned about suffering itself. Christians shouldn't be masochists, people who enjoy suffering. However, when suffering comes, as it will when we're faithful to Christ in this sinful world, we may learn to offer it to God with the assurance that he will use it to bring us to new depths of faith and new heights of service. Suffering humbles us and makes us dependent upon God. I've seen God use suffering to bring men such as my friend Assen to faith. Suffering in the life of Christians can make us more holy and usable by God, just as fire purges the impurities from gold (1 Peter 1:6-7) or as pruning makes a plant more fruitful (John 15:1-11).

Lastly, I discovered the joy of sharing in Christ's suffering in the sense that Paul speaks of it in Philippians 3:10. Paul writes, "I want to know Christ and the power of his resurrection and the fellowship of sharing in his sufferings."

To say that we share in Christ's suffering is not to imply that what Christ did on the cross is insufficient for our salvation. Not at all. Having died for our redemption, Christ invites us to join him in his ongoing redemptive work in our sinful, broken world.

That's why I'm convinced that my suffering in prison gave me extraordinary opportunities to witness for Christ. Even hardened criminals noticed that my Christian faith made a difference in how I responded to the hardships. They would have had nothing to do with preaching that was not practiced. But they did notice the serenity of a soul anchored in Christ and marveled when prayers were answered.

The Greatest Reversal

Signs of change were in the air. Even though the horrible economy in Bulgaria was getting worse, hopes were high that *glasnost* and its reforms would help. Local control of the economy, rather than party control, was now being promoted in the Soviet Union. Eastern European countries were following that example. Demonstrations by the minority Armenians in Nagorno-Karabakh asking for reunification with Armenia appeared to be on the verge of success. In the past demonstrations would have brought violent repression. Gorbachev had been made chairman of the USSR Supreme Soviet, strengthening his proposed reforms.

These political reversals gave hope to persecuted Christians. It would be harder for the Committee on Internal Religious Affairs to continue its abusive tactics under *glasnost*. With each passing day it was increasingly obvious that the hard-line Communists could never force a return to what had once been.

With these reversals came the promise of a new environment. The believers in our churches grew more bold in sharing their witness. Whereas repression had made it difficult to talk about religious beliefs, open speculation was now being made about the new policies and what religious practices would be tolerated. Young people, especially, were eager to ask questions that had been forbidden for generations.

My unconditional release was a personal reversal that was gratifying. It would be six months before Pavel Ivanov would step down at First Church, recognizing that *glasnost* made it impossible to use the ruthless tactics that had protected him. We patiently waited, knowing that our invisible God was at work.

My brother-in-law Marin and I continued to preach at churches such as the one at Banja each weekend. We continued faithfully, ministering wherever we could until Pavel Ivanov stepped down and the word came that the people of First Church were free to welcome me back as their minister.

It was a joyous day when I stepped back into the pulpit at First Evangelical Church of Sofia. I shall never forget those moments when I stood in the pulpit before the Scripture reading, with tears in my eyes and joy in my heart, saying, "Let us hear the Word of the Lord."

The message that day was from John 12:20–32. "What we all need to remember," I reminded the people, "is that ours is not a story of human interest or the reversal of personal circumstances. Neither is it a story of *glasnost* or political reversal, as intriguing a story as that is.

Rather, it's a story of God's grace, as seen in the cross and the Resurrection.

"It is the Lord Jesus Christ, crucified and risen again, that we follow faithfully. Our eyes are upon him and the glory he's preparing for us, not upon the trials we're passing through. That's why we must walk by faith and not by sight.

"When we serve our risen Savior faithfully, he will lead us from victory to victory, until that greatest and most glorious day of all when we shall be with him in eternity. He has promised, 'Where I am, my servant also will be' (John 12:26).

"When we suffer and are buried with Christ, Scripture promises us that we will be raised with him to new life. This is a story of divine mystery that we may not fully comprehend in this life, for it's the story of God's love submitting to hate and overcoming it; it's the story of divine goodness being seized by evil and repudiating its power; it's the story of God's Spirit converting a prison into a palace and making the darkest dungeon a haven of hope. Our hope is irrepressible, because we've experienced the truth of the Resurrection in our lives.

"Yes," I said, "the greatest reversal of all is the Resurrection of Jesus Christ."

EPILOGUE

In December 1999, I received a call from Mr. Blagoev, the director of religious programming for the Bulgarian National Television Network. "Rev. Kulichev, would you be willing to join other religious leaders from across Bulgaria in a television program called 'Prayer for Bulgaria'?" Stunned, I gratefully accepted the opportunity to publicly represent the evangelical churches of Bulgaria. The program was aired nationwide on Sunday, January 2, 2000.

And so it was that I was given the privilege of proclaiming the gospel of Christ to all of Bulgaria at the turn of the millennium. Men like Tzvetkov and Proinov had confidently predicted that free churches would be extinct by the year 2000. But by the power of God's Spirit, the gospel, which they had opposed with all the coercive power they could muster, was being preached with renewed vigor not only from pulpits across the land but from the National Radio and Television Network as well.

The message I proclaimed that day was not one of rancor or revenge against my captors but of a risen Christ who has promised to make all things new. It signaled another of those reversals of history that can only be explained by a God of grace and glory who died to save the world from sin, rose again to defeat the power of evil, and will one day return to take all those who love him to be with him forever.

> And now, all glory to God, who is able to keep you from stumbling, and who will bring you into his glorious presence innocent of sin and with great joy. All glory to him, who alone is God our Savior, through Jesus Christ our Lord. Yes, glory, majesty, power, and authority belong to him, in the beginning, now, and forevermore. Amen.
>
> JUDE 1:24-25

BIBLIOGRAPHY

The following volumes were helpful in articulating Christo Kulichev's views on various topics, particularly subjects related to God's sovereignty and human suffering.

Aulen, Gustav. *Christus Victor*. London: SPCK Publications, 1931.

Barth, Markus and Helmut Blanke. *The Anchor Bible: Colossians*. New York: Doubleday Publishing, 1994.

Bousfield, Jonathan and Dan Richardson. *Bulgaria*. London: Penguin Books, 1993.

Bruce, F. F. *The Epistles to the Colossians, to Philemon, and to the Ephesians*. Grand Rapids, Mich.: William B. Eerdmans Publishing Company, 1984.

Carnell, E. J. *Christian Commitment*. New York: The MacMillan Company, 1957.

Donchev, Anton. *Time of Parting*. New York: William Morrow and Company, Inc., 1968.

Frankl, Viktor E., ed. *Man's Search for Meaning*. New York: Simon and Schuster, Inc., 1984.

Gaebelein, Frank E., ed. *The Expositor's Bible Commentary*. Vol. 11, *Ephesians—Philemon*. Grand Rapids, Mich.: Zondervan Publishing House, 1978.

Gorbachev, Mikhail. *Memoirs*. New York: Doubleday Publishing, 1995.

Hall, Douglas John. *God and Human Suffering*. Minneapolis: Augsburg Publishing House, 1986.

Hafemann, Scott J. *Suffering and Ministry in the Spirit*. Grand Rapids, Mich.: William B. Eerdmans Publishing Company, 1990.

Hansel, Tim. *You Gotta Keep Dancin'*. Elgin, Ill.: David C. Cook Publishing Co., 1985.

Hauerwas, Stanley. *Suffering Presence*. South Bend. Ind.: University of Notre Dame Press, 1986.

Hengel, Martin. *The Atonement: The Origins of the Doctrine in the New Testament*. Translated by John Bowden. London: SCM Publishing, 1981.

Heschel, Abraham J. *The Prophets*. New York: Harper and Row Publishers, 1962.

Horbury, William and Brian McNeil, eds. *Suffering and Martyrdom in the New Testament*. London: Cambridge University Press, 1981.

Kittel, Gerhard. *Theological Dictionary of the New Testament*. 10 vols. Grand Rapids, Mich.: William B. Eerdmans Publishing Company, 1965.

Lewis, C. S. *The Problem of Pain*. London: Geoffrey Bles, 1956.

McGrath, Alister. *A Journey through Suffering*. London: Hodder and Stoughton, 1992.

McWilliams, Warren. *The Passion of God: Divine Suffering in Contemporary Protestant Theology*. Macon, Georgia: Mercer University Press, 1985.

Moltmann, Jurgen. *The Crucified God*. London: SCM Press, 1974.

Montefiore, C. G. and H. Loewe, eds. *A Rabbinic Anthology*. Philadephia: The Jewish Publication Society of America, 1998.

Nicoll, Robertson W., ed. *The Expositor's Greek Testament. Vol. 3.* Grand Rapids, Mich.: William B. Eerdmans Publishing Company, 1961.

Noll, Mark A. *Turning Points.* Grand Rapids, Mich.: Baker Books, 1997.

Ohlrich, Charles. *The Suffering God.* Downers Grove, Ill.: InterVarsity Press, 1982.

Plantinga, Cornelius Jr. *Not the Way It's Supposed to Be.* Grand Rapids, Mich.: William B. Eerdmans Publishing Company, 1995.

Sienkiewcz, Henryk. *Quo Vadis.*

Schlossberg, Herbert. *Called to Suffer, Called to Triumph.* Portland, Ore.: Multnomah Press, 1990.

Soelle, Dorothee. *Suffering.* Philadelphia: Fortress Press, 1973.

Tournier, Paul. *Creative Suffering.* San Francisco: Harper and Row Publishers, 1982.

Wright, N. T. *Jesus and the Victory of God.* Minneapolis: Fortress Press, 1996.

Yates, Roy. *The Epistle to the Colossians.* London: Epworth Press, 1993.

REV. CHRISTO KULICHEV
is the minister of the
First Evangelical Church of Sofia
and the president of the
Union of Evangelical Churches in Bulgaria.

MICHAEL HALCOMB
is a Congregational minister and writer.
He and his wife, Bonnie, live in
Whitefish Bay, Wisconsin.